VIKING SOCIETY

FOR NORTHERN RESEARCH

TEXT SERIES

General Editors
A. R. Faulkes and P. G. Foote

VOLUME VII (i)

HÁVAMÁL

Edited by David A. H. Evans

VOLUME VII (ii)

GLOSSARY AND INDEX

Compiled by Anthony Faulkes

The printing of this Book
is made possible by a gift
to the University of Cambridge
in memory of Dorothea Coke,
Skjaeret, 1951.

HÁVAMÁL

EDITED BY D. A. H. EVANS

WITH

GLOSSARY

AND

INDEX

COMPILED BY ANTHONY FAULKES

VIKING SOCIETY
FOR NORTHERN RESEARCH
UNIVERSITY COLLEGE LONDON

© VIKING SOCIETY FOR NORTHERN RESEARCH 1986, 1987

First published in two separate volumes in 1986–1987
Reissued as a single volume in 2017

Printed by Short Run Pess Limited, Exeter

ISBN: 978-0-903521-95-6

HÁVAMÁL

EDITED BY

DAVID A. H. EVANS

VIKING SOCIETY
FOR NORTHERN RESEARCH
UNIVERSITY COLLEGE LONDON

PREFACE

Hávamál is deservedly one of the most celebrated works to have survived from the early Norse world, and a very extensive scholarly literature, almost wholly in languages other than English, has accumulated around it over the past century and more. Yet no annotated edition of the complete text has been published since that of Finnur Jónsson in 1924 (in Danish, followed by a much briefer treatment, also in Danish, in the same scholar's *De Gamle Eddadigte* of 1932), and that to be found in the edition of the Poetic Edda by Hugo Gering and Barend Sijmons, of which the volume containing commentary (in German) on *Hávamál* appeared in 1927. For the English reader, the edition of D. E. Martin Clarke (Cambridge 1923) is helpful as far as it goes, but it was conceived on a modest scale, it is now over sixty years old and, like the works already mentioned, it has long been out of print. The only other treatment in English, that of Guðbrandur Vigfússon and F. York Powell in the first volume of their *Corpus Poeticum Boreale* (Oxford 1883), is too idiosyncratic to be reckoned an edition of the poem at all. A fresh presentation of this important and interesting work therefore seemed fully justified.

Recent discussion of *Hávamál* has tended less to the elucidation of individual textual cruces than to an attempt to place the poem (and more particularly its first, gnomic, half) in a cultural context. Some influential writers, notably Klaus von See in Frankfurt and Hermann Pálsson in Edinburgh, have argued forcefully that this context was not pagan Nordic antiquity, as has usually been supposed, but rather the learned Latin culture of the Christian middle ages. The reader of my Introduction will see that I have not found myself persuaded by their arguments, but I hope that he will not judge my opposition unreasoned.

Valuable corrections and suggestions have been contributed by several scholars. In Dublin, Bo Almqvist, long my friend and now my colleague, has offered the constant stimulus of his enthusiasm and wide learning. I am also grateful to R. W. McTurk and Ursula Dronke for sending me various studies not available in Ireland, and to the General Editors, Anthony Faulkes and Peter Foote, for erudite and judicious comment and practical assistance. That I have in a very few instances ventured to dissent from the judgments of these scholars is no doubt my readers' loss.

D.A.H.E.

CONTENTS

PREFACE vii

INTRODUCTION 1

HÁVAMÁL 39

COMMENTARY 75

BIBLIOGRAPHY AND ABBREVIATIONS 144

INTRODUCTION

I PRESERVATION

Hávamál is the second poem in the so-called Elder (or Poetic) Edda, a manuscript collection of anonymous Norse lays on mythological and heroic themes. The ms, which is in the same hand throughout, can be shown on palaeographic and linguistic grounds to have been written in Iceland *c.* 1270, but nothing is known of its history until it was brought to light (in Iceland, but where is not recorded) by the collector and antiquary Brynjólfur Sveinsson, bishop of Skálholt, who wrote his signature and the year 1643 on the first leaf. It was sent as a gift to the Danish king in 1662 and was preserved until recently in the Royal Library in Copenhagen; for which reason it is commonly known as the Codex Regius (CR) of the Elder Edda. This conventional designation is retained here, though it is no longer appropriate, for in 1972 the codex was returned home, to take its place as perhaps the greatest treasure of the new Arnamagnæan Institute in Iceland, *Stofnun Árna Magnússonar á Íslandi.*

Hávamál, like all the poems in CR, is written out continuously as though prose, but the scribe has sought to mark the beginning of each strophe by a capital initial (which is set out in the margin when this happens to begin a new line in the ms). The strophe-division and numbering established by Sophus Bugge in his edition of the poems in 1867, which has been adhered to by nearly all subsequent scholars and is followed here, is essentially based on the divisions implied in the ms; Bugge's st. 12, however, commences with a small initial in CR, doubtless through oversight, as do 74, 88, 114 and 123, which the scribe may well have taken as continuing the strophes that precede them; conversely, *fimbulfambi* in 103 and *ef* in 130/5 have capital initials as though to mark new strophes. In beginning new strophes at 86 *fljúganda* and 87 *sjúkum*, where the division is manifestly arbitrary, Bugge was simply following the ms, just as he was in making 143 a separate strophe even though it does not form a distinct sentence. The poem is headed in the ms by the title *Hávamál* and opens with a large capital initial; there are smaller capitals at 111 *Mál* and 137 *Veit*, plainly intended to mark the beginning of new sections.

Like the majority of the Eddaic poems, *Hávamál* is extant only in CR. The first strophe, however, also appears in Snorri's Prose Edda, near the beginning of *Gylfaginning*, where Gylfi's entry into the hall at Ásgarðr is described: *þá litaðisk hann um ok þótti margir hlutir ótrúlegir, þeir er hann sá. Þá mælti hann*: whereupon the strophe is quoted. Snorri's Edda is extant in three fourteenth-century mss and in the Utrecht ms of c. 1600. Further, the second half of st. 84 is cited in *Fóstbrœðra saga* ch. 21 (ÍF VI 225) where it is said of a thrall in Greenland who suspects his mistress of infidelity *kom honum þá í hug kviðlingr sá, er kveðinn hafði verit um lausungarkonur* and then the lines follow. This part of *Fóstbrœðra saga* is extant in two mss from the fourteenth century and in later copies of what is thought to have been another fourteenth-century ms. It is worth noting that neither the Prose Edda nor *Fóstbrœðra saga* attributes these quotations to a poem called *Hávamál*, which is indeed not named in any Old Norse document apart from CR itself. Lastly, it should be mentioned that chapters 6 and 7 of *Ynglinga saga* (in Snorri's *Heimskringla*) contain manifest echoes of st. 148 and some of the following strophes, showing that Snorri must have known this part (at least) of the poem; and in one place Snorri's wording is helpful in establishing the correct text (see the Commentary).

Though scholars have differed widely on the dates of the Eddaic poems, there can be little doubt that most of them are considerably older than CR and that they all, or almost all, were transmitted orally before being committed to writing. But CR cannot itself be the ms in which they were first set down: this is shown by errors which can hardly be explained except as misreadings of a text which was being copied (in *Hávamál*, for instance, *ǫlðr* 14 was first written *auðr, aflaðrom* 75 is plainly corrupt, the second occurrence of *ýta* in 164 can scarcely be right; the omission of necessary words, as after *ganga* 35 and *svági* 39, points in the same direction). That CR is not an original is further demonstrated by the existence of AM 748 I, 4to from the beginning of the fourteenth century, which contains some of the mythological poems in a text which, while clearly scribally related to the Codex Regius, is plainly neither derived from it nor the source of it; both these mss must then (at any rate as far as *these* poems are concerned) have a common ancestor, so these poems at least cannot have been drawn by the scribe of CR direct from oral recitation.

Gustaf Lindblad has made a valuable and acute study of the palaeography and orthography of CR (see the Bibliography for details of this and other works referred to in the present volume).

He shows that the scribe's practices are not uniform throughout but reflect a varying manuscript ancestry for the various poems or groups of poems it comprises. As for *Hávamál*, Lindblad was able to adduce a considerable number of features which mark it off both from its immediate neighbours, *Vǫluspá* and *Vafþrúðnismál*, and from the rest of the ms as a whole. For example, in the choice between *beztr* and *baztr* as the word for 'best', *Hávamál* has four instances with *a* against only one with *e*, whereas in the remainder of the ms *e*-forms occur ten times and *a*-forms are found only twice (counting n. pl. *bazt* (< *baztu*) in *Reginsmál* 19 as an *a*-form). There are two instances of *b* for *f*, in *halb* 53 and *hverb* 74; this is not found elsewhere in the ms, unless the mysterious *olubann* of *Hárbarðsljóð* 41 stands for *óljúfan* (which would not be a precise parallel anyway, the consonant here being intervocalic). The use of *ɐ* rather than *o* to signify the vowel normalized as *ǫ* is far commoner in *Hávamál*, with seventy-nine instances of *ɐ* against only eleven of *o*, than in the ms as a whole, where *ɐ* does indeed still markedly outnumber *o* but only in the proportion three to one. The use of *e* rather than *i* as a final vowel (as for instance *henne* 50, *missere* 60, *hlátre* 132, normalized in the present edition to *henni* etc.) is also much more frequent in *Hávamál*: though occupying only a tenth of the ms, it has almost a third of the examples. Some of these points (to which Lindblad adds a good many others) may not seem very weighty taken alone, but cumulatively they make it virtually certain that *Hávamál* was not transmitted in conjunction with any of the other poems in the Eddaic collection and joined them in the ms tradition only at a late stage, very possibly indeed only in CR itself. Now this is a very satisfying conclusion, since in content too *Hávamál* stands somewhat apart from the rest of the Edda: in the customary division, already implied in the ms itself, into mythological poems (or poems of the gods) on the one hand and heroic poems on the other, *Hávamál* must of course be placed in the former group and yet does not belong there very happily, for the great bulk of its subject-matter is secular and has a mundane and everyday spirit alien to that of the other mythological poems.

In the present edition the orthography has been normalized and modern conventions of punctuation, word-division and capitalization have been introduced. The orthography of the textual footnotes has, as a rule, been normalized also, though occasionally, as in the note on st. 60, it has been necessary to present the exact spelling of the ms. A diplomatic transcript can be found in the facsimile of CR edited by L. F. A. Wimmer and Finnur Jónsson, published at Copenhagen in 1891.

II CONTENTS AND COMPOSITION

The student who meets *Hávamál* for the first time may well find it a confusing, even bewildering, work. A great deal of it — most of the first 95 strophes, and 112 to 137 — is essentially occupied in giving advice (by means of precepts, gnomic remarks and illustrative examples) on how a man should conduct himself in this world. But between 96 and 110 the god Óðinn relates, in the first person, two tales of his fortunes in love, whose relation to the remainder of the poem is (to put it no stronger) not immediately apparent; 138-145, which seem particularly disjointed, mainly deal with runes and the rituals of pagan sacrifice, and 146-163 is a numbered sequence in which the speaker lists eighteen spells which he says he knows, and states what each of them is good for. Even within the long initial series of strophes on conduct, the train of thought is by no means always clear from one passage to the next, sometimes suggesting (to some modern scholars, at any rate) that the strophes have not been preserved in their original order, or that some have been interpolated and others lost; there are also strophes where the second half does not seem to follow very intelligibly from the first (e.g. 8, 28, 30, 63) and these have accordingly been suspected of some confusion or corruption. Metrically too the poem appears disordered in places: most of it is in *ljóðaháttr*, but *málaháttr* appears sporadically, at 73 and 144 for instance. St. 80 to 90 are especially irregular: 80 is not in any recognizable metre at all, 81-3 are in *málaháttr*, 84 is in *ljóðaháttr* (this is the strophe whose second half is quoted as a 'ditty' in *Fóstbrœðra saga*), 85-7 are twenty continuous lines of *málaháttr*, which would seem to be directly carried on in 89-90, also in *málaháttr*; 88, which is in *ljóðaháttr*, might appear to have been interpolated into this unbroken sequence but nevertheless, as our text stands, contains the verb on which all the datives of 85-7 are dependent. Even more chaotic are strophes 141 to 145: 141 begins as *ljóðaháttr* but ends irregularly, 142 and 143 do not constitute recognized strophe-forms at all, 144 is in *málaháttr*, and 145 begins as *ljóðaháttr* but ends in four lines of *fornyrðislag*. Or consider 137, which begins as *ljóðaháttr*, then passes into *málaháttr* and concludes with what looks like a *ljóðaháttr* 'full line'.[1] As for the *ljóðaháttr* strophes themselves, most of them are six lines long, but a number have nine lines (e.g. 6, 27, 102, 103), two (65 and 147) have only three (probably half the strophe has been lost in these instances), and others again have seven lines (e.g. 1, 61, 74, 109, 146, 149). Some editors have tried to restore uniformity by denouncing portions of the seven or nine-line strophes as interpolated, but some at least of the seven-line strophes (e.g. 105 and 155) are plainly examples of the sub-type of *ljóðaháttr* which Snorri in his Edda calls *galdralag*, characterized by parallelism and near-repetition, and in fact variation in strophe-length is typical of poems in *ljóðaháttr*, as is well exemplified elsewhere in the Elder Edda.

Hávamál opens with the arrival of a traveller at a farm. Cold and hungry from his journey over the mountain, he needs food and warmth, a wash and dry clothing, a kindly welcome and unhurried conversation. But not only a host has duties, there are things a guest too must remember: a traveller must have his wits about him in someone else's house ('at home everything is easy'); he must be watchful, ever on the alert, careful not to make a fool of himself by bragging talk; few words are best. Drunkenness is a ready trap: over ale-feasts hovers the 'heron of forgetfulness', in whose feathers 'I was fettered in the homestead of Gunnlǫð; I became drunk, extremely drunk, at the house of the wise Fjalarr'. Here, in st. 13-14, for the first time in the poem the pronoun *ek* appears, and the reference to Gunnlǫð shows that the speaker must be Óðinn, whose dealings with her are described more fully later in the poem (and in Snorri's Edda). After this little digression, the poet resumes his observations on conduct; most of the strophes still relate to the position of a guest in a strange house, or at any rate of a man in the company of his fellows (in one case, in st. 25, at the *þing*) whose scorn he must avoid arousing through gluttony, intoxication, reckless loquacity, sullen unsociability, picking on someone as a butt, and so on. Not all the strophes, however, presuppose this situation but offer more general advice (15, 16, 23) and after st. 35 the specific scene of a guest in another man's house is lost sight of, though it reappears sporadically, particularly at 66-7, and indeed some other strophes would also fit well enough into the 'guest-sequence' (e.g. 39, 57, 62-4). The poet now goes on

---

[1] The terminology used by scholars in describing *ljóðaháttr* is not always consistent. I speak of the lines which alliterate in themselves as 'full lines' and of each pair of lines which alliterate with each other as a 'long line'. Thus, in a normal six-line strophe, 3 and 6 are full lines, and 1 and 2 make one long line, as do 4 and 5.

to speak of friendship; one should cultivate one's friends with frequent visits and the exchange of gifts (41-4); the lot of a solitary man is wretched (47, 50). But untrustworthiness and falsehood you should repay with lies and deceit (45-6). It is better to be no more than moderately wise; a very wise man is seldom happy (54-6). After further miscellaneous advice we reach a series of strophes where the blessings of being alive are enumerated: a man may be lame but he can ride a horse, he may be deaf but he can fight; a corpse is no good to anybody (68-71). Then, after a few more strophes of variegated and partly obscure observations, come the celebrated lines in 76-7: cattle die, kinsmen die, one dies oneself, but what remains eternal is renown, a man's reputation. In all these strophes of precept and observation, the first person pronoun appears here and there (39, 47, 49, 66-7, 70, 73, 77) but not now identifiable with Óðinn or indeed with anybody in particular: it is simply the man of experience speaking in his own person.

76-7 are felt by many readers to form a climax to the 'gnomic' part of *Hávamál*, but nevertheless a further couple of strophes very similar to what has gone before follow (78-9). Next comes a strophe on runes (80), wholly out of context and somewhat obscure in itself, and then nine strophes, mostly in a different metre, taken up with lists of, first, suitable times and places to perform various actions and, second, things or persons that are not to be trusted (81-9). This leads into a series of reflections on the mutual faithlessness of the sexes and the irresistible power of love (90-5), and these themes are then illustrated by a tale where the speaker describes, in the first person, his deception by the woman he loved, the daughter (or possibly wife) of Billingr (96-102). This story is not known from any other source, but st. 98 identifies the narrator as Óðinn. After one strophe (103) of gnomic remarks comes a second tale of deception in love (104-10), but this time it is Óðinn who deceives the woman, Gunnlǫð, whose love for him he exploited to win the mead. Like the preceding tale, this too is narrated by Óðinn himself, though rather oddly it passes into the third person in the last two strophes.

A new section seems to begin at 111; so at least the scribe thought, who provided it with an extra-large capital initial. In this strophe the speaker proclaims, in grandiloquent if somewhat mysterious language, that the time has come to chant from the chair of the sage (*þulr*); silent himself, he heard, in the hall of Hávi, talk of runes, and counsels too, which he will now pass on. Then come 26 strophes (112-37), most of which consist of a four-line formula in which a certain Loddfáfnir is recommended to take heed of advice, followed by three or more lines in which the advice is stated. Who this Loddfáfnir can be is unknown to us: he is mentioned nowhere outside the poem. As for the advice itself, much of it is of the same general character as that offered in the first 80 or so strophes, though there are differences too, as we shall remark below. After the last of these Loddfáfnir strophes, an exceptionally long one listing medical remedies, the scribe indicates another new section with a large capital initial: here (138-41) Óðinn describes how he hung for nine days and nights 'on the windy tree', offered up to Óðinn, 'myself to myself', and won mystical wisdom. Four strophes follow (142-5), speaking in dark terms of runes and sacrificial rituals, and these are apparently *not* spoken by Óðinn, since he is mentioned in the third person, whether under his own name (143) or under pseudonyms for him (*fimbulþulr, Hroptr, Þundr*); so who the *ek* of 143 can be is obscure. Then (146-63) come eighteen strophes listing by number eighteen spells of which the speaker claims mastery, describing for what purpose each is to be used (but the spells themselves are not quoted). The *ek* here is not explicitly identified, but is evidently Óðinn: Snorri certainly understood it so (in the passages in *Ynglinga saga* ch. 6-7), and the powers which the speaker claims accord well with Óðinn as depicted in Old Norse literature generally. In the penultimate strophe in this section (162) Loddfáfnir, who has not been heard of since 137, suddenly reappears briefly and strangely. Then comes the final strophe of the poem (164): the words of Hávi, it says, have now been chanted in the hall of Hávi; good fortune to him who chanted them, to him who knows them, to those who listened!

It is inconceivable that these 164 strophes were originally composed as one poem: even if, *per impossibile*, they had been, a work so incoherent, so lacking in any evident thread of exposition, could not have been orally transmitted (over, in all probability, a fairly considerable stretch of time) without suffering a good deal of involuntary rearrangement and disruption. Plainly, what we have to do with is a conglomeration, a compilation of (mostly) didactic and gnomic matter brought together by a scribe (or 'editor') at a fairly late stage in the transmission — not, however, the scribe of CR itself (in view of Lindblad's findings) but a predecessor two or three stages further back in the ms tradition. The existing poem falls fairly clearly into several sections; the scribe himself, as we have noted, indicated breaks at 111 and 138, and, from the seventeenth century on, the Icelandic copyists who produced paper mss of the poem (all derived, ultimately, from CR[2]) marked off certain portions by inserting sub-headings: *Loddfáfnismál*, *Rúnatal* (or *Rúnaþáttur*); the name *Ljóðatal*, now generally used for 146-63, was first applied by Müllenhoff in the nineteenth century. Müllenhoff 250-88 was also first to recognize six more or less distinct segments, a division followed in principle by most subsequent scholars. They are:

I   Gnomic verses, covering the first 79 strophes or so.
II   Óðinn's adventure with *Billings mær*, running from 95 (or earlier?) to 102.
III   Óðinn's adventure with Gunnlǫð, from 104 (or 103?) to 110.
IV   *Loddfáfnismál*: 111 (or 112) to 137.
V   *Rúnatal*: 138-45.
VI   *Ljóðatal*: 146-63.

The boundaries between these segments are not all clear-cut, and some strophes seem to fall outside these divisions altogether. This applies particularly from about st. 80 to about st. 94: it is not entirely apparent, first of all, where the long gnomic segment ends or, secondly, where Óðinn's first love-adventure starts, for 91-4, and 84 as well, could be considered part of it, but they could also be independent gnomic observations of a general nature. The *málaháttr* st. 81-90 must surely be originally independent, yet they are interrupted by 84 and (especially curiously since it has been enmeshed in the grammatical structure of the *málaháttr* lines) by 88. There is st. 80 as well, which does not seem to belong anywhere here. Again, it is far from certain that the sonorous 111 can really have been originally composed to introduce the rather commonplace maxims of *Loddfáfnismál*; while *Rúnatal* is surely too incoherent, both in content and in metre, to have constituted one unit on its own from the start.

We should not, then, be justified in thinking of *Hávamál* as a more or less mechanical stringing together of some half-dozen distinct poems; it would come nearer the truth to say that, in the text as we now have it, we can glimpse the half-submerged hulks of such poems.

We shall now consider each of the 'segments' in turn.

---

[2] Note, however, Faulkes 88, who suggests that certain variant readings in *Hávamál* shared by two seventeenth-century paper mss and the first printed edition (by P. H. Resen, Copenhagen 1655) may possibly testify to contamination of the

III THE GNOMIC POEM

The primary question here is whether this was ever a real poem at all, a conscious original composition as one unit with a definite plan, or whether it is merely an anthology of already existing strophes, a heaping-up, as Schneider 77 put it, of ancient heathen lore from many centuries. Scholars have found it hard to come to a decision on this; it is instructive to find Professor Wessén writing in 1946 of 'the proverb poem proper, which itself, of course, in no way constitutes a unified poem but is rather a collection of strophes and strophe-sequences in the same metre and with the same sort of gnomic content' and then, thirteen years later, to come upon him stating the exact opposite: '*Hávamál* I is not really the work of an editor, a collection of strophes and strophe-groups of diverse origin, but, by and large, a unified work.'[3] Ultimately, no doubt, each reader has to decide this issue for himself, from the impression the strophes make on him, but at any rate it cannot be denied that a poem like *Málsháttakvæði*, which certainly is, indeed explicitly states itself to be, a 'heaping-up' of pre-existing proverbial matter, does seem very different from our Gnomic Poem.[4] There is, too, a certain unity in the tone and in the social and cultural background implied: that is, we cannot — in my view — assert that, while certain strophes must be pagan, certain others must be post-conversion, or that, if some were assuredly composed in Norway, others just as assuredly were composed in Iceland, or that some reflect a primitive and superstitious and others a sceptical and sophisticated outlook, or that some are evidently aimed at a different social class from others. A syntactical point also deserves mention here. In a poem concerned with giving advice one would naturally expect to find a good many verbs in the imperative mood (just as we do in *Loddfáfnismál*); but in fact there is not a single

CR tradition (to which these texts unquestionably belong) by some other medieval ms still surviving at that date. Faulkes in no way presses the suggestion, and indeed points out that some of the shared variants are clearly the result of misinterpreting scribal corrections in CR.
   [3] '. . . den egentliga ordspråksdikten, som ju själv ingalunda utgör någon enhetlig dikt, utan är en samling av strofer och stroffö1jder i samma versmått och med likartat, gnomiskt innehåll' (Wessén 1, 8). 'Háv. I är icke egentligen ett redaktions-arbete, en samling strofer och strofgrupper av olika ursprung, utan i stort sett ett enhetligt verk' (Wessén 4, 472).
   [4] *Málsháttakvæði* (or *Fornyrðadrápa* — the titles, both meaning 'Proverb Poem', are modern) is printed *Skj.* ii 138-45. It was probably composed by Bjarni Kolbeinsson, bishop of Orkney (died 1223); see Anne Holtsmark 'Bjarne Kolbeinsson og hans forfatterskap' *Edda* 37 (1937) 1-17, esp. 10-14.

imperative in the entire sequence. It is very hard to believe that this would be so if the origins of the strophes were as diverse as Schneider would make them.

Until recently, then, scholars were divided into those who thought that these 79 or so strophes were an original organized poem of some antiquity (albeit somewhat disrupted, perhaps, in CR) and those who thought them a mere anthology of traditional strophes collected and rather perfunctorily arranged by an editor, probably not very long before CR itself was written. But the most recent writer on this point, Professor Klaus von See, has taken a novel stand by combining elements of both views: the poem does indeed possess very considerable coherence of thought and design, far greater in fact (he argues at length) than any previous scholar has given it credit for; but this is not because it is an ancient original composition. On the contrary, this appearance of unity is the work of the thirteenth-century editor, who (like Schneider's editor) was bringing together 'a diffuse mass of strophes and strophe-sequences . . . from very different periods' but (very unlike Schneider's editor) was a deliberate artist who created a harmonious and coherent design by selection and arrangement and by himself composing strophes to smooth the transitions from one theme to the next. Some twenty strophes are regarded as the editor's own composition, though not all of these occur in the Gnomic Poem, since von See sees this same editor as having fused his collection of gnomes with the later sections of *Hávamál* (already existing in, by and large, their extant shape) so as to create one unified poem with an overall meaningful structure: the progressive revelation, by Óðinn to a disciple, of his own wisdom and power, ascending through the rules of everyday life through the mythical episodes to the mysteries of runes, cult and magic. (See von See 3, with critiques by Page, Wilson, de Boor and Beyschlag 2, and reply by von See 4.)

To the present writer, this view of the Gnomic Poem is as little convincing as Schneider's, though for the opposite reason: if it has too much coherence to be a mere anthology, it has at the same time too little for us to accept it as the conscious design of an editor working only some twenty years (as von See believes) before the Codex Regius was written. Where the subject-matter is so little abstruse as in the case of the Gnomic Poem, there is something initially suspect about an alleged unity which only an elaborate argument can bring to light. Also, the details of von See's argument are often unpersuasive: much of the postulated structure depends on supposed verbal echoes from one strophe to another, so that, for instance, *gott* in 12 (twice) is taken to refer back to *betri* in 10 and 11, and the occurrence of *ljúfr* and *leiðr* in 35 and again in 40 is alleged to demonstrate that 40 was composed by the editor, under the influence of 35. Yet, for all his readiness to resort to considerations as fine-drawn as these, von See has to make so many concessions as to suggest that the carefully designed composition he postulates is actually a mirage. He admits that 'der Kompositionswille des Redaktors' is 'oft nicht sehr geschickt und schwer durchschaubar' and that 'die ganze Komposition' is 'locker'; he concedes that the motivation he can provide for the extant succession of the strophes is 'gelegentlich nur schwache'; and for some strophes, where even this resource fails, he is driven to conjecture that the editor was given to inserting strophes and gnomes 'die nicht unmittelbar dazugehören und die er dennoch verwerten will, als Anhängsel und Einschübe dort unter, wo sie am besten passen' (quotations from von See 4, 102-4).

All in all, it seems safest to discern an original planned poem of some age behind these 79 or so strophes; if in places it seems rambling or disjointed, or to be returning to themes already dealt with earlier, this is explained easily enough as the consequence of confusion in oral transmission. Where there is no strong narrative thread to hold a poem together, strophes can very well be remembered in the wrong order, or left out entirely, and alien strophes can be interpolated, whether through the faulty memory of some reciter or as conscious additions. But to admit the likelihood that our text has been affected in these ways by no means implies that there is much profit in trying to restore it to its supposed original shape; though a number of scholars have indeed made just that attempt. Of the first 80 strophes, Müllenhoff, for instance, expelled 28 (four of them for no other reason than that they interfered with his belief that the Gnomic Poem falls into sections of ten strophes each) and Finnur Jónsson 23 (and even so felt obliged to postulate some losses and one displacement). Heusler contented himself with expelling only ten, and proposed instead a reshuffling of the strophes of a very far-going kind (his order runs, in part, 7, 18, 10, 11, 17, 19, 20, 21, 33, 63/1-3, 57, 28; see Heusler 2). Even more radical was the treatment imposed in the *Corpus Poeticum Boreale*, whose editors print a poem of 83 strophes which they call 'The Guest's Wisdom', consisting essentially of our Gnomic Poem, albeit very much rearranged (the concluding eleven strophes, for instance, run 63, 59, 58, 35, 38, 1, 33, 61, 6, 30, 40) with a good many strophes from later parts of *Hávamál* stirred in at various points: 84, 91-5 (though not in that order), 103, the two halves of 124 at different places, the second half of 133, the third line of 145. Other strophes have been allotted elsewhere: 44-6 are now to be found in *Loddfáfnismál*, 12-14 join (most of) 96-110 to form 'Woden's Love-Lessons', 73-4 are added to the other *málaháttr* verses and four stray lines from another ms to make the 'Song of Saws', and 78 finds itself despatched along with 118 and the second half of 70 (this last doing double duty, since it appears in 'The Guest's Wisdom' as well) to join a number of strophes extracted from *Sólarljóð* to compose a work entitled 'The Christian's Wisdom'. All this reconstruction, the editors cautiously remind us, 'can be no more than approximative'.

How the original poems could ever have become so disarranged neither Heusler nor the editors of CPB are able to explain. But Professor Ivar Lindquist, tackling the problem 'auf synthetischem Wege', had an answer: in its primal state, he tells us, *Hávamál* was a work in which a novice is initiated into Óðinn's wisdom. But the ms fell into the hands of a Christian zealot who, being interested in antiquity, abstained from destroying it but felt it his duty to emasculate this dangerous relic of paganism by jumbling it up into unrecognizability. Lindquist thereupon unjumbles it for us. Strophes containing *ek* are gathered up and put together as 'Block A': this is Óðinn addressing the visiting initiand. Some time later Óðinn returns the visit: this is 'Block B', where Óðinn vouchsafes impersonal information and avoids *ek*; most of our Gnomic Poem comes here. These blocks compose the *Ancient Hávamál*. Some 27 strophes, mostly from *Loddfáfnismál*, are left over: this is a different poem, the *Later Hávamál*. The entire text is heavily emended and is filled out with lines and strophes drawn from *Flóvents saga, Háttalykill, Gautreks saga, Heiðreks saga* etc. and with plentiful matter of Lindquist's own composition (including bad grammar and non-existent words). The monograph in which these insights are presented runs to nearly three hundred pages and appeared in 1956 in an official series of the University of Lund (Lindquist 3).

It is surely self-evident that comprehensive remodellings of the poem, which in any case are all wildly divergent, are too speculative to lead anywhere, and in fact they scarcely ever seem to convince anyone apart from their own authors. We have, in other words, no practical alternative to sticking, at any rate by and large, to the CR text. Even the matter of where exactly the Gnomic Poem ends is best left an open question: 76-7 would certainly form an admirable conclusion, but 78 sounds very much like part of the the Poem and so (unless one wishes to argue that relations between the sexes are a theme alien to it) do 79, 84 and perhaps 91-5. St. 103 could also very well have originally belonged to it.

Though preserved only in an Icelandic ms, the Gnomic Poem is clearly of Norwegian origin. This is shown by the references to cremation (71, and possibly also in 70), *bautarsteinar* (72), the use of bark for roofing (60), the wolf (58), the *þjóðann* (15), the solitary fir-tree (50) which stands *þorpi á* (whatever *þorp* means here, it is a word never used of Icelandic conditions): all these are unknown in Iceland. It may also be significant that the obscure *á brǫndum* (2) can perhaps best be explained by evidence from Norwegian rural life in later times, and the presence of a few verbs not otherwise recorded in Old Norse but which have parallels in modern Norwegian dialect points the same way: *kópa* (17 — though this is found occasionally in modern Icelandic), *glissa* (31), *glama* (31); and see also the Commentary on *snópa* (33) and *snapa* (62). The adjective *neiss* (49) is perhaps only Norwegian; if *dauðr* in 70 is taken to be a noun, this too has clear parallels only in Norwegian, and the use of *sær* to mean 'lake', which is probably the sense it bears in 53, is alien to Icelandic usage but evidently existed in Norway in pre-literary times, since it is found there in place-names.

The view generally held by scholars has been that the Gnomic Poem is purely heathen: 'there is no trace of Christianity', in Jón Helgason's words.[5] True, the only *explicitly* heathen allusions are those to cremation (the brief reference to Óðinn's adventure with Gunnlǫð cannot be counted, since tales of the pagan gods continued to be told for centuries after the Conversion, as Snorri's Edda shows, and in any case the strophes are very likely interpolated). But *bautarsteinar* also belong to the pre-Christian era, and a dating to that period is further supported by what appears to be an echo of st. 76-7 in the final strophe of *Hákonarmál*, an elegy on the Norwegian king, Hákon the Good, mortally wounded in battle c. 960, some forty years before the Conversion. (That it is the *final* strophe has been used to support the view that 76-7 were once, too, the final strophes of a poem.) This strophe runs (*Skj*. i 60):

       Deyr fé,
       deyja frændr,
       eyðisk land ok láð;

---

[5] 'Der findes ingen spor af kristendom' (Jón Helgason 2, 43).

síz Hákon fór
með heiðin goð,
mǫrg er þjóð of þéuð.

That there is a direct connection between these lines and the Gnomic Poem is not indeed absolutely certain, since *deyr fé, deyja frændr* could conceivably be a traditional alliterating cliché used independently in the two poems, but since the author of *Hákonarmál*, Eyvindr skáldaspillir, was notorious for plagiarism, as his nickname shows and as is plainly evidenced elsewhere in his work, the most natural view is that this is simply one of Eyvindr's borrowings (to suggest that, on the contrary, *Hávamál* borrowed from Eyvindr seems forced — so von See 3, 49). If this is accepted, the Gnomic Poem must antedate 960.[6]

This attribution of the poem to pagan times has led many scholars to value it highly as giving us an unadulterated view of ancient Nordic, or Germanic, life and values; as Hans Kuhn 1, 62 put it, 'es ist für die germanische Kultur- und Sittengeschichte von überragender Bedeutung, denn es ist nicht nur unberührt bodenständig, sondern auch das einzige grössere Denkmal rein bäuerlichen germanisehen Denkens' (cp. e.g. Jón Helgason 1, 30 and Finnur Jónsson 3, 230 for similar sentiments). This view of the poem as purely native and heathen has, however, been challenged sporadically, especially in recent years, by claims that some of the strophes betray Biblical or Classical influences, or can be paralleled by and therefore perhaps derive from medieval proverbs in the Continental vernaculars. Nore Hagman, for instance, brought together numerous supposed similarities with Ecclesiasticus as evidence that this Apocryphal text might have influenced *Hávamál*. But the examples adduced are fairly unimpressive, being only of a loose and general character, and are mostly not really saying the same thing at all: 'Better is the life of a poor man under a shelter of logs than sumptuous fare in another man's house' (Ecclus. 29.22) is quite different from 'a home of one's own, even a very modest one, is at any rate better than begging', which is the gist of *Hávamál* 36, and yet this is probably the closest of Hagman's

---

[o] A similar antedating is implied by the view (von See 1) that st. 17, 20 and 25 in Egill's *Sonatorrek* (c. 960) echo *Hávamál* 72, 22 and 15 respectively. (Von See can presumably only mean that these particular strophes antedate c. 960, since, as we saw, he does not believe that the Gnomic Poem ever existed as such.) Magnus Olsen, *Edda- og Skaldekvad* IV (Oslo 1962) 49, thought the use of *orðstírr* in Egill's *Hǫfuðlausn* echoed *Hávamál* 76.

parallels (as von See 4, 96 remarks, 'frappierend . . . das beste Beispiel'). Again, Régis Boyer detected striking resemblances with Proverbs and Ecclesiastes, all the more significant, he said, because such similarities are lacking for other books of Biblical wisdom such as Ecclesiasticus (Boyer 227; Hagman's article is absent from his otherwise comprehensive bibliography). But here too the parallels are not at all close, as when Proverbs 27.17 'Iron sharpeneth iron; so a man sharpeneth the countenance of his friend' is connected with st. 57, and sometimes they are not parallels at all, as when Proverbs 25.21 'If thine enemy be hungry, give him bread to eat; and if he be thirsty, give him water to drink' is associated with st. 3-4. It is true that both Proverbs and the Gnomic Poem lay stress on the connection between foolishness and loquacity; but need this be more than a coincidence? After all, the Book of Proverbs contains over eight hundred verses, practically all of them gnomic remarks based on observation and experience of life in a materially simple society; it would surely be startling if chance resemblances with our Gnomic Poem did *not* occur here and there.

Occasional derivation from Classical writers has also been alleged. Roland Köhne noted that in the *De Amicitia* Cicero speaks of a man's 'so mingling his mind with another's as almost to make the two of them one'[7] and wondered if this might be the ultimate source of st. 44 with its *geði . . . blanda*, and Rolf Pipping suggested that st. 21 could descend from Seneca, who in one of his letters draws a similar moralizing contrast between beasts, who know when they have eaten enough, and men, who do not, and in another letter actually uses the phrase *stomachi sui non nosse mensuram* in censuring gluttony (though not, on this occasion, in contrast to the habits of the beasts); this answers closely to the *kann ævagi síns um mál maga* of our poem.

St. 21 had earlier been assigned to a Biblical origin by Samuel Singer, who referred to Isaiah 1.3 and Jeremiah 8.7, where men and beasts are compared, to the former's disadvantage, though not in any connection with over-eating. In a section on early Germanic proverbial lore in his *Sprichwörter des Mittelalters* Singer adduces parallels, from the Scriptures and from medieval Latin and vernacular sources, to fifteen strophes, or portions of strophes, in our Gnomic Poem and assumes a genetic connection (though in three of the fifteen instances he thinks Norse culture may be the donor

---

[7] Köhne 1, 129. Cicero's remark, in *De Amicitia* 81, runs '. . . quanto id magis in homine fit natura, qui et se ipse diligit et alterum anquirit, cuius animum ita cum suo misceat, ut efficiat paene unum ex duobus'.

rather than the recipient).[8] Here once more the parallels are mostly of a fairly broad nature, and many of the sentiments in question are such as one might well suppose could arise spontaneously in different societies by anyone reflecting on the human lot. There is, too, one general consideration which should induce caution in approaching theories of widespread extra-Nordic influence on our poem. *Hávamál*, and not least the Gnomic Poem, is riddled with obseurities. Occasionally this is because a word is of uncertain meaning, or because the text is evidently corrupt; more often, though, the difficulty lies not so much in translating the text as in deciding what the drift of the strophe is supposed to be, what exact point the poet is seeking to make. Now, if *Hávamál* were significantly dependent on foreign sources, such as the Bible or medieval Continental matter, one might reasonably expect to find enlightenment in some, at least, of these difficulties by turning to these foreign sources; but in fact one finds such help only (as it seems to me) in two cases: in the 'wooden men' of st. 49 and in the first line (*tveir ro eins herjar*) of st. 73. This suggests that extra-Nordic influences have been at most marginal and that the great bulk of the poem is of native inspiration.

This last consideration can also be employed against the most recent, and perhaps most comprehensive, attempt to detach the Gnomic Poem from native heathen antiquity and associate it instead with the learned medieval tradition deriving from Scriptural and Classical sources. This is that of von See; as we have already seen, he does not believe that the Gnomic Poem existed as such until *Hávamál* was compiled by an editor in the mid-thirteenth century and, though he speaks of the gnomic strophes as being of very different ages, the whole tendency of his argument in practice is to detect as many links as he can with the vocabulary and outlook characteristic of twelfth- and thirteenth-century Christian moralizing (von See 2 and 4). A prominent part in his reasoning is played by the *Disticha Catonis*. This compendium of Latin verse maxims on conduct, dating perhaps from the third century A.D., was greatly celebrated in the Middle Ages and was widely translated into the vernaculars; in Icelandic there is a very free rendering, the *Hugsvinnsmál*, in 148 *ljóðaháttr* strophes, probably composed in the thirteenth century (I follow the strophe-number-

---

[8] Some of Singer's instances are noted in the Commentary. For a recent approach along somewhat similar lines see Köhne 2, who adduces a number of Middle High German parallels which reflect, he maintains, influence on *Hávamál* from medieval German proverb poetry and popular wisdom.

ing of *Skj.* ii 185 ff.). There are a number of verbal similarities between this work and *Hávamál* and, though they are in fact not very numerous and were dismissed by Gering (2, VIII note 3) as mere coincidences, the view usually taken by scholars has been that *Hugsvinnsmál* is consciously echoing *Hávamál* in these places.[9] Von See however maintains that the influence was in the reverse direction (he further believes that the *Disticha* also influenced *Hávamál* directly, though the two or three specific instances adduced are scarcely compelling). Now a comparison of the Gnomic Poem with *Hugsvinnsmál* is indeed instructive, but not for the reasons suggested by von See. What *Hugsvinnsmál* shows us is what a thirteenth-century Icelandic poet, working in the learned-clerical tradition, produced when he set out to compose a didactic poem on conduct; and the result is nothing at all like *Hávamál*. In the first place, *Hugsvinnsmál* (even though rendering a pagan Latin original) is soaked in allusions to Christian beliefs and ethics: God, *guð*, is mentioned repeatedly, 'Cato' is described as *heiðinn*, and pagan sacrifices are condemned; you do not win *sálubót* by slaughtering animals (118), for God prefers the scent of incense (138); you should be pure of life, *hreinlífr* (5), and believe in and love God the highest with a pure heart (17); there are references to 'heavenly things', to sin, and to atoning for one's sins by self-chastisement (*meinlæti* 139); you should renounce hatred, love your father and mother, let the poor profit from your money, urge your friend to do good, be merciful to your slaves and remember that they have the same earthly nature as the son of a prince; death is the end of ill (contrast that with the thoroughly pagan sentiment of *Hávamál* 71: 'it is better to be blind than to be cremated; a corpse is no good to anyone'). It should also be noted that books are referred to several times; advice for most things can be found *á fornum bókum* (57). How can we explain the total absence of allusions of this kind in the Gnomic Poem, if von See is right in attributing it, in a significant degree, to this period and to the learned-clerical tradition? And, in the second place, *Hugsvinnsmál* can be read straight through without any real difficulty of interpretation: its vocabulary is commonplace, not to say meagre, and the text is free of any obscurity beyond the most

---

[9] E. Noreen 1, 14f., drew up a list of eleven apparent echoes (only six of them in the Gnomic Poem); some of them are not very striking, but others seem to imply some real connection. Strangely, Noreen omits the most conspicuous resemblance: *af hyggjandi sinni skyldit maðr hrœsinn vera* (*Hugsv.* 73), which, with *skylit*, and *at* for *af*, is also in *Hávamál* 6.

trivial. The contrast with the Gnomic Poem could scarcely be sharper. Further, if so much of the Gnomic Poem is due to the Icelandic thirteenth century, why is all the distinctive local colouring Norwegian and not Icelandic? The only natural conclusion is that von See is mistaken and that the traditional view of the Gnomic Poem as essentially pagan, Norwegian and archaic is correct.[10]

The qualities counselled in the Gnomic Poem are moderation, sobriety, generosity, intelligence and above all prudence, caution, silent watchfulness. Much emphasis is laid on the importance of travel and of social intercourse in developing the mind. None of this will seem entirely strange to the reader who comes to *Hávamál* from the Icelandic Family Sagas, but he will nevertheless be struck by two substantial differences. First, the Gnomic Poem has very little to say of the heroic: there are no references to feuds or to the duty of vengeance, and only the most casual and passing allusions to weapons and fighting. St. 15 says that the 'son of a ruler' should be 'silent, thoughtful and bold in fighting', 16 mentions *víg* and *geirar*, warfare and spears, 38 advises one never to go out without one's weapons, 41 suggests weapons and garments as suitable gifts for friends to exchange, and 58 points out that it is necessary to rise early if you wish to take another man's money or life. Secondly, the *ætt*, the family, one's kinsmen, are barely mentioned at all: only st. 72 remarks that a son, a descendant, is the sole person likely to raise a stone to one's memory after one's death, and *frændr* are spoken of in passing in 69 and in the celebrated formula of 76-7. Conversely, much stress is laid on friendship. The dominant image in the Gnomic Poem, the implied recipient of the advice proffered, is that of the solitary, a man with no apparent attachments of family or kin, often travelling alone, playing no part in the social or political structure of the community (the *þing* is mentioned a couple of times, at 25 and 61, a ruler, *þjóðann*, once, at 15). Yet if, as has so often been believed, the

---

[10] Nothing in Hermann Pálsson's recent study *Áhrif Hugsvinnsmála á aðrar fornbókmenntir* (1985) weakens these arguments. He regards *Hávamál* and *Hugsvinnsmál* as contemporary creations from about 1150, which influenced each other reciprocally. A large number of supposed points of contact is adduced, the great majority of which concern alleged resemblances of sentiment rather than of wording (e.g. *Háv.* 20 and *Hugsv.* 83 both warn against gluttony; *Háv.* 78 says that rich men may be reduced to beggary, while *Hugsv.* 34 says that people may be unhappy though rich). Such similarities of wording as Hermann cites often seem to reflect no more than that both poems are written in the same language (e.g. *Háv.* 144 and *Hugsv.* 46 both have *biðja*, while *Háv.* 28 and *Hugsv.* 65 both have *leyna*; but in neither instance is there any resemblance whatever in the context).

poem is rooted in the world of the Norwegian smallholder, where the family lived on the ancestral farm from generation to generation, why does it simply ignore the *ætt*, so centrally present in the sagas and laws? And is it not also remarkable that there is no trace of the gradations of the class system of the Norwegian laws, with their *konungr, jarl, hǫlðr, lendr maðr* and so on, nor any trace either of superstition, of cult and ritual, of the gods who watched over the ancestral fields? To meet this difficulty, Sigurður Nordal (1, 152-3 and 3, 174-6) suggested that the poem mirrors, not the ancient world of the small farmer, but the new world of the Viking Age where men tore up their ancestral roots and abandoned their kin and their home-bound gods, and wandered at large over the northern hemisphere, free-ranging equals, knowing no tie but that of comradeship. Instead of the *ætt*, the *frændr*, we have the friend, the comrade: 'with half a loaf and a tilted bowl I got myself a comrade, *fekk ek mér félaga*' says st. 52, using the word which occurs repeatedly in runic memorials for a comrade in the Viking Age, as for example on the Sjörup stone: 'Saxi erected this stone in memory of Ásbjǫrn his comrade, *asbiurn sin filaga*, son of Tóki. He did not flee at Uppsala, but smote so long as he had a weapon'.[11] Nordal's hypothesis does, it is true, entail some difficulties of its own. The travelling on which the Gnomic Poem lays so much stress is all inland, and much of it plainly on foot; only the rather obscure st. 74 contains references to journeying by ship, and even here it is almost certainly sailing in coastal fjords rather than ocean voyaging that is in question. Foreign travel, the life of the warrior, how to behave at the king's court: these are conspicuously absent. So it is not Viking life itself, in the strict sense, which the poem reflects, but the life of Norway in a period tinged by the individualism and the loosening of inherited sanctities that the Viking expansion brought in its train.

Some scholars have spoken of the Gnomic Poem as a 'Proverb Poem' (*Spruchgedicht, Ordspråksdikt*), as though it were primarily a collection of pre-existing proverbs. Samuel Singer, as we have already seen, tried to detect parallels in extra-Nordic proverbial lore, from which he thought *Hávamál*'s gnomes were in not a few cases derived, and other investigators, leaving aside the question of *foreign* origin, have picked out lines or pairs of lines which they

---

[11] DR nr 279; Moltke 294. See also Jansson 65, who quotes another instance from the island of Berezanj in the Black Sea: 'Grani made this stone cist in memory of Karl his comrade [or partner]' — *iftir kal filaka sin*. On *félagi* as a word characteristic of the Viking Age see M. Olsen *Danske Studier* (1906) 23-4.

thought were ancient proverbs incorporated by the poet in the Gnomic Poem. But how can this ever be known? Certainly there are phrases in the poem which are employed as proverbs elsewhere in Icelandic (down to the present day in some cases), e.g. *sjaldan verðr víti vǫrum* 6, *sjaldan hittir leiðr í lið* 66, but there is always the possibility (to put it no stronger) that *Hávamál* itself is their ultimate source. Heusler, who claimed to identify 35 proverbs in the Gnomic Poem (including eight in strophes he thought interpolated), laid down several criteria for detecting them: they may betray themselves by lacking correct alliteration (as in *bú er betra þótt lítit sé* 35-6) or by fitting awkwardly into the strophe as a whole, so that they produce an anacoluthon (*sjaldan verðr víti vǫrum* 6 is a plausible instance of this) or so that the poet has evidently been obliged to fill out the proverb with vapid additions to complete his metrical strophe (thus Heusler thinks the second half of 12 may be an expansion, and dilution, of a pre-existing proverb *því færa veit er fleira drekkr*). Another criterion is the presence of the phrase in other sources, but here Heusler concedes that this is a strong argument only when the phrase occurs outside the 'Verbreitungsgebiet der eddischen Sittengedichte' (see Heusler 1). But how extensive was that? Both halves of st. 58 appear, in Latin, in Saxo Grammaticus (*c.* 1200); 41/4-5 appear in a closely similar form in a Faroese proverb recorded near the end of the eighteenth century; are these evidence that the Gnomic Poem was quoting ancient proverbs, or do they themselves merely descend ultimately from the Gnomic Poem?

In practice, Heusler seems to have found his criteria somewhat restricted in their helpfulness, and many of the entries on his list are there only because they sound as if they could well have been proverbs, e.g. *dælt er heima hvat* 5, *halr er heima hverr* 36, *glík skulu gjǫld gjǫfum* 46, *hálfr er auðr und hvǫtum* 59, *blindr er betri en brenndr sé* 71. Much the same approach was adopted by Wessén 4, who similarly believed the poet had made use of already existing proverbs, though (not surprisingly) his list by no means wholly coincides with Heusler's. He rejects as doubtful, on rather vague grounds, twelve of Heusler's 35 (e.g. *glík skulu gjǫld gjǫfum* 46, *hálf er ǫld hvar* 53, *mart um dvelr þann er um morgin søfr* 59) and adds a few of his own, such as *sýtir æ glǫggr við gjǫfum* 48, *opt kaupir sér í litlu lof* 52. In the last case, Wessén thought that this (alleged) proverb had provided the starting-point for the strophe, in which the poet exemplified the proverb with an invented anecdote in the first person; he saw the same process at work in 47 (*maðr er manns gaman*), 49 (*neiss er nøkkviðr halr*), 66 (*sjaldan hittir leiðr í lið*), 70 (*ey getr kvikr kú*) and 78 (where the supposed proverb is slightly more concealed: *auðr er valtastr vina*). Clearly, such a process could have taken place; equally clearly, there is no specific evidence that it did.

The whole question is manifestly one where we can do no more than speculate. My own inclination is to be fairly willing to accept that the poet is citing a proverb in those few instances where it occurs in other *old* native sources, or where an anacoluthon does seem to imply that an existing proverb has been dragged in, but otherwise to remain sceptical. But even if we wish to be a good deal more generous than this, the number of proverbs can never become so large as to allow us to speak of a 'Proverb Poem' in a full sense; even Heusler provides an average of fewer than one to every two strophes.

As it has come down to us in CR, the Gnomic Poem is presented as the utterance of Óðinn. This is plain, first, from st. 13, with its first-person reference to the Gunnlǫð story and, second, from the poem's inclusion in the collection which CR entitles *Hávamál*, 'The Words of Hávi': Hávi (on which more below) is certainly a name for Óðinn. But whether the Gnomic Poem was, in its original form, envisaged as proceeding from Óðinn's lips is another question, and one on which scholars are not agreed. Of course, if 13-14 are held to be integral to the Poem, that settles the matter; but the view that they are really a detached fragment of an 'Óðinn-adventure' similar to those in 96-110 and that they have been interpolated into the Gnomic Poem (not without some awkwardness) has enough plausibility to make it risky to rely on this consideration alone. Those who accept the attribution to Óðinn have therefore adduced three further arguments. First, it is said, the poem contains 'the sum of the fruits of human experience'[12] mediated by a speaker who makes it clear that he knows best what kind of understanding and knowledge must avail for human kind, and that his own understanding and knowledge are of a higher and more perfect sort; so he must himself be a being of a higher sort than the human: 'in other words,' writes Finnur Jónsson, 'the speaker must be a god'. And if a god, then Óðinn, for was not Óðinn regarded as the source of all knowledge? 'From him,' says *Ynglinga saga* chs. 6-8, 'they learnt all accomplishments, for he was the first to know them all, and more than anyone else . . . He

[12] 'summen af den menneskelige livserfaring' (Finnur Jónsson 3, 231).

knew how to transform himself into every sort of shape. He spoke so forcefully and fluently that all who listened thought that what he said was alone true . . . His words were all metrical, such as we now call poetry . . . He knew all kinds of runes and spells, and was the first lawgiver . . .' And in other sources he appears repeatedly, now under one pseudonym, now under another, dispensing information or defeating rivals in contests of knowledge, as Gagnráðr in *Vafþrúðnismál*, as Grímnir in *Grímnismál*, as Hnikarr in *Reginsmál*, as Gestumblindi in the riddles of Heiðrekr (in *Heiðreks saga*), almost certainly as Hǫrðr in *Sǫgubrot*.

Secondly, it is pointed out that, in several of these sources, Óðinn dispenses knowledge as a guest who has arrived, disguised, in a stranger's house (*Gestr* is indeed a quite common pseudonym for Óðinn). This is the situation in *Vafþrúðnismál*, in *Grímnismál*, in the Gestumblindi episode. But this, it is argued, is the position in *Hávamál* as well: here too the Gnomic Poem opens with the arrival of a *gestr* in a strange house and then moves on to retail advice and wisdom.

Thirdly, the ethics of the Gnomic Poem are, it is claimed, 'Odinic ethics': self-seeking, cynical, tough-minded, untrusting, unscrupulous. 'Repay falsity with lies' advises st. 45, just as in 110 Óðinn says of himself 'I think that Óðinn has sworn a ring-oath. How should one trust his pledges?'

These arguments are not convincing. In the first place, the knowledge of which Óðinn appears elsewhere as master and dispenser is mystical, magical, mythological; the mundane, even commonplace, counsels of the Gnomic Poem belong to a different world altogether. Secondly, it is far from clear that the guest who arrives at the beginning is supposed to be the speaker of the Gnomic Poem; in *Vafþrúðnismál* and the rest the disguised stranger turns up, displays his esoteric knowledge, and at the end is revealed in his true identity, but this is not at all what happens in our poem. Thirdly, the argument that the Gnomic Poem exhibits Odinic ethics surely exaggerates its unscrupulousness: the speaker is indeed a solitary, whose isolation makes him of necessity sceptical and wary, but there is very little in his recommendations that can be called self-serving or amoral in the sense which the argument requires.

The association of the Gnomic Poem with Óðinn is therefore almost certainly not original. For all that, it lent itself readily to such an association: its concern with knowledge and counsel (however mundane) and with the figure of the untrusting and worldly-wise wanderer easily permitted its incorporation in the

'Words of Hávi' by the later compiler or editor who shaped the text that now exists in CR.

Before leaving the Gnomic Poem, a few words should be said about the eighteen or so strophes that precede the tale of Óðinn and *Billings mær*, which begins, properly speaking, at 96. Whether any of these strophes are to be regarded as part of the Gnomic Poem is, as already remarked, obscure; the theme of sexual love, which is fairly prominent in them, has not previously been touched on in the poem, and there is something to be said for the opinion that their view of woman as faithless and deceitful (note especially st. 84) is alien to the pagan Nordic tradition and reflects the misogynist attitudes of medieval Christianity; this would suggest that they are of later origin than the Gnomic Poem. The strophes in *málaháttr* (81-3, 85-7, 89-90), with their lists of things to do and things to beware of, are reminiscent of the medieval German genre known as the *Priamel* and have for this reason sometimes been regarded as of foreign inspiration. The German *Priamel* itself, however, appears to belong to the very end of the Middle Ages, so it can hardly be the direct source of the form in Norse, and so elementary a poetic mode as a list could arise spontaneously in many different cultures. The emphasis on the untrustworthiness of things has been taken by von See as a Christian theme, 'die Unsicherheit alles Irdischen' (4, 99), thus linking *Hávamál* yet again with the learned-Biblical tradition of the Middle Ages.[13] But mutability becomes a Christian theme only when it is brought into contrast with the security and permanence of Heaven; von See has achieved this contrast by inserting the word *Irdischen*, but there is no warrant for this in the text of the poem. It is going rather far to claim that a piece of advice like 'Don't praise ale until you have drunk it' (81) implants the Christian moral of the transience and unreliability of this poor fleeting life! (This very strophe, as a matter of fact, contains a pagan allusion in what is manifestly a reference to cremation.) As in the Gnomic Poem, the scene implied is Norwegian, or at any rate non-Icelandic: besides the cremation, note the wolf (85), the snake, the bear and the king (86), and the reindeer (90).

IV ÓÐINN'S ADVENTURE WITH BILLINGS MÆR

This story, not recorded elsewhere, is told by Óðinn in the first

---

[13] This view consorts uneasily with von See's belief (1, 28-9) that 89/7-8 influenced Egill's *Sonatorrek* (so also, independently, Einar Ól. Sveinsson 2, 299 note 2). If this is right, these lines must be older than c. 960.

person in st. 96-102. Some of the preceding strophes may also belong to it; indeed, 96 can hardly be the absolute beginning, since its opening word, *þat*, evidently refers back to something that precedes. As the text stands, this can only be 95, but since the story makes it plain that what in fact Óðinn learned to know was the irresistible power of love and the deceitfulness of women, better sense would be obtained if we were to suppose that 84 was designed to precede 96 or (as Finnur Jónsson 3, 235 advocated) that the tale properly consisted of 84, 91, 93 and then 96-102. Conceivably, 79 and 92 also belong to it.

It is difficult to say anything definite about the date of the poem. Paasche put it well back in the pagan period, on the ground that its uncomplimentary view of Óðinn suggested a time earlier than the tenth century, when paganism was fighting for survival, and Finnur Jónsson 3, 235 also gave it a relatively early date, mainly, as it seems, because he believed that the second half of 84 (which he thought was part of the poem) really had been quoted by a thrall in Greenland in the early eleventh century. De Vries 6, 53, on the other hand, remarked that the poem was 'usually' considered an imitation of a medieval comic tale and could therefore be attributed to the Christian period, and von See (4, 97) saw the influence of medieval Christianity's condemnation of fleshly lust in the use of *lǫstr* (98) and *flærð* (102) to characterize Óðinn's relationship with the woman, since these expressions are principally met with in Icelandic Christian contexts.

V ÓÐINN'S ADVENTURE WITH GUNNLǪÐ

This occupies st. 104-10, to which 103 can be taken as an introduction. De Vries (6, 53) seems to be almost alone in sharply differentiating this tale from its predecessor, for, whereas he considered that humorous and 'medieval', he thinks that the Gunnlǫð story is told in a form which 'makes an archaic impression' and that the use of *galdralag* metre (in 105) suggests that the author wished to give his poem an air of ritual solemnity. Most scholars have been struck rather by the similarity in the atmosphere of the two tales and in their structure as well (in that both begin with a general gnomic observation which is then exemplified through an anecdote) and have therefore assigned them to the same date, even to the same poet; Paasche suggested that they might in fact all be one poem, illustrating the two aspects implied by *bæði* in 91. There is no specific internal evidence to help us date these strophes, unless we accept Einar Ól. Sveinsson's view (2, 299 note 2) that Egill's poetry shows the influence of 107 and 110. In that case these strophes would have to be older than *c.* 960.

VI LODDFÁFNISMÁL

St. 112 to 137 is a sequence in which a certain Loddfáfnir is addressed and given advice on conduct. In notable contrast to the Gnomic Poem, this advice is couched in the imperative mood, a circumstance which in itself imbues this poem with a rather different air: admonitory rather than contemplative. The strophes are normally introduced by a repeated four-line formula in which Loddfáfnir is addressed by name and recommended to lay to heart counsels which will profit him. This formula is absent from six strophes, but all but one of these (136) merely expand what has gone before and do not contain imperatives (two, 114 and 123, are not in fact marked as distinct strophes in CR); there is therefore no need to follow Finnur Jónsson 3, 238 in dismissing these strophes as 'not genuine'. The length of the strophes which do have the formula varies a good deal: sometimes the formula is prefixed to a mere three lines in *ljóðaháttr*, as in 112, 115 and 116, but there are also cases where it is followed by a full six-line *ljóðaháttr* strophe (e.g. 117, 119, 126) and there are other varieties too (e.g. 129, 134, 137). It is impossible to avoid the suspicion that all these strophes may once have existed without the Loddfáfnir formula, which has been added (perhaps in an attempt to endow the advice with the solemnity of ritual) at the cost of some disruption of the original poem. It looks very much as if a didactic poem consisting (like the Gnomic Poem) essentially of six-line strophes has been revised by an adaptor who prefixed the formula, now to a mere half of an original strophe, now to a whole one, and sometimes did not add it at all; and very possibly he modified the text in other ways as well. De Vries 2, 25 points out that 122/5-7 and the first half of 123 could well have originally formed one strophe; when the formula had been added the adaptor may well have supplied the somewhat flat and otiose second half of 123 to complete the new strophe. 132/5-7 and 133/1-3 were also very possibly one strophe originally; as von See 3, 59 has observed, this would have been of the type seen in 20, 40 and 93, where a general rule in the first half is provided in the second half with an illustrative justification introduced by *opt*.

As with the Gnomic Poem, scholars disagree whether *Loddfáfnismál* was intended from the beginning as the utterance of Óðinn. The first person pronoun appears twice, in 118 and 131, but in neither case does the speaker appear to possess Odinic characteristics, and the poem's advice is in general of a mundane, even petty, kind (particular offence has been taken at the notion that the last line of 112 could proceed from the lips of a deity; Müllenhoff even thought a touch of burlesque was intended here). The question is complicated by the problem of how 111 is to be understood. As the text stands in CR, this strophe introduces *Loddfáfnismál*, but its grand mystical tone, in contrast to the not very elevated contents of the poem that follows, makes it doubtful that it was originally composed for this purpose. A further objection has been seen in the reference in line 7 to runes, which are not in fact dealt with in *Loddfáfnismál* (apart from a very cursory allusion in 137). The strophe would in fact be more appropriately placed among the miscellaneous fragments of *Rúnatal*; it is also conceivable that it was at one time intended to introduce *Ljóðatal*. Even if we accept it as the opening strophe of *Loddfáfnismál*, its implications are far from clear. Who is the *ek* who saw and was silent in the hall of Hávi, pondering and listening to counsels and talk of runes? Certainly a god, says Finnur Jónsson 3, 237, for only a god would have been admitted to such exalted surroundings, and so most naturally Óðinn, and it is Óðinn (Finnur continues) who utters *Loddfáfnismál* in the disguise of an aged *þulr*, giving an exaggerated portrait of himself in 134. This may be so; but in the hall of Hávi it would seem reasonable that Hávi, i.e. Óðinn, would be the speaker rather than that he would be the listening *ek*. Müllenhoff believed that 111-137 were the utterance not of Hávi but of the *þulr* Loddfáfnir recounting what he claims has previously been addressed to him in Hávi's hall (Müllenhoff emended *manna mál* in 111/6 to *Háva mál* — but that leaves *þǫgðu* with no apparent pl. subject), and that 164 was the original conclusion of this poem; in that strophe he expelled *Háva* before *hǫllu í* and took the hall to be the one in which the *þulr* gave his performance; *heill sá er kvað* is his praise of Hávi and *heill sá er kann* his praise of himself. This is ingenious, but obviously very speculative, and is still vulnerable to the charge that the advice, taken as a whole, is too trifling for its grandiose frame. The most plausible conclusion is that what we have here originated, like the Gnomic Poem, as an independent set of impersonal didactic strophes of six *ljóðaháttr* lines each; at some date it was adapted to the Loddfáfnir formula and thereby somewhat disrupted; and it was then (like the Gnomic Poem) incorporated in the 'Words of Hávi', only at that stage acquiring a connection with Óðinn. Who Loddfáfnir can have been, and why the formula was ever added at all, are totally mysterious; the name also occurs, equally mysteriously, in st. 162, where it has perhaps been inserted to provide a link between *Ljóðatal* and what has gone earlier in the collection (though it is possibly just conceivable that the occurrence there is the primary one, from which the composer of the formula took the name).

The poem is often felt by readers to be less lively and memorable than the Gnomic Poem: 'mere versified prose' according to Heusler 2, 134. The content of the advice, however, is often very similar: the cultivation of friendship is a prominent theme in both poems, and so are guest-host relationships, though *Loddfáfnismál* confines itself to the duties of the host whereas the Gnomic Poem is more concerned with those of the guest. The note of caution, of watchful suspiciousness, which is so striking in the Gnomic Poem, is less conspicuous, though it does appear (e.g. 131). There are differences as well: relationships with women are the subject of a number of strophes in *Loddfáfnismál*, and these are not referred to in the Gnomic Poem, unless some of the strophes after 77 are taken as belonging to it. But the most notable difference is in the allusions to magic and superstition: Loddfáfnir is urged to beware of sleeping with sorceresses (113-4), of incurring a curse (126,136), and of being bewitched into frenzied madness (129); note also the reference to *galdr* in 120 and the apparent allusion to sorcery in 118. The various 'medical' remedies of 137 are also of course largely of a magical nature. This kind of thing is completely absent from the Gnomic Poem.

Much of the discussion devoted to *Loddfáfnismál* has run along the same lines as that bearing upon the Gnomic Poem. Müllenhoff and Finnur Jónsson denounced considerable portions of the work as interpolations; Heusler radically reshuffled the strophes. Heusler also claimed to detect half a dozen pre-existing proverbs in the poem. *Opt er gott þat er gamlir kveða* 134 is cited (in the form *þat er opt gott, er gamlir kveða*) as an 'old proverb' (*Búit þar komi at gǫmlum orðskvið*) in *Þorleifs þáttr jarlsskálds* ch. 5 (ÍF IX 222); this *could* of course be a direct quotation from our poem (but note that it also occurs in modern Norwegian: *D'er ofta godt, som dei gamle kveda*). In 124 Heusler 1, 44 suggested that *era sá vinr ǫðrum er vilt eitt segir* revealed itself as not composed for its present place, and therefore presumably a proverb, since its length makes it more suitable for a *ljóðaháttr* 'long line' than for a single 'full line' as it now stands. Heusler also observed that the structure of 125, ending as it does in two 'full lines', is very unusual, and suggested that this was because *opt inn betri bilar þá er inn verri vegr* was a proverb which the author of *Loddfáfnismál* incorporated in his work.

As for the localisation of the poem, there is very little to go on, but *þjóðann* in 114 is a non-Icelandic reference, and *orrosta* 129 is a word rarely applied to events in Iceland; still, it would be going much too far to claim that an Icelandic poet could not have used these words. The dating is similarly elusive; there is no specific reference to heathen cult or ritual, but neither is there anything that is unquestionably Christian. *Gjalti* in 129 is an Irish loanword, but this by no means rules out an early date, since the Norsemen were in close contact with the Irish from the beginning of the Viking Age. The metaphorical use of *api*, which occurs in 122 (and earlier in 75), has been claimed as a sign of learned-clerical influence; von See 4, 109 calls attention to E. R. Curtius' demonstration of the popularity of *simia* in Latin school poetry of the twelfth and thirteenth centuries.[14] On the other hand, the *þulr* referred to in 134 (and in 111, if that is taken as part of *Loddfáfnismál*) is a highly archaic figure, manifestly obsolescent at the time of our oldest records (for which reason his status and functions are comparatively obscure to us) and so fits most naturally a poem of relatively early date. The sentiments of *Loddfáfnismál* have sometimes been regarded as tinged by Christianity, on the grounds that they seem in places milder, less nakedly self-interested, than those of the Gnomic Poem; 130, for instance, may be contrasted with 45 (and has indeed been interpreted as a conscious reply to it — though 45 does not actually speak of relations with women), and note for instance *get þú váluðum vel* 135 and *illu feginn verðu aldregi en lát þér at góðu getit* 128. All in all, a tenth-century date would seem to do no violence to the facts, but this can be advanced only very tentatively.

---

[14] Curtius 538-40. The word itself, however, must be older than this in Norse: see Frank Fischer *Die Lehnwörter des Altwestnordischen* (Palaestra LXXXV, Berlin 1909) 12, who points out that the suffix of the feminine *apynja* (as in the native words *ásynja*, *vargynja*) indicates an early formation, in contrast to later loans like *hertoginna*, *keisarinna*.

VII RÚNATAL

Between the strophes addressed to Loddfáfnir, which end at 137, and the numbered list of spells which opens at 146 occur eight fairly obscure and incoherent strophes concerned with runes, ritual and myth. The first four (138-41) evidently form a sequence: here Óðinn recounts, in the first person, how he hung on a 'windy tree' for nine days and nights without food or drink, wounded with a spear and 'given to Óðinn, myself to myself'; shrieking, he 'took up' runes (or perhaps 'secrets', for *rúnar* can also bear that meaning) and fell from the tree. From the renowned son of Bǫlþórr he learnt nine 'mighty songs' and he got 'a draught of the precious mead'; then he grows and flourishes, becomes powerful in word and deed.

These first four strophes have given rise to an immense amount of discussion and argument among students of Norse paganism.[15] The fundamental difference of opinion is whether the notions they present are of undiluted heathen origin or whether they owe something (or, it may be, a great deal) to Christianity. The picture of the god who hangs on a tree, wounded with a spear and sacrificed (or possibly 'dedicated') to himself cannot but remind us of the self-sacrifice of Christ on the 'tree' on Calvary; he too was wounded with a spear, he thirsted and Óðinn received neither food nor drink, Christ's tree has no roots and Óðinn's has roots whose mystery none can pierce. It is not surprising that Sophus Bugge, who devoted much of his long and productive scholarly life to arguing that Norse culture and religion had been very heavily interpenetrated by Classical, Christian and Gaelic elements (supposedly mediated to the North via the British Isles in the Viking Age), should have leapt upon these strophes as a perfect illustration of his great theme.[16]

Yet there is also much here that finds no parallel in the Christian tale. The *nætr allar níu*, the nine days and nights for which Óðinn hung, are not of Christian origin; true, a fairly recent follower of Bugge, Reichardt (28 note 26), has suggested that they reflect 'the nine *hours* of the Gospels', but all that Matthew, Mark and Luke say is that Jesus called out at the ninth hour and soon afterwards

---

[15] In addition to the studies mentioned below, see the Bibliography under Chadwick, Eiríkr Magnússon 4, Fleck, van Hamel, Hunke, Kauffmann, Turville-Petre 2 (42ff.), and de Vries 4 (§§ 336, 583).

[16] Bugge 4, 291-541. Similar views were expressed in this period by E. H. Meyer *Germanische Mythologie* (Berlin 1891) 250 and Wolfgang Golther *Handbuch der Germanischen Mythologie* (Leipzig 1895) 348-50.

gave up the ghost. None of them says that Jesus hung for nine hours; Mark indeed explicitly states that he mounted the Cross at the third hour, and John has him sentenced at about the sixth hour. In fact, the number nine occurs repeatedly in Norse in contexts of myth and magic, and was plainly felt to have some mystical significance. St. 140, for example, speaks of the nine mighty songs that Óðinn learnt, the sibyl in *Vǫluspá* says she remembers nine worlds, Heimdallr was the son of nine sisters, there are nine charms in *Grógaldr*, Vafþrúðnir claims to have visited nine subterranean worlds, the great heathen festival at Uppsala was held every nine years and lasted nine days.[17] Nor does the crucifixion of Christ present any parallel to Óðinn's 'taking up' runes, falling from the tree, learning nine mighty songs, and commencing to flourish and thrive. Another advocate of Christian derivation of these lines, F. Ohrt, has linked this passage to the medieval Christian folk-legend that, while he hung on the Cross, Christ created or discovered herbs of medicinal or magical healing powers. But runes are not the same thing as herbs; Ohrt believed that at some point in the Nordic tradition the substitution was made and suggests that *œpandi* 'shrieking' originally modified not the subject *ek* but the object, the herbs which supposedly preceded the *rúnar* of our text. This would give us a legend of the mandrake type. All this is manifestly wholly speculative, and far-fetched at that.

As for the spear, which reminds us so strikingly of the Gospel story, this was in fact the weapon associated above all others with Óðinn in Norse tradition, just as the hammer was with Þórr. In *Sonatorrek* Egill calls him 'lord of the spear', *geirs dróttinn*, and in *Vǫlsunga saga* ch. 11 he makes a characteristic entry, a one-eyed man with drooping hood and a spear in his hand. In Snorri's euhemerizing account in *Ynglinga saga* ch. 9 Óðinn, here represented as an early Swedish king, has himself 'marked with the point of a spear' on his death-bed and 'assigned to himself all those who died fighting', and his successor Njǫrðr similarly had himself

---

[17] For further examples see Fritzner 2 and LP s.v. *níu*, Läffler 1, 635, and de Vries 4 (Index under *Neunzahl*). See also the comprehensive study of Karl Weinhold *Die mystische Neunzahl bei den Deutschen* (Abh. der königlichen Akademie der Wissenschaften zu Berlin, 1897). For editions of the texts mentioned here and in the next two paragraphs, see *Edda* for *Vǫluspá*, *Grímnismál* and *Helgakviða Hundingsbana* II; for *Grógaldr* and *Fjǫlsvinnsmál* see Bugge 1 or Briem; *Sonatorrek* is in *Skj.* i 34-7; *Ynglinga saga* is in ÍF XXVI; *Styrbjarnar þáttr* is in Flat. II 70-3; and the remaining sagas and *Norna-Gests þáttr* are in *Fornaldar Sögur Norðurlanda* I-IV ed. Guðni Jónsson (Akureyri 1954) with index of names in Volume IV. On names for Óðinn see also Falk 6.

'marked for Óðinn' when he in turn lay dying. In *Norna-Gests þáttr* an elderly man in a green cloak and with a spear in his hand appears on a sea-crag and gives his name as Hnikarr (known elsewhere as a name for Óðinn); later he disappears and 'people think that that must have been Óðinn'. This reminds us of the man with a long red beard, hooded and blue-cloaked, carrying a reed-cane, who appears in *Qrvar-Odds saga* calling himself Rauðgrani (also known as an Óðinn-name); he too later disappears and 'people realized that this must in fact have been Óðinn'. In *Helgakviða Hundingsbana* II Dagr, anxious to avenge his slain father, sacrifices to Óðinn; the god lends him his spear, and with this he kills Helgi. In *Styrbjarnar þáttr* King Eiríkr of the Swedes, on the eve of his last day of battle on Fýrisvellir, went into Óðinn's temple and 'gave himself' to the god, in return for victory; shortly afterwards he saw a big man with a drooping hood who handed him a reed-cane and told him to hurl it over the enemy host, at the same time proclaiming 'Óðinn has you all'. When he did this, it turned into a javelin as it flew; at once the enemy host was struck blind, and then overwhelmed by a sudden avalanche. A very similar action had been performed by Óðinn himself, according to *Vǫluspá* 24, at the first battle in the history of the world. The most important parallel to our *Hávamál* passage, however, is to be found in *Gautreks saga* ch. 7. The casting of lots decrees that King Víkarr must be sacrificed to Óðinn, to win a favourable wind for his stormbound host. His disconcerted councillors resolve on a 'symbolic' sacrifice: the guts of a calf are attached to the twig of a fir-tree and placed round the neck of the king as he stands on a tree-stump. Starkaðr, the king's favourite champion, has in his hand a spear which he had received the previous night from Óðinn, who had assured him it would look like a reed-cane and had instructed him to send Víkarr to him. 'Then Starkaðr pricked the king with the cane and said, "Now I give you to Óðinn". Then Starkaðr released the fir twig. The reed-cane became a spear and pierced through the king. The stump fell from beneath his feet and the calf-guts turned into a stout withy, and the twig rose up and lifted the king into the branches, and there he died.'

This is the fullest description extant of a sacrifice to Óðinn and, in its combination of stabbing with a spear and hanging, it provides a very close parallel to the account in st. 138. The only difference is that in our poem Óðinn is not only the recipient but also the victim of the sacrifice, a notion which probably reflects the widespread tendency among practitioners of a sacral rite to postulate that the rite is a re-enactment of an archetypal occasion when the god himself was the protagonist. Reichardt, however, has argued, in favour of the Christian derivation of this passage, that this depiction of Óðinn as himself hanged stands isolated in our records; this shows, he says, that it has no roots in genuine Norse tradition. That Óðinn had *some* connection with hanging is indeed well evidenced, not only by the story of Víkarr just mentioned, but also by the names and kennings for him in poetry and in Snorri's Edda: *Hangaguð, Hangatýr, hanga Dvalinn, hanga heimþinguðr, galga valdr*. All these, however, are presumably references either to Óðinn as the recipient of hanged victims or to his power to resurrect the hanged and hold converse with them (as described in st. 157 and in *Ynglinga saga* ch. 7). Now Reichardt is indeed correct to this extent, that there is no *explicit* statement outside our poem that Óðinn was himself hanged, but there is nevertheless a number of scattered allusions which reveal by implication a knowledge of this myth. Eyvindr skáldaspillir speaks of Óðinn as *galga farmr* 'burden of the gallows' and Tindr Hallkelsson calls him *Hangi* 'the hanged one'; *Váfuðr*, a common Óðinn-name, means 'dangler' and is surely a reference to the story, and *Geiguðr* may well belong here too (cp. *geiga* 'to sway').[18] Furthermore, it is highly probable that the name of the mighty ash *Yggdrasill*, the 'world-tree' spoken of in *Vǫluspá* and *Grímnismál* and described in detail in Snorri's Edda, also contains an allusion to this same myth. *Yggr* is a well-evidenced name for Óðinn and *drasill* means 'horse', and *Yggdrasill* is therefore most naturally to be explained as 'Óðinn's horse'.[19] Now the gallows is sometimes spoken of in Norse poetry as a horse;[20] *Yggdrasill* would therefore appear to be the gallows, or tree, on which Óðinn hung — that is to say, the 'windy tree' of st. 138 is the famous world-tree, which has taken its name from this event. This hypothesis receives some support from the closing

---

[18] LP, however, takes both *Vófuðr* and *Geiguðr* as 'wanderer'; this has little plausibility in the former case. Falk 6, 32 suggested that *Þunnr*, found three times as an Óðinn-name, alluded to his fasting on the tree (but see de Vries 3, 48 and Sturtevant 5, 486-7).

[19] Admittedly, this view is not entirely free from difficulty (one would rather expect *Yggsdrasill*). For some alternative etymologies, all however highly speculative, see the entry in de Vries 5.

[20] For examples see LP s.v. *hestr, jór, Sleipnir*, and cp. the use of the verb *ríða* of the victim who hangs (so also *rīdan* in Old English, e.g. *Beowulf* 2445). Note too the story of the thrall Karkr, whose dream that Óláfr Tryggvason gave him a very large horse is interpreted by his master Hákon jarl to mean that Óláfr will hang Karkr on the loftiest gallows he can get (Finnur Jónsson 8, 82-3).

words of the strophe *er manngi veit hvers hann af rótum renn*, remarkably similar as they are both to the phrase *en þat manngi veit, af hverjum rótum renn* applied to the world-tree (though here called *Mímameiðr*) in *Fjǫlsvinnsmál* 20, and also to the expression *cuius illa* [sc. *arbor*] *generis sit, nemo scit* in Adam of Bremen's description (*c*. 1075) of the enormous tree beside the temple at Uppsala. Green winter and summer alike, and adjoining a spring in which sacrificial victims were drowned, this Uppsala tree seems to have been a kind of image of the world-tree, or rather perhaps it served as the model from which the Norse picture of the world-tree developed in myth and poetry (on the Uppsala tree see especially Läffler 1).

Why did Óðinn hang fasting on the tree in this way? The reasons are supplied in 139-141. These strophes evidently describe his acquisition of occult wisdom through self-imposed ascetic disciplines: rapt into an ecstatic trance, he wins insight into the hidden depths of nature and attains mastery of runes and poetry. The underlying notion is that self-imposed privations and torments will, if continued long enough, induce an exalted visionary state in which the seer transcends the mundane limits of time and space and is granted a revelation of the hidden secrets of the universe. This is the procedure described in *Orkneyinga saga* ch. 36 by a Swedish 'wise man': *er ok svá, at þeim, er á slíkt stunda, er undarliga farit, fara með fǫstur ok vǫkur, ok ætla, at þar af myni þeim veitask þeir hlutir, er þeim er forkunni á at vita.*[21] It is probable that such mortifications were thought to bring the seer to the critical border between life and death, or perhaps to take him, by means of his own symbolic death, right into the world of the dead. This was where occult wisdom was to be acquired: in *Vafþrúðnismál* 43 the giant Vafþrúðnir explains that he learnt all the fates of the gods, the secrets of the giants and of all the gods, in his journeyings through the 'nine worlds' of the underworld inhabited by the dead and, as we have already noticed, Óðinn is stated to have been able to arouse the hanged and converse with them, doubtless to learn their secrets; some lines by the poet Bjarni Kolbeinsson seem to imply a legend that Óðinn acquired the art of poetry in this way.[22]

The figure of Óðinn, the arch-magician of Norse myth, fasting

---

[21] ÍF XXXIV 91. The speaker is describing, not his own methods, but those of his Christian rivals, whom he disdains. *Grímnismál*, where Óðinn reveals much hidden cosmic lore after being tormented by being placed between two fires for eight nights, without food, has often been thought to reflect the same notion.

[22] *ǫllungis namk eigi Yggjar feng und hanga* 'I did not learn the art of poetry

and windswept for nine nights on the world-tree until he is restored to this world, bearing hidden wisdom from the land of the dead, has much resemblance here to those traditional magicians of the Lapps and other North Asiatic and Arctic peoples, the shamans, who in a very similar way practised disciplines to induce trances in which, while the shaman's body lay lifeless on the ground, his soul (so it was thought) wandered at large elsewhere, acquiring occult knowledge. That the portrayal of Óðinn in *Ynglinga saga* ch. 7 as able to change his shape, travelling in a moment to distant lands in the form of a bird, a fish etc., while his body lay seemingly dead or asleep, is of shamanistic derivation is hardly open to dispute, and it seems likely that the same is true of the notions that lie behind our passage in *Hávamál*.[23] Indeed, the very concept of a world-tree may itself have been taken by the Norsemen from their Finno-Ugric neighbours; at any rate, this concept is prominent and central in Finno-Ugric mythology, whereas it seems fairly marginal in Norse tradition and not entirely reconcilable with other Norse cosmological beliefs.

The succeeding four strophes of *Rúnatal* (142-145) are very miscellaneous (not least metrically) and are plainly a jumble of fragments. Here Óðinn is spoken of in the third person, under his own name in 143 and under what are more or less certainly pseudonyms for him in 142 and 145; Hroptr, Þundr and *fimbulþulr* (this last occurs elsewhere only in st. 80 of *Hávamál*; since that too deals with runes and has no apparent connection with its present context, it may very well be another stray fragment of the same sort as we find here in *Rúnatal*). Who the *ek* of 143 can be is therefore quite unclear. The last four lines of 145 could possibly be another reference to the immolation and resurrection of Óðinn, but cannot belong with the first four strophes of *Rúnatal*, not only because Óðinn is here alluded to in the third person but also because they are not in *ljóðaháttr* but in *fornyrðislag*.

VIII LJÓÐATAL

This numbered sequence of eighteen strophes (146-163) is the most clearly demarcated of all the segments of *Hávamál*, and is

beneath a hanged man' (implying that somebody else [Óðinn?] did), *Jómsvíkinga drápa* 2 (*Skj*. ii 1). On the subject in general see Ström.

[23] See R. Pipping 2 and Bruhn. For the whole question of shamanistic influences on Norse beliefs about shape-changing and *seiðr* see Strömbäck 1, 115ff.

doubtless an originally independent poem incorporated, seemingly with little or no modification, into the *Hávamál* collection. The speaker lists in turn eighteen *ljóð*, magic charms or spells, of which he claims (146) a unique knowledge, and describes what function (usually an apotropaic one) each possesses. The fourteenth and fifteenth *ljóð* (159-60) stand somewhat apart, however: the fourteenth is not a spell but a catalogue of mythological information, and knowledge of the fifteenth was evidently *not* peculiar to the speaker, since it was, he says, originally chanted by 'the dwarf Pjóðreyrir' when he magically inspired the Æsir with might, the *álfar* with prowess, and Hroptatýr (a name for Óðinn) with intellect.

Although Óðinn is thus mentioned at this point in the third person, there can scarcely be any doubt that he is the *ek* who utters the poem. As already mentioned, this was certainly Snorri's understanding when he made use of the work in *Ynglinga saga* ch. 6-7. Furthermore, the final strophe, in which the speaker darkly refers to secret knowledge which he will never impart to another, is reminiscent of the climaxes in *Vafþrúðnismál* and in the riddle sequence in *Heiðreks saga*, in both of which the disguised Óðinn finally betrays his true identity by posing a question to which he alone knows the answer.

Ljóðatal seems well preserved textually, though the second half of 147 has evidently been lost, and it may well be, as many scholars believe, that 162 has been interfered with: the abrupt reappearance of Loddfáfnir is puzzling, and, as remarked above, the lines have very possibly been interpolated to provide a link with an earlier part of *Hávamál*.

The contents of *Ljóðatal* make an attribution to the pagan period likely.

IX THE COMPILATION OF HÁVAMÁL

If, then, the *Hávamál* of CR is a conglomeration of originally independent poems, by what process were they brought together, and at what date? And what can have been the reasons for making such a compilation?

Some scholars have tried to identify one of the constituent segments as the 'real' or the 'original' *Hávamál*; this, they suppose, is the core of the work, to which alone the name *Hávamál* originally belonged, and this was then transformed into our present text by a process of accretion. Each one of the six segments has had its champion: Finnur Jónsson thought that the real *Hávamál* was the Gnomic Poem, because it is the longest and comes at the beginning; de Vries and Magnus Olsen thought it was *Ljóðatal*, prefaced by 111; Schneider took it to be the three Óðinn-adventures plus 138-141 and 164; Müllenhoff thought it was *Loddfáfnismál* with 164 as its end; and Einar Ól. Sveinsson too inclined to believe that *Loddfáfnismál* was the original *Hávamál*.

Some of these suggestions are more plausible than others — Finnur Jónsson's is incompatible with the view adopted above that the Gnomic Poem was not originally intended as the utterance of Óðinn at all — but in fact there is no reason to assume that such a process, of accretion round an initial core, was actually what occurred. It is at least equally conceivable that none of the segments, in independent form, bore the name *Hávamál* and that all of them were brought together at the same moment by one man — we may call him the editor. Very possibly he composed 164 himself to round off the compilation and thus created the name by which it is headed in CR. The disparate character of the segments makes the motives of such an editor something of a puzzle, it is true; it hardly seems possible to say more than that, in a broad sense, they are all concerned with *wisdom*, the imparting of secular advice and the display of esoteric lore, and that they could all more or less plausibly be put in the mouth of Óðinn, either because they had actually been composed in that way from the start or, failing that, because Óðinn was the god with whom wisdom and cunning were above all associated. This is evidently how the scribe of CR (or his predecessor, if it was he who put the poems in their present order) understood the situation, since he followed *Hávamál* with *Vafþrúðnismál* and *Grímnismál*: all three of them didactic 'Óðinn-poems' in which the god dispenses wisdom.

Whether the act of editing the segments to form one work also marked the moment when they were written down for the first time, or whether some or all of them already existed in writing, cannot be determined. We are little better placed in trying to decide when this editing took place. Certain noteworthy similarities that exist between *Hávamál* and Snorri's *Gylfaginning* have sometimes been regarded as significant in this connection. First of all, the hall in which *Gylfaginning* is set is referred to at one point as *Háva hǫll*;[24] apart from its appearance in a metrical list of names

---

[24] *Heimill er matr ok drykkr honum sem ǫllum þar í Háva hǫll* (*Gylfaginning* ch. 2, Finnur Jónsson 9, 10).

for Óðinn (*Skj.* i 673), this is the only occurrence of *Hávi* as a proper name outside our poem. Second, as already mentioned, Gylfi utters the first strophe of *Hávamál* as he enters the hall at the beginning of the episode and, third, at the end, after his final question has been answered, Gylfi is enjoined *ok njóttu nú, sem þú namt*, a phrase reminiscent of *njóti sá er nam* in the last strophe of our poem. From these facts Wessén 1, 9 and 3, 9 drew the inference that the editor of *Hávamál* was Snorri himself. Von See drew a different conclusion: the very notion of using *Hávi* as a name for Óðinn originated in *Gylfaginning*, he holds, and must have been taken by the editor of the poem (along with his opening strophe) from there.[25] Now *Hávi* can only be the weak form of the adjective *hár* 'high', and von See's argument is that using 'high' as a name for Óðinn (whether in its weak or its strong form) was an invention of Snorri and has no roots in Norse tradition.[26] This of course entails dating the editor's work later than *c*. 1230.[27] But can it be thought at all probable that Snorri's use of *Hávi* once only, and merely in passing, would suffice to establish it so firmly that our editor could employ it without explanation and expect it to be understood? The way in which *Hávi* appears in his text suggests rather that, even if not very old, the name was of sufficient age to have acquired some authority and general recognition as a term for the god. But in that case how are we to explain the apparent contacts with *Gylfaginning*? Possibly some might wish to dismiss them as mere coincidences, but the most natural explanation, it seems to me, is that Snorri knew *Hávamál* and was consciously echoing it, citing the opening strophe near the beginning of his work and alluding to the closing strophe near the end. This

[25] von See 4, 116. He has to suppose, of course, that the strophes in which Hávi is named (109, 111, 164) were composed, or at any rate modified, by the editor.

[26] A form *Hár*, if it existed at all, can be disentangled only with difficulty in the mss from *Hárr*, a well-established Óðinn-name; only the genitive *Hás* is in practice distinctive, but that occurs seldom and could always be explained as a scribal error for *Hárs* (which in most instances actually occurs as a textual variant). In any case, *Hár*, if it really was a genuine and long-established Óðinn-name, can plausibly be explained not as the adjective 'high' but as a cognate of Gothic *haihs* 'one-eyed' (which would of course be a very suitable name for the god). For the form compare *fár* 'coloured' = Gothic *-faihs*. (See Detter, PBB 18 [1894] 202.) Snorri, though, almost certainly intended his *Hár* and *Jafnhár* to be understood as 'High' and 'Equally High'.

[27] von See, it will be remembered, believes that some twenty strophes were actually composed by the editor. But if so many strophes are no older than the mid-thirteenth century, it is likely that some of them would betray their late date more obviously than, even on von See's showing, they do.

implies that our poem existed as a unified text by c. 1220. Further evidence for the existence of the unified text has been seen in *Sólarljóð*: quite a large number of resemblances between the two poems has been adduced, not merely in wording and in metre (*Sólarljóð* is the only Christian poem in *ljóðaháttr*) but, more significantly in the present context, in overall structure as well,[28] and Paasche went so far as to speak of *Sólarljóð* as 'an attack on the *Hávamál*, whose form the poem has made use of. For the Eddaic poet, death is the greatest evil, and the thought of renown is the only consolation . . . The truth is that life and its pleasures are shadows, what constitutes reality is death and the next world.'[29] Unfortunately, the date of *Sólarljóð* is quite uncertain: some scholars have thought it older than 1200, but Falk (3, 56f.) has argued powerfully for placing it in the second half of the thirteenth century. This would make it of roughly the same age as CR itself, so it is of no assistance in dating the compilation of *Hávamál*.

[28] See the edition of *Sólarljóð* by Björn Magnússon Ólsen in *Safn til sögu Íslands og íslenzkra bókmenta* V (Reykjavík 1915) 66 and passim. A few further points are added by Erik Noreen 1, 16. Bjarne Fidjestøl, in his *Sólarljóð: Tyding og tolkningsgrunnlag* (Bergen 1979) 32-4, accepts this view that *Hávamál* essentially set the pattern for the poem.

[29] 'Solarljod er et angrep på det Håvamål hvis form kvadet har nyttet. Eddaskalden ser i døden det største onde, tanken på ryet blir det eneste som trøster . . . Sannheten er at livet og dets lyst er skygger, døden og det annet liv det egentlige' (Paasche 428).

HÁVAMÁL

1. Gáttir allar
   áðr gangi fram,
   um skoðask skyli,
   um skyggnask skyli,
   því at óvíst er at vita
   hvar óvinir
   sitja á fleti fyrir.

2. Gefendr heilir!
   Gestr er inn kominn.
   Hvar skal sitja sjá?
   Mjǫk er bráðr,
   sá er á brǫndum skal
   síns um freista frama.

3. Elds er þǫrf
   þeims inn er kominn
   ok á kné kalinn;
   matar ok váða
   er manni þǫrf,
   þeim er hefir um fjall farit.

4. Vatns er þǫrf
   þeim er til verðar kømr,
   þerru ok þjóðlaðar,
   góðs um œðis,
   ef sér geta mætti,
   orðs ok endrþǫgu.

---

1. *Also in Snorri's Prose Edda; see Commentary for variants.*

5. Vits er þǫrf
   þeim er víða ratar;
   dælt er heima hvat.
   At augabragði verðr
   sá er ekki kann
   ok með snotrum sitr.

6. At hyggjandi sinni
   skylit maðr hrœsinn vera,
   heldr gætinn at geði;
   þá er horskr ok þǫgull
   kømr heimisgarða til,
   sjaldan verðr víti vǫrum,
   því at óbrigðra vin
   fær maðr aldregi
   en mannvit mikit.

7. Inn vari gestr,
   er til verðar kømr,
   þunnu hljóði þegir,
   eyrum hlýðir
   en augum skoðar;
   svá nýsisk fróðra hverr fyrir.

8. Hinn er sæll
   er sér um getr
   lof ok líknstafi;
   ódælla er við þat
   er maðr eiga skal
   annars brjóstum í.

9. Sá er sæll
   er sjálfr um á
   lof ok vit meðan lifir,
   því at ill ráð
   hefir maðr opt þegit
   annars brjóstum ór.

10. Byrði betri
 berrat maðr brautu at
 en sé mannvit mikit;
 auði betra
 þykkir þat í ókunnum stað;
 slíkt er válaðs vera.

11. Byrði betri
 berrat maðr brautu at
 en sé mannvit mikit;
 vegnest verra
 vegra hann velli at
 en sé ofdrykkja ǫls.

12. Era svá gott
 sem gott kveða
 ǫl alda sonum;
 því at færa veit
 er fleira drekkr
 síns til geðs gumi.

13. Óminnishegri heitir
 sá er yfir ǫlðrum þrumir;
 hann stelr geði guma;
 þess fugls fjǫðrum
 ek fjǫtraðr vark
 í garði Gunnlaðar

14. Ǫlr ek varð,
 varð ofrǫlvi,
 at ins fróða Fjalars;
 því er ǫlðr bazt
 at aptr of heimtir
 hverr sitt geð gumi.

11. 4 verra] vera *CR*.   12. 3 sonum] sona *CR*.   14. 4 ǫlðr] *first written* auðr *CR*.   bazt] baztr *CR*.   5 of] vf *CR*.

15. Þagalt ok hugalt
    skyli þjóðans barn
    ok vígdjarft vera.
    Glaðr ok reifr
    skyli gumna hverr
    unz sinn bíðr bana.

16. Ósnjallr maðr
    hyggsk munu ey lifa
    ef hann við víg varask;
    en elli gefr
    honum engi frið,
    þótt honum geirar gefi.

17. Kópir afglapi,
    er til kynnis kømr;
    þylsk hann um eða þrumir.
    Allt er senn
    ef hann sylg um getr:
    uppi er þá geð guma.

18. Sá einn veit
    er víða ratar
    ok hefir fjǫlð um farit,
    hverju geði
    stýrir gumna hverr.
    Sá er vitandi vits.

19. Haldit maðr á keri,
    drekki þó at hófi mjǫð,
    mæli þarft eða þegi;
    ókynnis þess
    vár þik engi maðr,
    at þú gangir snemma at sofa.

18. 6 vitandi] + er *CR*.

20. Gráðugr halr,
   nema geðs viti,
   etr sér aldrtrega;
   opt fær hlœgis
   er með horskum kømr
   manni heimskum magi.

21. Hjarðir þat vitu
   nær þær heim skulu
   ok ganga þá af grasi;
   en ósviðr maðr
   kann ævagi
   síns um mál maga.

22. Vesall maðr
   ok illa skapi
   hlær at hvívetna.
   Hittki hann veit
   er hann vita þyrfti,
   at hann era vamma vanr.

23. Ósviðr maðr
   vakir um allar nætr
   ok hyggr at hvívetna;
   þá er móðr
   er at morni kømr;
   allt er víl, sem var.

24. Ósnotr maðr
   hyggr sér alla vera
   viðhlæjendr vini;
   hittki hann fiðr,
   þótt þeir um hann fár lesi,
   er hann með snotrum sitr.

21. 6 mál] máls *CR*.   22. 6 era] er *CR*.

25. Ósnotr maðr
hyggr sér alla vera
viðhlæjendr vini;
þá þat finnr
er at þingi kømr,
at hann á formælendr fá.

26. Ósnotr maðr
þykkisk allt vita,
ef hann á sér í vá veru;
hittki hann veit,
hvat hann skal við kveða,
ef hans freista firar.

27. Ósnotr maðr
er með aldir kømr,
þat er bazt, at hann þegi;
engi þat veit
at hann ekki kann,
nema hann mæli til mart.
Veita maðr,
hinn er vættki veit,
þótt hann mæli til mart.

28. Fróðr sá þykkisk
er fregna kann
ok segja it sama;
eyvitu leyna
megu ýta synir,
því er gengr um guma.

27. 1 maðr] ÷ CR.

29. Œrna mælir
sá er æva þegir
staðlausu stafi;
hraðmælt tunga,
nema haldendr eigi,
opt sér ógott um gelr.

30. At augabragði
skala maðr annan hafa,
þótt til kynnis komi;
margr þá fróðr þykkisk
ef hann freginn erat
ok nái hann þurrfjallr þruma.

31. Fróðr þykkisk
sá er flótta tekr
gestr at gest hæðinn;
veita gǫrla
sá er um verði glissir,
þótt hann með grǫmum glami.

32. Gumnar margir
erusk gagnhollir
en at virði vrekask;
aldar róg
þat mun æ vera:
órir gestr við gest.

33. Árliga verðar
skyli maðr opt fá,
nema til kynnis komi;
sitr ok snópir,
lætr sem sólginn sé,
ok kann fregna at fá.

32. 3 vrekask] rekask *CR*.

34. Afhvarf mikit
	er til ills vinar,
	þótt á brautu búi;
	en til góðs vinar
	liggja gagnvegir,
	þótt hann sé firr farinn.

35. Ganga skal,
	skala gestr vera
	ey í einum stað;
	ljúfr verðr leiðr
	ef lengi sitr
	annars fletjum á.

36. Bú er betra
	þótt lítit sé;
	halr er heima hverr;
	þótt tvær geitr eigi
	ok taugreptan sal,
	þat er þó betra en bœn.

37. Bú er betra
	þótt lítit sé;
	halr er heima hverr;
	blóðugt er hjarta
	þeim er biðja skal
	sér í mál hvert matar.

38. Vápnum sínum
	skala maðr velli á
	feti ganga framarr;
	því at óvíst er at vita
	nær verðr á vegum úti
	geirs um þǫrf guma.

35. 1 skal] ÷ *CR*.

39. Fannka ek mildan mann
    eða svá matar góðan
    at ei væri þiggja þegit,
    eða síns féar
    svá gjǫflan
    at leið sé laun ef þegi.

40. Féar síns,
    er fengit hefr,
    skylit maðr þǫrf þola;
    opt sparir leiðum
    þats hefir ljúfum hugat;
    mart gengr verr en varir.

41. Vápnum ok váðum
    skulu vinir gleðjask;
    þat er á sjálfum sýnst;
    viðrgefendr ok endrgefendr
    erusk lengst vinir
    ef þat bíðr at verða vel.

42. Vin sínum
    skal maðr vinr vera
    ok gjalda gjǫf við gjǫf;
    hlátr við hlátri
    skyli hǫlðar taka
    en lausung við lygi.

43. Vin sínum
    skal maðr vinr vera,
    þeim ok þess vin,
    en óvinar síns
    skyli engi maðr
    vinar vinr vera.

39. 4 féar] fiár *CR*.   5-6 svá gjǫflan at] svági at *CR*.
40. 1 Féar] Fiár *CR*.

44. Veiztu, ef þú vin átt,
þann er þú vel trúir,
ok vill þú af honum gott geta,
geði skaltu við þann blanda
ok gjǫfum skipta,
fara at finna opt.

45. Ef þú átt annan,
þanns þú illa trúir,
vildu af honum þó gott geta,
fagrt skaltu við þann mæla
en flátt hyggja
ok gjalda lausung við lygi.

46. Þat er enn of þann
er þú illa trúir
ok þér er grunr at hans geði:
hlæja skaltu við þeim
ok um hug mæla;
glík skulu gjǫld gjǫfum.

47. Ungr var ek forðum,
fór ek einn saman;
þá varð ek villr vega;
auðigr þóttumk
er ek annan fann;
maðr er manns gaman.

48. Mildir, frœknir
menn bazt lifa,
sjaldan sút ala,
en ósnjallr maðr
uggir hotvetna,
sýtir æ glǫggr við gjǫfum.

49. Váðir mínir
    gaf ek velli at
    tveim trémǫnnum;
    rekkar þat þóttusk
    er þeir ript hǫfðu;
    neiss er nøkkviðr halr.

50. Hrørnar þǫll,
    sú er stendr þorpi á;
    hlýrat henni bǫrkr né barr;
    svá er maðr,
    sá er manngi ann;
    hvat skal hann lengi lifa?

51. Eldi heitari
    brennr með illum vinum
    friðr fimm daga,
    en þá sloknar
    er inn sétti kømr
    ok versnar allr vinskapr.

52. Mikit eitt
    skala manni gefa:
    opt kaupir sér í litlu lof;
    með hálfum hleif
    ok með hǫllu keri
    fekk ek mér félaga.

53. Lítilla sanda,
    lítilla sæva,
    lítil eru geð guma;
    því at allir menn
    urðut jafnspakir;
    hálf er ǫld hvár.

49. 2 ek] *repeated at line division CR.*   5 ript] rift *CR.*
50. 3 hlýrat] hlyrar *CR.*   53. 4 at] ÷ *CR.*

54. Meðalsnotr
skyli manna hverr,
æva til snotr sé;
þeim er fyrða
fegrst at lifa
er vel mart vitu.

55. Meðalsnotr
skyli manna hverr,
æva til snotr sé;
því at snotrs manns hjarta
verðr sjaldan glatt,
ef sá er alsnotr er á.

56. Meðalsnotr
skyli manna hverr,
æva til snotr sé;
ørlǫg sín
viti engi fyrir;
þeim er sorgalausastr sefi.

57. Brandr af brandi
brenn, unz brunninn er,
funi kveykisk af funa;
maðr af manni
verðr at máli kuðr,
en til dœlskr af dul.

58. Ár skal rísa
sá er annars vill
fé eða fjǫr hafa;
sjaldan liggjandi úlfr
lær um getr
né sofandi maðr sigr.

56. 5 engi] + m-*rune* (= maðr) *apparently cancelled by scribe CR.*
58. 1-2 rísa sá er] ri sa er *with line division after* ri *CR.*

59. Ár skal rísa
    sá er á yrkendr fá,
    ok ganga síns verka á vit;
    mart um dvelr
    þann er um morgin sefr;
    hálfr er auðr und hvǫtum.

60. Þurra skíða
    ok þakinna næfra,
    þess kann maðr mjǫt,
    ok þess viðar
    er vinnask megi
    mál ok misseri.

61. Þveginn ok mettr
    ríði maðr þingi at,
    þótt hann sét væddr til vel;
    skúa ok bróka
    skammisk engi maðr,
    né hests in heldr,
    þótt hann hafit góðan.

62. Snapir ok gnapir,
    er til sævar kømr,
    ǫrn á aldinn mar;
    svá er maðr
    er með mǫrgum kømr
    ok á formælendr fá.

63. Fregna ok segja
    skal fróðra hverr,
    sá er vill heitinn horskr;
    einn vita
    né annarr skal;
    þjóð veit ef þrír ro.

60. 3-4 mjǫt, ok] miotvǒc *with* v *cancelled* CR.
63. 6 þrír ro] þriro CR.

64. Ríki sitt
    skyli ráðsnotra hverr
    í hófi hafa;
    þá hann þat finnr,
    er með frœknum kømr,
    at engi er einna hvatastr.

65. Orða þeira
    er maðr ǫðrum segir
    opt hann gjǫld um getr.

66. Mikilsti snemma
    kom ek í marga staði,
    en til síð í suma;
    ǫl var drukkit,
    sumt var ólagat;
    sjaldan hittir leiðr í lið.

67. Hér ok hvar
    myndi mér heim of boðit
    ef þyrftak at málungi mat,
    eða tvau lær hengi
    at ins tryggva vinar
    þars ek hafða eitt etit.

68. Eldr er beztr
    með ýta sonum
    ok sólar sýn,
    heilyndi sitt
    ef maðr hafa náir,
    án við lǫst at lifa.

67. 2 of] vf *CR*.

69. Erat maðr alls vesall,
 þótt hann sé illa heill:
 sumr er af sonum sæll,
 sumr af frændum,
 sumr af fé œrnu,
 sumr af verkum vel.

70. Betra er lifðum
 en sé ólifðum,
 ey getr kvikr kú;
 eld sá ek upp brenna
 auðgum manni fyrir,
 en úti var dauðr fyr durum.

71. Haltr ríðr hrossi,
 hjǫrð rekr handarvanr,
 daufr vegr ok dugir;
 blindr er betri
 en brenndr sé;
 nýtr manngi nás.

72. Sonr er betri,
 þótt sé síð of alinn,
 eptir genginn guma;
 sjaldan bautarsteinar
 standa brautu nær
 nema reisi niðr at nið.

73. Tveir ro eins herjar;
 tunga er hǫfuðs bani;
 er mér í heðin hvern
 handar væni.

70. 2 en sé ólifðum] ok sæl lifðum CR.
71. 2 handar-] hundar- CR.

74. Nótt verðr feginn
    sá er nesti trúir;
    skammar ro skips rár;
    hverf er haustgríma;
    fjǫlð um viðrir
    á fimm dǫgum,
    en meira á mánuði.

75. Veita hinn
    er vættki veit:
    margr verðr af aurum api;
    maðr er auðigr,
    annarr óauðigr;
    skylit þann vítka vár.

76. Deyr fé,
    deyja frændr,
    deyr sjálfr it sama;
    en orðstírr
    deyr aldregi
    hveim er sér góðan getr.

77. Deyr fé,
    deyja frændr,
    deyr sjálfr it sama;
    ek veit einn
    at aldri deyr:
    dómr um dauðan hvern.

78. Fullar grindr
    sá ek fyr Fitjungs sonum;
    nú bera þeir vánarvǫl;
    svá er auðr
    sem augabragð;
    hann er valtastr vina.

74. 4 hverf] hverb *CR*.   75. 3 af aurum] afla/ðrom *CR*.

79. Ósnotr maðr,
 ef eignask getr
 fé eða fljóðs munuð,
 metnaðr honum þróask
 en mannvit aldregi:
 fram gengr hann drjúgt í dul.

80. Þat er þá reynt
 er þú at rúnum spyrr,
 inum reginkunnum,
 þeim er gørðu ginnregin
 ok fáði fimbulþulr;
 þá hefir hann bazt ef hann þegir.

81. At kveldi skal dag leyfa,
 konu er brennd er,
 mæki er reyndr er,
 mey er gefin er,
 ís er yfir kømr,
 ǫl er drukkit er.

82. Í vindi skal við hǫggva,
 veðri á sjó róa,
 myrkri við man spjalla;
 mǫrg eru dags augu;
 á skip skal skriðar orka,
 en á skjǫld til hlífar,
 mæki hǫggs,
 en mey til kossa.

83. Við eld skal ǫl drekka,
 en á ísi skríða,
 magran mar kaupa
 en mæki saurgan,
 heima hest feita
 en hund á búi.

84. Meyjar orðum
 skyli manngi trúa
 né því er kveðr kona,
 því at á hverfanda hvéli
 váru þeim hjǫrtu skǫpuð,
 brigð í brjóst um lagit.

85. Brestanda boga,
 brennanda loga,
 gínanda úlfi,
 galandi kráku,
 rýtanda svíni,
 rótlausum viði,
 vaxanda vági,
 vellanda katli,

86. fljúganda fleini,
 fallandi báru,
 ísi einnættum,
 ormi hringlegnum,
 brúðar beðmálum
 eða brotnu sverði,
 bjarnar leiki
 eða barni konungs,

87. sjúkum kálfi,
 sjálfráða þræli,
 vǫlu vilmæli,
 val nýfelldum,

88. akri ársánum
 trúi engi maðr
 né til snemma syni;
 veðr ræðr akri
 en vit syni;
 hætt er þeira hvárt.

86. 8 eða] eð CR.

89. Bróðurbana sínum,
þótt á brautu mœti,
húsi hálfbrunnu,
hesti alskjótum —
þá er jór ónýtr
ef einn fótr brotnar —
verðit maðr svá tryggr
at þessu trúi ǫllu.

90. Svá er friðr kvenna,
þeira er flátt hyggja,
sem aki jó óbryddum
á ísi hálum,
teitum, tvévetrum,
ok sé tamr illa,
eða í byr óðum
beiti stjórnlausu,
eða skyli haltr henda
hrein í þáfjalli.

91. Bert ek nú mæli,
því at ek bæði veit,
brigðr er karla hugr konum;
þá vér fegrst mælum
er vér flást hyggjum;
þat tælir horska hugi.

92. Fagrt skal mæla
ok fé bjóða
sá er vill fljóðs ást fá,
líki leyfa
ins ljósa mans;
sá fær er fríar.

93. Ástar firna
    skyli engi maðr
    annan aldregi;
    opt fá á horskan
    er á heimskan ne fá
    lostfagrir litir.

94. Eyvitar firna
    er maðr annan skal
    þess er um margan gengr guma;
    heimska ór horskum
    gørir hǫlða sonu
    sá inn mátki munr.

95. Hugr einn þat veit
    er býr hjarta nær;
    einn er hann sér um sefa;
    øng er sótt verri
    hveim snotrum manni
    en sér øngu at una.

96. Þat ek þá reynda
    er ek í reyri sat
    ok vættak míns munar;
    hold ok hjarta
    var mér in horska mær;
    þeygi ek hana at heldr hefik.

97. Billings mey
    ek fann beðjum á
    sólhvíta sofa;
    jarls ynði
    þótti mér ekki vera,
    nema við þat lík at lifa.

94. 4 horskum] horskann *CR*.

98. 'Auk nær aptni
    skaltu, Óðinn, koma,
    ef þú vilt þér mæla man;
    allt eru óskǫp,
    nema einir viti
    slíkan lǫst saman.'

99. Aptr ek hvarf
    ok unna þóttumk
    vísum vilja frá;
    hitt ek hugða,
    at ek hafa mynda
    geð hennar allt ok gaman.

100. Svá kom ek næst,
     at in nýta var
     vígdrótt ǫll um vakin
     með brennandum ljósum
     ok bornum viði;
     svá var mér vílstígr of vitaðr.

101. Ok nær morni,
     er ek var enn um kominn,
     þá var saldrótt um sofin;
     grey eitt ek þá fann
     innar góðu konu
     bundit beðjum á.

102. Mǫrg er góð mær,
     ef gǫrva kannar,
     hugbrigð við hali;
     þá ek þat reynda
     er it ráðspaka
     teygða ek á flærðir fljóð;
     háðungar hverrar
     leitaði mér it horska man,
     ok hafða ek þess vættki vífs.

98. 1 aptni] apni *CR*.   102. 9 vættki] vętkis *CR*.

103. Heima glaðr gumi
ok við gesti reifr,
sviðr skal um sik vera,
minnigr ok málugr,
ef hann vill margfróðr vera,
opt skal góðs geta;
fimbulfambi heitir
sá er fátt kann segja:
þat er ósnotrs aðal.

104. Inn aldna jǫtun ek sótta;
nú em ek aptr um kominn;
fátt gat ek þegjandi þar;
mǫrgum orðum
mælta ek í minn frama
í Suttungs sǫlum.

105. Gunnlǫð mér um gaf
gullnum stóli á
drykk ins dýra mjaðar;
ill iðgjǫld
lét ek hana eptir hafa
síns ins heila hugar,
síns ins svára sefa.

106. Rata munn
létumk rúms um fá
ok um grjót gnaga;
yfir ok undir
stóðumk jǫtna vegir;
svá hætta ek hǫfði til.

107. †Vel keypts litar†
hefi ek vel notit;
fás er fróðum vant;
því at Óðrerir
er nú upp kominn
á alda vés jaðar.

107. 6 jaðar] jarðar CR.

108. Ifi er mér á
 at ek væra enn kominn
 jǫtna gǫrðum ór,
 ef ek Gunnlaðar ne nytak,
 innar góðu konu,
 þeirar er lǫgðumk arm yfir.

109. Ins hindra dags
 gengu hrímþursar
 Háva ráðs at fregna
 Háva hǫllu í;
 at Bǫlverki þeir spurðu,
 ef hann væri með bǫndum kominn
 eða hefði honum Suttungr of sóit.

110. Baugeið Óðinn
 hygg ek at unnit hafi;
 hvat skal hans tryggðum trúa?
 Suttung svikinn
 hann lét sumbli frá
 ok grœtta Gunnlǫðu.

111. Mál er at þylja
 þular stóli á
 Urðar brunni at;
 sá ek ok þagðak,
 sá ek ok hugðak,
 hlýdda ek á manna mál;
 of rúnar heyrða ek dœma
 né um ráðum þǫgðu
 Háva hǫllu at,
 Háva hǫllu í,
 heyrða ek segja svá:

109. 7 sóit] sótt *corrected to* sóitt *CR.*

112. Ráðumk þér, Loddfáfnir,
en þú ráð nemir,
njóta mundu, ef þú nemr,
þér munu góð ef þú getr:
nótt þú rísat,
nema á njósn sér
eða þú leitir þér innan út staðar.

113. Ráðumk þér, Loddfáfnir,
en þú ráð nemir,
njóta mundu, ef þú nemr,
þér munu góð ef þú getr:
fjǫlkunnigri konu
skalattu í faðmi sofa
svá at hon lyki þik liðum.

114. Hon svá gørir
at þú gáir eigi
þings né þjóðans máls;
mat þú villat
né mannskis gaman,
ferr þú sorgafullr at sofa.

115. Ráðumk þér, Loddfáfnir,
en þú ráð nemir,
njóta mundu, ef þú nemr,
þér munu góð ef þú getr:
annars konu
teygðu þér aldregi
eyrarúnu at.

116. Ráðumk þér, Loddfáfnir,
en þú ráð nemir,
njóta mundu, ef þú nemr,
þér munu góð ef þú getr:
á fjalli eða firði
ef þik fara tíðir,
fásktu at virði vel.

112. 2, 113.2 en] at *CR*, but 116.2 has en; *in the other strophes the formula is so abbreviated that the word does not appear.*

117. Ráðumk þér, Loddfáfnir,
en þú ráð nemir,
njóta mundu, ef þú nemr,
þér munu góð ef þú getr:
illan mann
láttu aldregi
óhǫpp at þér vita,
því at af illum manni
fær þú aldregi
gjǫld ins góða hugar.

118. Ofarla bíta
ek sá einum hal
orð illrar konu;
fláráð tunga
varð honum at fjǫrlagi
ok þeygi um sanna sǫk.

119. Ráðumk þér, Loddfáfnir,
en þú ráð nemir,
njóta mundu, ef þú nemr,
þér munu góð ef þú getr:
veiztu, ef þú vin átt,
þanns þú vel trúir,
farðu at finna opt,
því at hrísi vex
ok hávu grasi
vegr er vættki trøðr.

120. Ráðumk þér, Loddfáfnir,
en þú ráð nemir,
njóta mundu, ef þú nemr,
þér munu góð ef þú getr:
góðan mann
teygðu þér at gamanrúnum
ok nem líknargaldr meðan þú lifir.

121. Ráðumk þér, Loddfáfnir,
    en þú ráð nemir,
    njóta mundu, ef þú nemr,
    þér munu góð ef þú getr:
    vin þínum
    ver þú aldregi
    fyrri at flaumslitum;
    sorg etr hjarta
    ef þú segja ne náir
    einhverjum allan hug.

122. Ráðumk þér, Loddfáfnir,
    en þú ráð nemir,
    njóta mundu, ef þú nemr,
    þér munu góð ef þú getr:
    orðum skipta
    þú skalt aldregi
    við ósvinna apa,

123. því at af illum manni
    mundu aldregi
    góðs laun um geta,
    en góðr maðr
    mun þik gørva mega
    líknfastan at lofi.

124. Sifjum er þá blandat,
    hverr er segja ræðr
    einum allan hug;
    allt er betra
    en sé brigðum at vera;
    era sá vinr ǫðrum er vilt eitt segir.

125. Ráðumk þér, Loddfáfnir,
en þú ráð nemir,
njóta mundu, ef þú nemr,
þér munu góð ef þú getr:
þrimr orðum senna
skalattu þér við verra mann;
opt inn betri bilar
þá er inn verri vegr.

126. Ráðumk þér, Loddfáfnir,
en þú ráð nemir,
njóta mundu, ef þú nemr,
þér munu góð ef þú getr:
skósmiðr þú verir
né skeptismiðr,
nema þú sjálfum þér sér;
skór er skapaðr illa
eða skapt sé rangt:
þá er þér bǫls beðit.

127. Ráðumk þér, Loddfáfnir,
en þú ráð nemir,
njóta mundu, ef þú nemr,
þér munu góð ef þú getr:
hvars þú bǫl kannt,
kveðu þat bǫlvi at
ok gefat þínum fjándum frið.

128. Ráðumk þér, Loddfáfnir,
en þú ráð nemir,
njóta mundu, ef þú nemr,
þér munu góð ef þú getr:
illu feginn
verðu aldregi
en lát þér at góðu getit.

127. 6 þat] þ *with abbreviation sign CR; see Commentary.*

129. Ráðumk þér, Loddfáfnir,
en þú ráð nemir,
njóta mundu, ef þú nemr,
þér munu góð ef þú getr:
upp líta
skalattu í orrostu
— gjalti glíkir
verða gumna synir —
síðr þik um heilli halir.

130. Ráðumk þér, Loddfáfnir,
en þú ráð nemir,
njóta mundu, ef þú nemr,
þér munu góð ef þú getr:
ef þú vilt þér góða konu
kveðja at gamanrúnum
ok fá fǫgnuð af,
fǫgru skaltu heita
ok láta fast vera;
leiðisk manngi gott, ef getr.

131. Ráðumk þér, Loddfáfnir,
en þú ráð nemir,
njóta mundu, ef þú nemr,
þér munu góð ef þú getr:
varan bið ek þik vera
en eigi ofvaran;
ver þú við ǫl varastr
ok við annars konu
ok við þat it þriðja,
at þjófar ne leiki.

129. 9 þik] þitt *CR*.

132. Ráðumk þér, Loddfáfnir,
  en þú ráð nemir,
  njóta mundu, ef þú nemr,
  þér munu góð ef þú getr:
  at háði né hlátri
  hafðu aldregi
  gest né ganganda.

133. Opt vitu ógǫrla
  þeir er sitja inni fyrir,
  hvers þeir ro kyns, er koma;
  erat maðr svá góðr
  at galli ne fylgi,
  né svá illr at einugi dugi.

134. Ráðumk þér, Loddfáfnir,
  en þú ráð nemir,
  njóta mundu, ef þú nemr,
  þér munu góð ef þú getr:
  at hárum þul
  hlæðu aldregi;
  opt er gott þat er gamlir kveða;
  opt ór skǫrpum belg
  skilin orð koma,
  þeim er hangir með hám
  ok skollir með skrám
  ok váfir með vílmǫgum.

135. Ráðumk þér, Loddfáfnir,
  en þú ráð nemir,
  njóta mundu, ef þú nemr,
  þér munu góð ef þú getr:
  gest þú ne geya
  né á grind hrekir;
  get þú váluðum vel.

135. 5 geya] geyia CR.   6 hrekir] hrǫkir CR. Cf. Commentary.

136. Rammt er þat tré
 er ríða skal
 ǫllum at upploki;
 baug þú gef
 eða þat biðja mun
 þér læs hvers á liðu.

137. Ráðumk þér, Loddfáfnir,
 en þú ráð nemir,
 njóta mundu, ef þú nemr,
 þér munu góð ef þú getr:
 hvars þú ǫl drekkr,
 kjós þú þér jarðar megin,
 því at jǫrð tekr við ǫlðri,
 en eldr við sóttum,
 eik við abbindi,
 ax við fjǫlkynngi,
 hǫll við hýrógi
 — heiptum skal mána kveðja —
 beiti við bitsóttum,
 en við bǫlvi rúnar;
 fold skal við flóði taka.

138. Veit ek, at ek hekk
 vindga meiði á
 nætr allar níu,
 geiri undaðr
 ok gefinn Óðni,
 sjálfr sjálfum mér,
 á þeim meiði
 er manngi veit
 hvers hann af rótum renn.

139. Við hleifi mik sældu
 né við hornigi,
 nýsta ek niðr,
 nam ek upp rúnar,
 œpandi nam,
 fell ek aptr þaðan.

140. Fimbulljóð níu
 nam ek af inum frægja syni
 Bǫlþórs, Bestlu fǫður,
 ok ek drykk of gat
 ins dýra mjaðar,
 ausinn Óðreri.

141. Þá nam ek frævask
 ok fróðr vera
 ok vaxa ok vel hafask;
 orð mér af orði
 orðs leitaði,
 verk mér af verki
 verks leitaði.

142. Rúnar munt þú finna
 ok ráðna stafi,
 mjǫk stóra stafi,
 mjǫk stinna stafi,
 er fáði fimbulþulr
 ok gørðu ginnregin
 ok reist Hroptr rǫgna,

143. Óðinn með ásum,
 en fyr álfum Dáinn,
 Dvalinn dvergum fyrir,
 Ásviðr jǫtnum fyrir;
 ek reist sjálfr sumar.

139. 1 sældu] seldo *CR; see Commentary.* 6 þaðan] þatan *CR.*
143. 3 Dvalinn] + ok *CR.*

144. Veiztu hvé rísta skal?
Veiztu hvé ráða skal?
Veiztu hvé fá skal?
Veiztu hvé freista skal?
Veiztu hvé biðja skal?
Veiztu hvé blóta skal?
Veiztu hvé senda skal?
Veiztu hvé sóa skal?

145. Betra er óbeðit
en sé ofblótit;
ey sér til gildis gjǫf;
betra er ósent
en sé ofsóit.
Svá Þundr um reist
fyr þjóða rǫk,
þar hann upp um reis
er hann aptr of kom.

146. Ljóð ek þau kann
er kannat þjóðans kona
ok mannskis mǫgr;
hjálp heitir eitt,
en þat þér hjálpa mun
við sǫkum ok sorgum
ok sútum gǫrvǫllum.

147. Þat kann ek annat
er þurfu ýta synir,
þeir er vilja læknar lifa.

148. Þat kann ek it þriðja:
ef mér verðr þǫrf mikil
hapts við mína heiptmǫgu,
eggjar ek deyfi
minna andskota,
bítat þeim vápn né velir.

148. 1 it] ÷ *CR*.

149. Þat kann ek it fjórða:
ef mér fyrðar bera
bǫnd at bóglimum,
svá ek gel
at ek ganga má;
sprettr mér af fótum fjǫturr
en af hǫndum hapt.

150. Þat kann ek it fimmta:
ef ek sé af fári skotinn
flein í fólki vaða,
flýgra hann svá stinnt
at ek stǫðvigak,
ef ek hann sjónum of sék.

151. Þat kann ek it sétta:
ef mik særir þegn
á rótum rams viðar,
ok þann hal
er mik heipta kveðr,
þann eta mein heldr en mik.

152. Þat kann ek it sjaunda:
ef ek sé hávan loga
sal um sessmǫgum,
brennrat svá breitt
at ek honum bjargigak;
þann kann ek galdr at gala.

153. Þat kann ek it átta,
er ǫllum er
nytsamligt at nema:
hvars hatr vex
með hildings sonum,
þat má ek bœta brátt.

151. 3 rams] rás *CR*.

154. Þat kann ek it níunda:
ef mik nauðr um stendr
at bjarga fari mínu á floti,
vind ek kyrri
vági á
ok svæfik allan sæ.

155. Þat kann ek it tíunda:
ef ek sé túnriður
leika lopti á,
ek svá vinnk
at þær villar fara
sinna heimhama,
sinna heimhuga.

156. Þat kann ek it ellipta:
ef ek skal til orrostu
leiða langvini,
undir randir ek gel,
en þeir með ríki fara
heilir hildar til,
heilir hildi frá,
koma þeir heilir hvaðan.

157. Þat kann ek it tólpta:
ef ek sé á tré uppi
váfa virgilná,
svá ek ríst
ok í rúnum fák
at sá gengr gumi
ok mælir við mik.

155. 5 þær villar] þeir villir *CR*.   6-7 heimhama, heimhuga] *written* heim hama, heim huga *CR*.

158. Þat kann ek it þrettánda:
ef ek skal þegn ungan
verpa vatni á,
munat hann falla,
þótt hann í fólk komi;
hnígra sá halr fyr hjǫrum.

159. Þat kann ek it fjórtánda:
ef ek skal fyrða liði
telja tíva fyrir,
ása ok álfa
ek kann allra skil;
fár kann ósnotr svá.

160. Þat kann ek it fimmtánda
er gól Þjóðreyrir,
dvergr, fyr Dellings durum:
afl gól hann ásum
en álfum frama,
hyggju Hroptatý.

161. Þat kann ek it sextánda:
ef ek vil ins svinna mans
hafa geð allt ok gaman,
hugi ek hverfi
hvítarmri konu
ok sný ek hennar ǫllum sefa.

162. Þat kann ek it sjautjánda,
at mik mun seint firrask
it manunga man;
ljóða þessa
mun þú, Loddfáfnir,
lengi vanr vera,
þó sé þér góð ef þú getr,
nýt ef þú nemr,
þǫrf ef þú þiggr.

163. Þat kann ek it átjánda,
er ek æva kennik
mey né manns konu
— allt er betra
er einn um kann;
þat fylgir ljóða lokum —
nema þeiri einni
er mik armi verr
eða mín systir sé.

164. Nú eru Háva mál kveðin
Háva hǫllu í,
allþǫrf ýta sonum,
óþǫrf jǫtna sonum.
Heill sá er kvað!
Heill sá er kann!
Njóti sá er nam!
Heilir þeirs hlýddu!

164. 4 jǫtna] ýta *CR,* with iotna *as a later correction in the margin.*

COMMENTARY

1

This strophe is quoted near the beginning of Snorri's Prose Edda, without attribution; see above, p. 2. Only the Utrecht ms has line 3; Worm's ms lacks *at vita* in 5, and the Uppsala ms has the awkward *Skatnar allir áðr né gangim fram* as 1-2 and the pl. *fletjum* for *fleti* in 7. The text in Snorri is evidently somewhat corrupt, though *fletjum* is perfectly possible (as in st. 35).

1-4 Although the general sense is clear, the construction is disputed. Some editors take *gáttir* as acc. object of *skoðask um* and *skyggnask um*, but this is hardly right, since these verbs are equivalent to *skoða (skyggna) um sik* and cannot have an object; they are of the same type as *sjásk um, lítask um, leitask fyrir* etc., see Nygaard 2, §154. (*Skyggnask um* occurs in prose, always intransitively; cp. Fritzner 2 s.v. *skygna*.) Others understand *gáttir* as nom.; this entails taking the infinitives as passives (with *um* as the particle). So FJ. It has been denied (e.g. Olson 540, Lindquist 2,1) that refl. with passive sense occurs in the Poetic Edda, and indeed it is true that in Norse as a whole this usage is common only in the Latin-influenced 'learned style' and is otherwise largely confined to a few verbs such as *spyrjask, fásk, byggjask* (Nygaard 2, §161); yet there are a few Eddaic instances which come very close to passives (*ǫll muntu lemjask* Helg. Hj. 21, *á gengusk eiðar* Vsp. 26) and early scaldic verse also supplies examples (*eyðisk land ok láð* and *troddusk torgur*, both in Eyvindr's Hákonarmál, cp. FJ 5, 275). This is certainly therefore a defensible interpretation, but it is perhaps safer to take the infinitives as intransitive, with *gáttir* as acc. object of *gangi*; for this construction cp. *Þorkell ok þeir báðir fǫrunautar gengu út skyndilega aðrar dyrr en þeir hǫfðu inn gengit* Hkr. ii 166 and other instances in Nygaard 2, §96.

7 *sitja . . . fyrir* probably 'are present' (as in 133) rather than specifically 'lie in ambush' (as von Friesen), though *sitja fyrir* can have this sense with a dat. object. CPB 461 insists that *gangi fram* must mean 'go to the door' (from inside), as indeed it commonly does; but this involves the impossible 'lurk *round* one's house' for the last line, and Snorri's use of the strophe shows that he took it to refer to entry from without.

2

1 is spoken by the visitor as he enters.

6 *síns um freista frama* means 'to try one's luck', but lines 4-5

are difficult: the problem, essentially, is that the context is not sufficiently precise to determine which of the many meanings of *brandr* is required. These are: (1) sword; (2) blazing log (in the pl. this is virtually 'the fire'); (3) raised prow, ship's beak; (4) in pl., ships' beaks used over, or on each side of, the door of a farm, e.g. Grettis saga ch. 38 (ÍF VII 128), where they function as weather-vanes, and cp. compound *brandadyrr*; (5) piece of (as yet unkindled) firewood. The only clear occurrence of the last in ON is at Lndn. 222, where a servant sent to a farm to spy out whether a wanted man was in hiding there *sá fatahrúgu á brǫndum, ok kom undan rautt klæði* (for other possible instances see Valtýr Guðmundsson 156ff.), but the sense is well evidenced in modern Norwegian dialects and perhaps also underlies the modern Icelandic expression *að standa á bröndunum*, used in the nineteenth century of someone standing between door and hearthstones and thus obstructing the draught (cp. Finnur Jónsson á Kjörseyri *Þjóðhættir og Ævisögur frá nítjándu öld* [Akureyri 1945] 282).

Bellows chooses 'swords', supposing the lines to be misplaced, and renders 'Swift shall he be who with swords shall try the proof of his might to make'; but this would require *skal* or *skyli* for *er* in 4, and *bráðr* is not so much 'swift' as '*too* swift, hasty, rash'. From sense (4) Sveinbjörn Egilsson deduced the rendering *juxta postes* (so also CPB 2 'at the gate-post' and Kock 2, 26, who compares the situation in Vafþr. 11). As SG remark, this would require *at* rather than *á*, and furthermore the visitor appears to be already inside; this last consideration also rules out Falk's (8, 225) rendering with *brandr = slagbrandr*: 'He is impatient who has to try his fortune on the door-bar, i.e. whether it will be opened for him or not'. There is a Norwegian expression *koma ut på brannan* 'get into severe difficulties, plumb the depths of misery', which FJ derives from sense (3), arguing that in a sea-battle this was where the fight was toughest, and renders here 'Very eager (to receive help or hospitality) is he who is (has been) in extreme distress'. Another Norwegian expression, *det er på brannom med han* 'it is almost up with him, he is on the verge of disaster' is cited by A. Moe (see Skulerud 571) to support the translation 'He is in hot haste who is reduced to his last remnants to get by on'. Some editors follow sense (2), but *á* cannot give the sense *at* the hearth (so Clarke) and recognition of this leads to extravagancies, e.g. Guðmundur Finnbogason 2, 104 thinks the guest is impatient to see, *from* the fire (i.e. whether the host heaps it up or not), what reception he will receive, and H. Pipping 2, 6 translates 'Very hasty, rash, is that (guest) who takes it on himself to poke the fire', the sacred place of the household; see also Richert 1-4. Lie 219 also follows sense (2), interpreting 'The man who is unlucky enough to find himself on burning logs exerts himself speedily to escape'. This does not cope well with line 6 and, as Lie admits, does not fit the context. BMÓ 1, 223-26 follows sense (5): the stranger modestly takes up his place on the pile of firewood and waits impatiently to see what reception he will get. This is not paralleled from the ON world, but can be supported from modern Norwegian rural custom: 'Folk som var bljuge av seg, kom vanleg ikkje lenger enn till "brondo" . . . Det er ei herma um nokre gjentor som eg høyrde: "Du e liksom Røyslandsgjentunn; du kjem barre at brondo" (ell. "du set deg barre i brondo")', Heggstad 165. If a host wishes to honour a guest especially, he will say, 'Nei, du skal ikkje sitja i brondo; set deg innar', Hannaas 232; see also Skulerud 547-8. Those who follow this interpretation, which seems clearly the best, mostly take *bráðr*, probably rightly, as 'impatient, anxious, on edge', but Raknes thinks it implies 'will depart speedily' if he is left to occupy a humble seat, and will thus bring disgrace on the host. But the following strophes suggest the guest was hardly in a position to adopt so lofty an attitude.

4

3 *þjóðlaðar* 'friendly invitation'; for this sense of *þjóð*- cp. *þjóðdrengr*, *þjóðmenni* etc., *þýðr* 'kind, affectionate', Gothic *þiuþ* : τὸ ἀγαθόν.

4 *góðs œðis* most simply taken, with FJ and BMÓ, as 'good disposition, friendliness' on the part of the host. M. Olsen 7, 7 took it to be a needful quality of the *guest*, but his only reason for this is that in Vafþr. 20 and 22 the same word is used (*ef þitt œði dugir*) of the demands made on the guest (so Olsen says, but this is untrue).

6 *endrþǫgu* — only the interpretation 'silence in return' makes reasonable sense; *þaga* is admittedly not otherwise recorded, but is formed regularly on *þegja* 'be silent' like *saga* : *segja*. The sense is that the guest needs conversation (*orðs*) from his host, and then silence in turn from the host while he himself speaks. The CR spelling *-þǫ́go* can equally well be interpreted as *-þǫgu*, which is read by Eiríkr Magnússon 2, 4 and Lindquist 2, 7, supposed to be genitive of *þega* (the vowel ǫ is left unexplained by Eiríkr; Lind-

quist refers it to *u*-umlaut in a syllable bearing secondary stress, cp. *-tøgr* and A. Noreen §77.3). But *þega* means 'acceptance' and cannot give the postulated sense '(renewed) invitation'. Lindquist denies that *endr-* can mean 'reciprocated', but cp. *endrgjalda* 'repay', *endrvinda* 'wind back' and modern Icelandic *endurborga*, *endurfallinn*, *endurhljómur*.

6

1-2 *hrœsinn at hyggjandi sinni* is commonly rendered 'boastful of his intellect', but the preposition *at* seems strange; one would expect *af*, which is what we find in the virtually identical lines in Hugsvinnsmál (Skj. ii 197): *Af hyggjandi sinni skyldit maðr hrœsinn vera*. FJ renders *at* 'with regard to'. E. Noreen 2, 41 takes *at hyggjandi* as parallel to *at geði*, for, while *hyggjandi* normally means 'intellect, wisdom' (the only sense in Fritzner 2), twice in the Icelandic Homily Book what is evidently the identical formation *hyggendi* (Torp 26/44) renders *anima* 'soul'. So we might translate 'a man should not be showy in his mind'. The weakness of this view is the poor support for such a rendering of *hyggjandi*; it is probably better to emend to *af*.

6 The usual sense of *víti* (the only one in Fritzner 2 and Cl-Vig) is 'punishment, penalty, fine'. But the sense 'harm, misfortune' seems to be present in Reginsmál 1 (*kannat sér við víti varask*) and perhaps elsewhere in poetry (see LP); OE *wīte* also has this meaning at times. This would make good sense here ('misfortune seldom befalls the wary') and is cogently argued for by Kock, NN §1921. Most editors, however, prefer to follow Falk 8, 231, who suggests that *víti* 'penalty' passed into denoting the offence itself; so also LP ('deed deserving punishment, blameworthy conduct'). This is certainly better evidenced than the sense 'harm' and is still alive in modern Icelandic. Thus 'the wary man seldom commits a culpable blunder'. The line is now proverbial; Heusler 1,110 remarks that if it was a pre-existing proverb this would explain the anacoluthon.

7-9 are bracketed by many editors; their sense is inappropriate, for they do not really supply a reason for what precedes.

7

3 *hljóð* is probably used here in its primary sense 'hearing' (cognate with κλύω 'I hear') preserved in such expressions as *biðja* (or

kveðja) hljóðs 'to ask for a hearing', *hann kom á hljóð at* . . . 'he heard, learnt that . . .', *í heyranda hljóði* 'in the hearing of all'. For the adj. Kock 2, 107 compares OE *þynne andgyt* and Latin *tenuis sensus*. FJ believes that *hljóð* has here developed the concrete sense 'ear', comparing the proverb *þunnt er móðureyrað*. But such a sense of *hljóð* would be unique. (*Heimdallar hljóð* Vsp. 27 is too dubious to build on; DH interpreted 'ear' here, but Snorri, like most modern scholars, plainly took it as 'sound', i.e. 'horn', cp. Gylfaginning ch. 27 [FJ 9, 33].)

8

The two halves do not fit well together, for, as Guðmundur Finnbogason 2, 105 points out, 'praise' and 'favour, warm judgments' — as *lof* and *líknstafi* are customarily rendered respectively — are precisely things which one inevitably has *annars brjóstum í*. Lindquist 2, 8ff. holds that *lof* is etymologically related to OE *lufu* etc. (but this is uncertain) and that a sense 'love, affection, esteem' fits better than 'praise' both here and in some other Eddaic instances (the best case is st. 52 below). He takes *líknstafir* as 'words (magically) calculated to win help from other persons', a sense that also fits its only other occurrence, Sigrdr. 5: *fullr er hann ljóða ok líknstafa, góðra galdra ok gamanrúna*. Other editors take *líknstafir* as = *líkn*, with *-stafir* as a mere derivative ending (so SG, comparing *bǫlstafir* = *bǫl, flærðarstafir* = *flærð* Sigrdr. 30 and 32).

4 Eiríkr Magnússon 1, 25 and 2, 67 emends *við* to *vit* and renders 'less tractable is the wit (wisdom) which one owns in another's breast = borrowed wisdom is a property difficult to manage'; he thinks that st. 9 has expanded on this idea while *vit* was still uncorrupted. This is perhaps over-ingenious; 4-6 in CR are in themselves fully acceptable. For the sentiment Eiríkr well compares Konráðs saga ch.2: *þat ræð ek þér, at þú trúir betr þér en honum. Enda segi ek þat, at hallkvæmra þyki mér þér vera þat, er þú berr í brjósti þér, en þat, er hann veit ok þú átt undir honum.*

10-11

brautu at, velli at — for this sense of *at* 'along, down through' see Fritzner 2, s.v. *at* 17. In this sense the prep. seems likely to descend from the *aft* (later *at*, with loss of *f* in weak-stressed position) often found in runic inscriptions, cognate with *eptir* and distinct in origin from the usual preposition *at* (= OE *æt*, Latin *ad*). See S. Bugge in ANF XVIII (1902) 5-6 and his *Der Runenstein von Rök* (Stockholm 1910) 211-12, also Jansson 23. It should however be noted that in the inscriptions the word governs the acc. and means 'in memory of'.

13

1 *Óminnishegri* — the heron does not appear to be connected with forgetfulness elsewhere, and the exact point of the expression is unclear. FJ points out that the heron's habit of standing motionless for long periods, in seeming oblivion, might account for the image, though he surely goes too far in proposing that this oblivion could have been thought to infect the beholders. Von Hofsten 25-6 asserts that what is emphasized here is not forgetfulness *per se* but rash actions under the influence of alcohol, and connects this with the way in which the heron, after waiting motionless, can suddenly strike out with his terrible 'harpoon'. But this does not sort well with the actual word *óminni* in the text. Dronke points out that the heron, in fact and in modern proverbial lore, is associated with vomiting, which (though not in herons) is often a consequence of excessive drink; but it is again some way to the *óminni* of the text. Holtsmark 1 believes the reference is to an ale-ladle in the form of a heron and renders *yfir ǫlðrum þrumir* 'floats on the surface of the ale'. *Ǫlðr* can mean both 'ale' (as in 137 below) and 'ale-party' (which is how most editors take it here); in the former sense it is normally singular, but the plural occurs in a verse of Egill (*ǫlðra dregg* Skj. i 50). Ladles in the form of birds (*øland, ølgås, ølhane*) are known in Norway, though no instance of a heron-ladle seems to have come to light. Elmevik has objected that a ladle would not repose silent and motionless, as implied by *þrumir*, but would be continually raised and lowered; a perhaps weightier objection is that there is no actual evidence for bird-ladles in Norway before *c.* 1500, though of course they might have existed earlier. If Holtsmark's suggestion is rejected, 2 should be rendered 'he who hovers over ale-feasts'.

3 *guma* is probably acc., not gen.; for the construction cp. *stela mik eign minni* Laxdœla saga ch. 84 (ÍF V 239).

6 Gunnlǫð is known in Norse legend only as the daughter of the giant Suttungr, who had acquired the sacred mead of poetry from the dwarfs Fjalarr and Galarr; Óðinn wins the mead by seducing her. The story is related in 104-110 below, and in Snorri's Prose

Edda (Skáldskaparmál ch. 5-6). Presumably this is the story referred to here and in st. 14, and *ek* must accordingly be Óðinn; but if so it is clearly a variant version, for nothing is told elsewhere of Óðinn's being drunk nor of his visiting Fjalarr. St. 14 reads most naturally as though in this version Fjalarr, not Suttungr, was the name of Gunnlǫð's giant father, and Fjalarr is indeed recorded as a giant-name (Hárb. 26, and in a *þula*, Skj. i 659).

14

3 For Fjalarr see on 13 above.

4 *því* is correctly explained by Fritzner 2 s.v. *því* 4 as 'i det Tilfælde', that is 'in this case': the best sort of drinking party is one which is not excessive, one where everyone leaves still in possession of his right senses, or easily able to reclaim them. (So also Schneider 63: 'nur das Gelage taugt, von dem der Mann seine Sinne mit heimbringt'.) Many editors take *því* as 'therefore, for this reason' (thus FJ: 'It is ale's best quality that everyone recovers his senses') but this contradicts the context and gives feeble sense in itself.

5 The particle *of* is written *vf* in CR here, as also in 67 below and in Grímnismál 34; similarly for *of* prep. in Guðrúnarkviða II 2.

16

1 *ósnjallr* also occurs in 48, where it is opposed to *mildir, frœknir menn*. 'Cowardly' seems to be what is mainly implied, though some editors render 'foolish'; the positive *snjallr* can mean both 'bold' and 'wise'.

4-6 mean of course that death is inescapable — even if you manage to avoid a violent death, you will die of old age in the end — and not, as preposterously suggested by Vesper 28, that the man who in his youth skulks away from battle will have an uneasy conscience in his old age. 'This sentence had needed no commentary, had not a commentator darkened it.'

17

1 *kópa* 'stare, gaze', only here in ON, but found in Norwegian and in Danish and Swedish dialects, and occasionally in later Icelandic; BMÓ 52 testified in 1915 that it was common in this sense in Árnessýsla in southern Iceland.

3 Collinder 1, 17, followed by FJ and SG, holds that *þylsk um*

and *þrumir* are contrasted: either the fool prattles endlessly or he is sullenly speechless. This is based on the sense 'proclaim ceremonially' for *þylja*, as e.g. in 111 below; but this verb is also well evidenced in the sense 'mumble' and the use of the reflexive, which is found only here and must have the force of 'to oneself' shows that this is the meaning in this passage.

4 For *allt senn* to denote simultaneous occurrence cp. María saga (ed. Unger, 210): *er þá mjǫk allt senn, at kertit brotnar ok húsfrú vaknar* (another instance in Sverris saga ch. 10 [ed. Indrebø, 11]).

6 *uppi er þá geð guma*. Guðmundur Finnbogason 2, 105 explains 'the moment he gets a drink, he reveals the whole contents of his mind', i.e. taking *uppi* as 'displayed, visible', and similarly many editors. But *uppi* can also mean 'finished, exhausted', as in *er þá uppi hverr penningr fjárins* Msk. 182, and other instances in Fritzner 2, s.v. *uppi* 5c. The last line would then mean 'the man's sense is at an end, is no more'. (For *geð* = *vit* cp. *lítil eru geð guma* in st. 53.) There is no way of deciding between these two possibilities. The rendering of the line in Cl-Vig (s.v. *geð* 2 — otherwise in CPB 3) as 'then folk are in high spirits' is eccentric and does not fit the context.

18

3 *Fjǫlð* is in effect adverbial, cp. *fjǫlð um viðrir* 74 and *fjǫlð ek fór* Vafþr. 3.

6 This line, which in CR reads *sá er vitandi er vits*, has caused difficulty, as is shown by the variations among translators. Since *vita* with gen. normally means 'to know, know of' (*margs vitandi* Vsp. 20, *barna veiztu þinna* Atlamál 84), Brate understood it as 'He knows what sense is'. But in Flat. ii 76 we read *má hverr maðr [sjá], sá er vits er vitandi, at þessi augu hafi í einum hausi verit bæði*, where the phrase clearly means 'anyone who has got any sense'. Cp. Fritzner 2, s.v. *vit* 5, where it is associated with such expressions as *varð ek svá feginn at ek þóttumst varla vita vits míns* Heilag. i. 489, *þeir lágu sem dauðir menn en vissu vits síns* Heilag. i 527. *Vitandi vits* is still used in Icelandic, in the sense 'with one's eyes open, knowing what one is about'.

Some editors take the line as conditionally modifying *sá einn* in line 1, e.g. Heusler 2, 110-11: 'nur der Vielgereiste hat die Kenntnis der mennschlichen Sinnesart, sofern er nämlich *vitandi er vits*'. But, as E. Noreen 2, 43 remarks, this is syntactically unbelievable:

if the last line is relative, it must modify the immediately preceding *gumna hverr*, and so Noreen explains that not even the travelled and experienced connoisseur of human nature can comprehend those who have *not* got sense. But this alternative is also unsatisfactory: the meaning proposed is most implausible and, as Sijmons (in SG) observes, after the absolute *gumna hverr* one expects no limitation. The only escape from the dilemma is to turn the line into an independent sentence by expelling the second *er* and then render '*He* (i.e. the much-travelled man) is a person of sense, knows what he is talking about' (thus Lindquist 3, 64).

19

1-2 The sense of these lines is much disputed. Many of the earlier editors printed *haldi* and rendered 'A man may grasp the bowl, yet he should drink moderately'. But CR clearly reads *haldit* with the suffixed negative, and it is unsafe to emend, especially as *haldi* gives feeble sense to the first line. But what does *haldit* mean? *Halda á e-u* cannot mean 'abstain from sth.', as numerous nineteenth-century editors believed. Cl-Vig s.v. *halda* A V β groups this passage with expressions like *halda á sýslu, halda á ferð sinni, halda á hinni sǫmu bœn*, where the verb means 'to be busy about, stick to, persist in', and renders 'to go on drinking, carousing', taking *ker* as figurative for *drykkja*; so also Eiríkr Magnússon 2, 8 and Wisén 109. FJ objects that this would be a strange way to utter so simple a rule, and it is doubtful if *halda á* could have this meaning when followed by a concrete object (cp. Fritzner 2, s.v. *halda á* 7). Magnus Olsen 4 compares an Icelandic pre-Reformation wedding-toast which begins *Heilags anda skál skulum vér í einu af drekka, ok halda eigi lengi á* and thinks the first line means 'Don't sit for a long time with your bowl in your hand, but drain it off at a gulp'. But this leaves far too much to be read into the text. It is much more likely that the scene implied in our poem is one of *sveitardrykkja*, where the bowl goes round from man to man; the idea would then be 'Don't hold on to the bowl (drinking greedily, but pass it on to the next man)'. This seems plainly the most natural way of taking the line in itself, but does it give a clear contrast to the next line? (and contrast there must be, as *þó* shows). Not if *at hófi* implies 'a moderate amount as opposed to a great deal', but we would get reasonable sense if we can take it as suggesting 'a moderate amount as opposed to nothing or next to nothing'. It certainly was regarded as bad conduct to drink too little; this was called *drekka sleituliga* or *við sleitur*.

3 This line is also found in Vafþr. 10.

5 *vár* is evidently from a verb *vá* 'to blame', only found here, though some insert it by emendation into st. 75. SG, following a suggestion of Bugge 1, 45, connect with Gothic *unwahs* 'blameless'; otherwise de Vries 5.

20

3 *aldrtrega* 'life-sorrow' is taken by LP, both here and in its only other occurrence (Skj. i 442), to mean 'death': the glutton eats himself to death. More probably it means 'life-long misery' (CPB 4), perhaps here specifically 'grave illness'. Cp. NN §949, comparing OE *ealdorcearu*.

21

On the question of whether this strophe owes something to a Biblical or a Latin source (as argued respectively by Singer 7f. and Rolf Pipping 3) see p. 15 above.

6 The *máls* of CR is defended by DH and by Bugge 1, 394, but is plainly an error induced by the preceding *síns*.

22

1 *Vesall* has been attacked on two grounds:

(1) allegedly, it fails to alliterate. This raises the question whether *v* can alliterate with a vowel; Gering thought it could, and adduced 17 examples from the Edda, as well as a few from scaldic verse. Some of the examples have been criticized as corrupt, but some seem sure enough, e.g. *óhǫpp at þér vita* 117 below, *svaf vætr Freyja átta nóttum* Þrymskviða 28. The view that *v* can alliterate with a vowel was defended by Gering PBB 13 (1888) 202-9 and ZFDPh 42 (1910) 233-5, by Hildebrand ZFDPh (Ergänzungsband 1874) 109 and by Läffler SNF IV, 1 (1913) 27. It was attacked by Mogk *Indogermanische Forschungen* 26 (1910) 209-21 and by E. Noreen SNF III, 5 (1912).

(2) on grounds of sense. This is a more cogent attack, for *vesall* means 'wretched, miserable', which does not fit. CPB 461 suggested emending to *ósnotr* (though apparently only on grounds of alliteration), BMÓ advocated *ósviðr*, as in the preceding and following

strophes, and Collinder 1, 17, objecting that this failed to explain the intrusion of *vesall*, suggested the initial lines of st. 22 and 23 had been reversed; this would certainly give a more pointed meaning to 23. *Vesall* is defended by M. Olsen 7, 11, who says it can be used of someone of a low, coarse mentality. He does not however adduce any instance of this sense, though a case of *vesalingr* in Hávarðar saga ch. 15 (ÍF VI 342) comes fairly close; cp. also Fritzner 2, s.v. *veslingr* 3. Hannaas 234 says that *vesalmann* can be used in modern Sætesdal dialect of one with poor wits and low moral character.

2 *illa* is an adv.; FJ explains the phrase as elliptical for *illa skapi farinn*, for which cp. Harðar saga ok Hólmverja ch. 24: *mikill maðr ok sterkr ok illa skapi farinn, ójafnaðarmaðr um alla hluti*. Bugge 1, 45 compares Vatnsdœla saga ch. 29 (ÍF VIII 76): *hann var fjǫlkunnigr mjǫk ok þó at ǫðru illa*.

24

5 *fár* 'mischief, malice'; *lesa fár um e-n* evidently means 'speak ill of someone, utter malicious slanders about someone', cp. Stock. Homil. 52: *þat kann enn verða, at maðr vensk á þat, at lesa of aðra ok hafa uppi lǫstu manna*, and note *umlestr* 'slander', *umlassamr* 'slanderous', *umlesandi, umlesmaðr, umlestrarmaðr* 'slanderer'; it is interesting that these words are found only in religious texts.

The sentiments of this and st. 25 can be paralleled in a number of Continental proverbs (though none of them restrict their application to the *unwise* man). Singer 8 asserts there can be no doubt of a connection; in default of a Biblical or Classical model, he wonders if the origin could be Arabic (mediated via Viking raiders in Spain).

25

5 *er at þingi kømr* — most editors understand *hann* as the implied subject, but the verb may conceivably be impersonal, as in *er at morni kømr* 23 and other instances in Fritzner 2, s.v. *koma at* 7. So BMÓ and von See 3, 27.

26

3 *vera* 'refuge, resort', as in 10 above. *Vá* may well be the common word 'woe, calamity' (as recently argued by von See 3, 23). But

Sigsk. 29 has . . . *at kváðu við kálkar í vá*, where 'woe' is clearly impossible, and from which scholars have deduced the existence of a noun of this form meaning 'nook, corner', either as a mere textual corruption of *vrá* (Bugge 1, 394, who thinks the word may have baffled the scribe after the loss of *v* before *r* in West Norse) or alternatively as a dialectal by-form of it (Cl-Vig 673 postulates a rare sound-change *vr*-> *v*-, supposedly exemplified in *veita* 'to trench', *veina* 'to whinny', alleged to be from **vreita*, **vreina*, but these etymologies are more than dubious) or, thirdly and most likely, as a distinct word cognate with OE *wōh* 'crooked, crookedness' (so de Vries 5, 637 and Fritzner 2, iii 835-6, who adduces Norwegian place-names in support). The rendering 'corner' gives better sense here than 'woe' and should be adopted.

27

maðr is a necessary insertion in 1. On the supposed Biblical origin of the exposure of folly by loquacity see p. 15.

de Boor 373 plausibly suggests that lines 4-6 and 7-9 are interchangeable 'tradition-variants'.

28

6 *gengr um* — either 'befalls', as in 94, or 'is said about', see Fritzner 2, s.vv. *ganga um* 4 and *ganga* 19. Whichever view is taken, the connection between the two halves of the strophe is obscure; the 'explanations' of Heusler 2, 112 and von See 3, 24 are somewhat obscure in themselves. It may well be, as many editors have thought, that the two halves did not originally belong together, though it is certainly curious that, as von See points out, what appears to be the same combination of notions also occurs in 63 (whose two halves Heusler 2, 117, interestingly enough, sought to sever).

29

3 *staðlausu* is generally taken as a defining gen. sg. of a noun *staðlausa* 'baselessness, senselessness', though the possibility that it is weak acc. pl. of an adj. *staðlauss* cannot be excluded. The noun does not occur elsewhere (though *staðleysi* is found); *staðlauss* is found once, rendering Latin *pavidus* 'fearful'. *Stafi* 'words', cp. *sagði sanna stafi* Sigrdr. 14.

5 *haldendr* may be either nom. subject or acc. object of *eigi*.

30
The two halves fit poorly together.
3 *þótt* is virtually 'when'.
5-6 For the co-ordination of two conditional clauses, where the first has *ef* with indicative and the second has subjunctive without *ef*, cp. *ef þú kannt með at fara, ok bregðir þú hvergi af* Njáls saga ch. 7 (ÍF XII 24) and numerous other instances in Nygaard 2, §185, Anm. c.
6 *þurrfjallr* 'with dry skin', i.e. in dry clothes.

31
1-3 The drift of this half is not clear, and there is a metrical difficulty in 3, since (as was shown by Bugge 3) the first syllable of a disyllable at the end of a *ljóðaháttr* 'full line' must be short. (A long vowel followed immediately by a short vowel, as for instance in *búa*, counts as short for this purpose.) A few counter-instances are adduced by DH in their note on this strophe, but they are mostly unconvincing, being either textually dubious (*jarðar* 107, *þægi* 39) or not in true *ljóðaháttr* strophes (*rǫgna* 142, *sorgum* 146, *hlýddu* 164). Interpretations which take *hæðinn* as nom. can remove the difficulty by reading *hæðinn gestr at gest* (FJ) or *gestr hæðinn at gest* (SG, presumably on the ground that the *first* of the *nomina* should bear the alliteration; but there are counter-examples, cp. H. Pipping 2, 8-9); FJ also suggested reading *heðinn*, taken as an adj. formed from *hǫð* and meaning 'militant'.

The most usual interpretation is that a guest who mocks a fellow-guest is then wise to take to flight. This makes sense, but it reduces *þykkisk* in effect to *er*, it takes *fróðr* as 'prudent, sensible', which is hard to parallel, and it assumes an expression *taka flótta* 'take to flight' that does not seem to appear elsewhere despite the frequent occurrence of the notion in the sagas. All these objections also apply to Kock's view (NN §§18, 1508 B) that the person who takes to flight is the mocked guest, with *at gest hæðinn* seen as analogous to phrases like *at Hrungni dauðan* Hárb.14, *at liðinn fylki* Helg. Hj. 42 (Fritzner 2, s.v. *at* 1, LP s.v. *at* B). So 'That guest seems to be (= is) wise, who takes to flight after another guest has mocked (him)'. This seems a pusillanimous sentiment. In view of all the difficulties, it is likely that there is a deep-seated corruption in the text; an interesting emendation is that of Guðmundur Finnbogason 2, 106, who reads *flátta* 'to sneer at' (not recorded, but cp. *flåtta* in this sense in modern Norwegian dialects). Thus 'A mocking guest who starts to sneer at a guest thinks he is being clever'.

5-6 *glissa* and *glama* do not occur elsewhere in Icelandic, but are well evidenced in modern Norwegian and Swedish dialects, meaning respectively 'to mock, sneer' and 'to be rowdy, talk noisily'. Cp. Flom 262-5.

32

2 *erusk* — refl. forms of *vera* (with reciprocal sense) are very rare, but cp. 41 below, and further instances in Cl-Vig s.v. *vera* B IV; a runic inscription on a comb found in Trondheim (*c.* 1100?) is normalized *Liut*[*ge*]*r ok Jóhan erusk vinir*, NIYR V 31.

3 *virði* is also found as a dat. in 116; the Staðarhólsbók version of Grágás (ed. V. Finsen, 1879, 352) has the alliterating doublet *at verði eða at virði*; and a scaldic poet uses the phrase *á ulfs virði* (Skj. i 196). This is perhaps a noun *virði* n. distinct from *verðr* m. (Bugge 1, 394), but is more probably an old dat. of *verðr* showing *i*-mutation (A. Noreen §63.3 and §395 Anm.1), later replaced by a form with -*e*- levelled from the other cases; for if there really was a word **virði* it is odd it is found only in the dat. *Vrekask* — the restoration of this early form for CR *rekask* is required by the alliteration, as in *þess mun Víðarr vreka* (CR *reka*) Vafþr. 53. See A. Noreen §288 and, for other instances in the Edda, FJ 5, 264.

4 *aldar róg* 'strife of (i.e. among) men'. M. Olsen 7, 12 reads *aldarróg* in one word and suspects *at* or *ef* has dropped out before *órir*; he renders 'Eternal strife will there ever be, if guest disputes with guest' (cp. Wessén 3, 29). Olsen compares *aldartryðir ok ævintrygðir er æ skulu haldask* from Tryggðamál (Grágás, Staðarhólsbók 406), where the first word clearly means 'pledges that shall last for ever'. But Olsen is wrong to say that in the Edda *ǫld* means 'men' only when in the pl., cp. *aldar ørlǫg* Lokasenna 21 and *hálf er ǫld hvár* 53 below.

6 *óra* only here in West Norse, but in Old Swedish we find the same expression *óra við e-n* 'to show hostility to someone', which occurs several times in the laws of Östergötland (but with present *órar*, not *órir*), and also the subst. *óran* 'feud'. R. Pipping 1 denies

the identity of the two verbs, because of the difference of inflection; but this can be paralleled. See Richert 5-6 and SGL II 54-5.

33

2 *opt* probably means 'as a rule, regularly', cp. NN §309 and Fritzner 2, comparing *oft an wīg gearwe* Beowulf 1247; see also S. Bugge in *Tidskrift for Philologi og Pædagogik* 8 (1868-9) 70. Richert 21-4, followed by SG, thought he could demonstrate a sense 'plentifully' for this word; but, as well as being etymologically dubious, such a sense would fit poorly here, where the emphasis seems to be on eating *early* rather than on eating *well*. A. Kock implausibly postulated (ANF XX [1904] 69) a distinct word *opt* 'certainly, without fail', cognate with Gothic *auftô, uftô* and separate from the homonym meaning 'often'.

Some editors have understood 1-3 to imply 'Eat early, unless you are going on a visit — in which case don't eat at all, but wait until you reach your host'. Since this contradicts 4-6, Bugge 1, 47, followed by BMÓ and SG, emended *nema* to *né án*, supposed to mean 'nor come on a visit without (having eaten)'. But, as FJ observes, this is a very strained expression. He himself read *skylit* (FJ 1, 46): 'Don't eat early, unless you are going on a visit'. But why should one not eat early? This seems in fact to have been the regular practice. Much the best explanation is that of M. Olsen 5, who renders 'Normally eat early, unless you are going on a visit (in which case you should eat somewhat later, so as not to arrive famished)'.

4 *snópa* is found only once elsewhere in ON, in a verse in Gautreks saga (*snauðr mun ek snópa* Skj. ii 342), where the context is not decisive. It occurs in modern Icelandic in the sense 'hang around idly, kill time' and in Norwegian dialects, meaning 'sit around waiting, like a beggar, or staring dully' and 'nose about after something'. See BMÓ 55 and Flom 266-7, and cp. *snapir* 62. In the present passage it must mean something like 'hang around hungrily, restlessly craving food'.

5 *sólginn* probably means 'famished'. It was taken by Richert 6-8 as 'with something stuck in the throat', a sense found for *svulgen* in modern Swedish dialects. But this cannot be paralleled elsewhere in Scandinavian, ancient or modern, whereas a sense 'hungry' is found both in modern Icelandic (*sólginn í e-ð* 'hungry for something') and apparently in a verse in Þjóðólfr's Haustlǫng (Skj. i 17), while in a verse of Einarr Skúlason (Skj. i 454) the billow is described as *brimsolginn* ('hungry for the surf' LP).

34

6 'Though he is gone further off'. It may be, though, that FJ is right to suppose that we have here an instance of *fara* transitive with acc. object: 'to come upon, overtake, meet'; thus, 'though he is (to be) met with further off' (so also Cl-Vig s.v. *fara* B I 2).

35

The omission of *skal* in 1 is a clear instance of haplography. For the sentiment editors compare Egils saga ch. 78 (ÍF II 272): *þat var engi siðr, at sitja lengr en þrjár nætr at kynni.*

36

2 lacks alliteration. Heusler 1, 111 and Kuhn 3, 21 accept the text on the supposition that 1-2 are an old proverb incorporated in the poem without alteration, and Wessén 2, 21 suggests that *lítit* gives such perfect meaning (which is true enough) that the poet decided for once to dispense with alliteration. But lack of parallels makes this implausible. No wholly persuasive emendation, however, has yet been advanced. Among suggested substitutions for *lítit* are *búkot* (Bugge 1, 394 and CPB 5; the word occurs in prose), *borlítit* (Kock 2, 277, a non-existent word; *bor-* is a strengthening prefix in OHG), *bjarglítit* (M. Olsen 7, 15; found only in modern Icelandic) and *búð* (M. Olsen 8, inferring the sense 'very small farm' from the use of *búðsetumaðr* in Grágás; but *búð* itself is never found alone in this sense, and the concept is unknown to the Norwegian laws, which must be more relevant than the Icelandic Grágás). Lindquist 3, 245 proposed *þótt séi bragðlítit* (not in ON, and in modern Icelandic only in inapt senses, but ON has *bragðmikill* 'of imposing appearance', of a person). Lie 217 reads *Bú, þótt sé lítit, betra er*; but why should this ever have been corrupted? Nordenstreng suggested *þótt breitt sét* 'though it is not broad', comparing the name *Breiðibólstaðr*, but a *bú* 'household' is less concrete than a *bólstaðr* and can hardly be described by this adj. FJ 1, 46 replaced 2 by *en biðja sé*, which is rewriting rather than emending, and the same can be said of BMÓs version: *Bæn* (dat. of comparison) *es betra / bú þót lítit sé*, which is awkward into the bargain.

5 *taugreptan* (only here) evidently refers to a house whose *raptar* 'rafters' are of *taug*, 'ropes' or perhaps 'withies', instead of timber. For the characterization of the poorest type of household, compare

Rígsþula, where Þræll and Þír tend pigs and goats (12) while the farmer Karl is depicted as breaking in oxen and erecting buildings of timber (22).

38

2 *velli á* probably means no more than 'out of doors' (surely not 'on the battlefield' as Holtsmark 4, 147 suggests).

39

1-2 Jansson 122-3 and 144 notes similar expressions in Swedish runic epitaphs: at Hagstugan in Södermanland (SR nr 130) four sons erected a stone in memory of their father *Dómara, mildan orða ok matar góðan*, and the Ivla stone in Småland (SmR nr 44) commemorates one Sveinn, *mildan við sinna ok matar góðan* (spelling normalized). Both these inscriptions are in verse.

3 Most scholars appear to take this line as conveying the idea 'that he would not accept a gift if it were offered to him', e.g. Bellows: 'that gladly he took not a gift'; Collinder 2: 'att han avslog alla gåvor'; Guðni Jónsson *Eddulyklar* 163: 'að hann þægi ekki að þiggja laun eða gjafir'. But this follows poorly on 1-2 (for it is no denigration of a man's generosity that he is also willing to accept a gift) and, as FJ 1, 47 observes, it is hard to see how such a meaning can be deduced from the text. 1-3 must rather mean: 'I never met a man so generous, or so liberal with food, that *þiggja* was not *þegit*, to accept was not (reckoned as) accepted, i.e. that accepting (of hospitality from him) was not (in his eyes) a gift (and therefore demanding repayment)'. Cp. M. Olsen 7, 16.

5 An adj. in the acc. sg. m. has evidently been omitted after *svági* (there is no gap in CR). The general sense of 4-5 must be something like 'or so generous with his money'. Most editors insert *gjǫflan*, others *ǫrvan*, though they differ as to retaining or omitting *-gi*. SG argue that the clause would most naturally begin with *né*, but in fact it begins with *eða* and *-gi* merely negates that word and so is needed; other scholars, more plausibly holding that *-gi* would negate the adj., omit it, or else (as FJ) read *svági glǫggvan* 'so unniggardly'. H. Pipping 1, believing that covetousness (seeking more) rather than miserliness (keeping what one has) is what the sense requires, reads *svági fíkinn*. But, as he half-admits, this is incompatible with *síns*.

6 The last word reads *þegi* in CR, interpreted by many editors as *þægi*, pret. subj. (cp. *mælum* 91, *svæfik* 154, written *melom*,

svefic); but the 'full line' should not end in a trochee (cp. on 31 above). CPB 460 suggests *þegin* for *ef þegi*, FJ reads *þiggr*, M. Olsen 7, 16 conjectures *geti*. But *þegi* as a form for the present subjunctive can be paralleled in Norwegian laws: *engi scal til annars mæla at hann þegi scömm* NGL I 181/23, cp. A. Noreen §498, Anm.7, and Jón Þorkelsson *Supplement til Islandske Ordbøger* Fjerde Samling (København 1899) 186, who postulates a strong verb *þega* of the same meaning as *þiggja*.

40

Von See 2, 11-12 takes the sense of 1-3 to be 'Be generous (to others)'. But 'one should not endure need of one's money, which one has acquired' would be a very tortuous, even impossible, way to express this simple notion, and it is not the case, as he avers, that 4-5 impose this interpretation. The sense is rather 'Don't hesitate to make use of your money; for, after all, if you do save it, it may very well end up in the hands of someone you wouldn't have chosen'.

41

3 'That is most manifest on oneself' or '. . . on themselves' (*sjálfum* may be sg. or pl.). What can this mean? Richert 8-9 understood it as 'One knows this best from one's own experience', and this has been widely followed (FJ, Bellows, Collinder 2). But CPB 12 renders 'such as may shew about one's body'. This goes back to Sveinbjörn Egilsson's 'haec (arma vestesque) in ipsis sunt maxime conspicua', and is far more plausible; as BMÓ 61 says, it is very difficult to see how Richert's interpretation can be deduced from the words of the text. BMÓ well compares Haraldskvæði: *Á gerðum sér þeira / ok á gullbaugum / at þeir eru í kunnleikum við konung* 'One sees from their garb and their rings of gold that they are on familiar terms with the king' (Skj. i 24-5). *Þat* refers to the whole content of 1-2: the idea is that the reciprocally exchanged gifts which they bear on their bodies give the most manifest testimony to their mutual generosity.

4-5 FJ and SG expelled *ok endrgefendr* as tautologous and as making the line over-long. But Matras drew attention to a Faroese proverb recorded by Svabo (1746-1824): *Endigjeer o Vüɡjeer eru laangstir Vinir*, which Matras renders in 'normalised Norse form' as *endrgerð ok viðrgerð eru lengstir vinir*. Svabo translated the proverb as 'Tjeneste og Gjentjeneste holder længst Venskab, officia redintegrata amicitiam diutissime conservant'. It is clear that this is in some way related to the lines in our poem; very possibly the strophe has incorporated a proverb which survived independently in the Faroes (with -*gefendr* corrupted into -*gerð*, as Matras suggests, after this type of agent noun became extinct in Faroese). That the lines were a pre-existing proverb had already been argued by Heusler 1,111, on the grounds of their alliterative irregularity and the pointlessness of the final line ('if it endures to turn out well'), as if it had been added merely to round off the strophe.

47

6 may well be a proverb; it also occurs in the Icelandic Runic Poem (ed. Bruce Dickins *Runic and Heroic Poems* [Cambridge 1915]), though as this is of late medieval date it might have drawn the line direct from our poem.

48

4 For *ósnjallr* see on 16 above.

6 is rendered by Bellows 'And not gladly the niggard gives' (so also Fritzner 2 s.v. *sýta* and von See 3, 34). This is probably wrong; it most likely means 'the niggard is ever apprehensive about gifts' i.e. he does not want to receive them, because that obliges him to make gifts in return. FJ compares *sýta við dauða*, as in Krákumál 25 (Skj. i 655).

49

2 *velli at*: if this means 'in a field', as most editors take it, we may cite *hrafn at meiði* Brot 5 as a near enough parallel to the use of *at*, though it is true we might rather expect *á*, as in 38. M. Olsen 7, 20, comparing st. 10-11 above, argues for the sense 'passing over open country'.

3 *trémǫnnum* — images of men carved in wood. CPB 460 suggests these were way-marks, but there is no evidence for the existence of such in early Scandinavia. Elsewhere *trémaðr* always appears to have a cultic or magical connection: in Þorleifs þáttr jarlsskálds (ÍF IX 225ff.) Hákon jarl constructs a *trémaðr* into which the heart

of a slaughtered man is inserted, and which then functions as a robot, and in Flat. I 403 Óláfr Tryggvason speaks of the Freyr-idol worshipped by the Prœndir as *eigi kvikr maðr, heldr einn trémaðr* — one of two *trémenn* whom, he explains, the Swedes had buried along with their dead king Freyr and whom they later exhumed and worshipped. In the last chapter of Ragnars saga loðbrókar we hear how Qgmundr arrives with five ships at Sámsey, where some of his party go off into the woods and come upon *einn trémann fornan*, forty ells high and covered with moss; they speculate who can have worshipped *þetta it mikla goð. Ok þá kveðr trémaðrinn*, and then follow three stanzas. (See further on strophe 50.) The Arab traveller Ibn Fadlan, describing the Rus (Swedish vikings) of the middle Volga whom he encountered in 921-2, tells how they prostrate themselves in worship before 'a long upright piece of wood that has a face like a man's ... surrounded by little figures (idols)', praying to them for aid and sacrificing sheep and cattle to them (Smyser 97).

5 *ript* 'cloth, clothing', only here and in a verse by Óláfr hvítaskáld, who has *vinda ript* as a kenning for 'sail'; it also constitutes the second element of *valaript* Sigsk. 66 and of *lérept* 'linen' (< *lín* + *ript*). A by-form *ripti* occurs a few times. The word still exists in modern Norwegian dialects, as *ryft, rift, ryfte* etc. (Hannaas 235) and has cognates in OE *rift, rifte* 'cloak, curtain, veil'.

6 *neiss* only here in poetry, but recorded in two prose passages (see Fritzner 2 s.v. *hneiss*); in one the alliterative association with nakedness similarly occurs: *þá hǫfðu borgarmenn hina sǫmu siðvenju við konung sinn ok sendu hann til sǫmu eyjar nøktan ok neisan sem alla aðra* (Barlaams ok Josaphats saga, ed. Magnus Rindal [Oslo 1981], 53, here normalized). So also in English, into which *neiss* was borrowed: *nais and naked* (c. 1300), *nakid and nais* (c. 1325), see OED s.v. *nais*. It is commonly rendered 'ashamed' or the like on the assumption that it is related to *hneisa* 'shame, disgrace' and should properly be *hneiss (whence Fritzner's spelling; SG explain the loss of *h* as a Norwegianism) but this etymology is far from certain (Holm 157-8), and Holtsmark 4, 148 plausibly proposes instead a sense 'defenceless, destitute of help'. Neg. *óneiss* occurs several times (only in the Poetic Edda) as an epithet of princes and warriors; it may also occur in a runic inscription at Gårdstånga in Skåne (DR nr 330, Moltke 312, 526), applied to *drengir . . . í víkingu*, but this depends on a conjectural restoration. *Neiss* is possibly a distinctively Norwegian word; as Holtsmark

notes, the Icelandic version of Barlaams saga replaces it by a past participle. See further Harris 324-8.

The drift of the strophe has sometimes been thought obscure; most probably it reflects the notion 'clothes make the man; clothe a pillar and it will have the appearance of a gentleman'. Cp. the German proverb 'Kleider machen Leute'. Line 6 could have been a pre-existing proverb, as Heusler 1, 112 and Wessén 4, 456 hold.

50

1-3 Wessén 2 takes 3 as conditional ('a fir withers, if neither bark nor needles protect it') and regards 2 as a mere adjectival space-filler: *þorp* has been selected only to alliterate with *þǫll* and has no real significance. But this is biologically unsatisfactory, for it is only *after* a fir has died that its bark and needles fall away. *Þorpi á* must in fact define the situation which is unpropitious for the fir; but what it means here is much disputed. The problem is closely involved in the very extensive general debate about the etymology, primary sense, and relation between the various attested and apparent senses of *þorp (torp, Dorf* etc.) in the Germanic languages, where it occurs both as an appellative and as a common place-name element; see KLNM s.v. *-torp*, A. H. Smith *English Place-Name Elements* ii (English Place-Name Society XXVI [Cambridge 1956]) s.vv. *þorp, þrop*, and the entries in the Bibliography below under Eriksson, Foerste, Knudsen and Rooth.

The following senses have been proposed for *þorp* here:

(1) 'Bare, rocky hillock' or the like; perhaps the commonest rendering (most recently von See 3, 35). But the evidence that *þorp* can bear this meaning is far from strong; essentially it depends on an episode in the second chapter of Hálfs saga ok Hálfsrekka, in which a man on his way to settle in Iceland puts in at Ǫgvaldsnes, where King Ǫgvaldr had fallen and been buried in a mound and, on his asking how long ago this had happened, a voice from the mound speaks a verse which ends *þá varð ek þessa þorps ráðandi.* There is, however, nothing in the verse itself, as distinct from the accompanying prose, to imply that 'this *þorp*' refers to a mound, and furthermore the same verse occurs elsewhere, as the first of the three spoken by the *trémaðr* in Ragnars saga (see on 49 above) and *here there is no mound.* The only other evidence adduced for this sense is a rocky islet in Lake Vättern called Torp, and a rock platform in a field in Bohuslän referred to in 1775 as Torpet.

(2) 'Ledge, shelf of rock in a hillside' (Rooth), on the somewhat random assumption that it is related to *þrep* 'ledge'; the use of *torp* in modern Central Swedish dialects to mean 'an upper bunk' is seen as deriving from such a sense.

(3) 'Field, bare exposed area', e.g. Konráð Gíslason in *Njála* II 43: '(nærmest en skovlös men dertil i det hele) en åben plads, uden ly og læ'. This rests on the solitary occurrence of *þaúrp* in Gothic, rendering ἀγρός in Nehemiah 5.16, which has naturally led many scholars to suppose that the Gothic (and therefore perhaps the primary Germanic) sense was 'field', a sense which might be thought to survive in the use of *torp* on Bornholm to mean 'elevated dry meadowland with thin grass' (see Knudsen, and note also *geirþorp* as a shield-kenning beside *geirvangr* and *geirfit*). But Eriksson has powerfully argued that in rendering ἀγρός Wulfila rather had in mind the sense 'estate, farmstead' (Latin *villa*) which it sometimes has in late Greek (though Foerste has retorted that in that case Wulfila would have written *weihs*).

(4) Some scholars have believed that *þorp* is cognate with Latin *turba*, and, whether this be accepted or not, there is some evidence of a sense 'group' in ON: Snorri says in the Prose Edda (FJ 9, 188) that a single man is called *maðr*, two are called *tá* and three are called *þorp*, and in a *þula* (Skj. i 662) *þorp* occurs as a *heiti* beside such words as *folk, fundr, drótt, samnaðr*. One may compare the verb *þyrpask* 'to crowd', and the use of *torp* in modern Norwegian dialects to denote 'flock (of animals or children)'. Foerste has suggested that late Latin *troppus* 'flock, herd' (the ultimate source of English *troop, troupe*), which has no obvious etymology, is an adoption of a metathesized form of the Germanic word in this sense. On this basis, Stefán Karlsson emends to *þorpi án*, supposed to mean 'without company, i.e. not sheltered by other trees, all alone'. But this seems a tortuous way to express so simple a sense, and it has the disadvantage that it requires an alteration of the text.

(5) 'Pen, fold', supposed by Foerste to be the primary sense from which 'flock, group', as above, developed ('that which encloses' coming to mean 'that which is enclosed', cp. *tún, garðr*). This is clearly speculative and, while it is doubtless true that a fir shut in with animals would not flourish, the scene evoked is too specialized to furnish the everyday image we need here.

(6) 'Habitation, farmstead, hamlet'. This has the advantage of being the usual sense of the word in ON; whatever the ultimate etymology and prehistoric sense(s) of *þorp* may have been, there

is no doubt that in ON, and indeed elsewhere in Germanic, it normally refers to an inhabited building or group of buildings of some kind. In West Norse it is not used of native Icelandic circumstances (where it is also virtually non-existent in place-names), but occurs in the Kings' Sagas of farms in Norway and in religious texts as a rendering of *villa, vicus, castrum* (see Cl-Vig and Fritzner 2). In East Norse it mostly denotes a little farm, a croft, especially a secondary settlement, a dependent steading erected on newly-won land. In modern Norwegian and Swedish it means 'minor farm, smallholding', and cp. Swedish compounds like *fiskartorp, soldattorp*. The sense 'farm' has naturally developed into 'village' (cp. Latin *villa* > French *ville*), as in German and Dutch (already in OHG). As a place-name element, it appears to have spread from Germany into Denmark and thence into Sweden and eastern Norway and into the Danelaw, apparently in the sense 'secondary settlement'.

The picture of the lonely fir on mound or hillside, as evoked by all the first four explanations, appeals to modern taste, but, apart from the philological weaknesses of the first three, there is a fundamental botanical objection to this interpretation, which is that firs do *not* wither in such conditions; on the contrary, they thrive. Where they waste away is in the neighbourhood of human habitation. So we should follow (6): the fir stands among farm buildings, its roots nibbled by animals, its shoots and bark eaten by goats and, perhaps, its lower bark flayed off to make flour (a practice followed in periods of hardship in Scandinavia until recent times; there is a reference to the consumption of bark and fir-sap in Sverris saga ch. 13 [ed. Indrebø, 13]). See Lindquist 1, 129 and Holtsmark 1, 24-29.

Line 3 surely means 'It has lost the bark and needles which would have protected it' rather than 'It has bark and needles, but they do not suffice to protect it' (as Lindquist and FJ), which seems pointless.

6 *hvat* probably means 'how', as in 110, rather than 'why', which, as Lindquist 1, 131 observes, would be anachronistic.

It is a curious fact that the passage in Ragnars saga alluded to under 49 above seems to have some relation to st. 49-50 here: both refer to a wooden man, or men, both contain the fairly unusual word *þorp*, and the verses in the saga end *hlýr hvárki mér hold né klæði*, a phrase somewhat reminiscent of 50/3. But how this circumstance is to be interpreted is very difficult to see (for a speculative discussion see M. Olsen 7, 19ff.).

51

3 For *friðr* see on st. 90. The reference to *five* days (also in 74) may be connected with the frequent occurrence of this period in the Old Norwegian laws, which has led some to infer that the pre-Christian week was one of five days; cp. Cl-Vig s.v. *fimt*.

52

1-2 For *eitt* meaning 'only' cp. 124 below and *við vín eitt . . . lifir* Grímnismál 19 (Cl-Vig s.v. *einn* A III β). Sveinbjörn Egilsson, followed by FJ, takes the neg. suffix of *skala* closely with *mikit*, to mean 'only small gifts should be given'. But 'one should not give large gifts only' makes more natural sense in itself and is a less strained interpretation of the wording of the text.

3 For the suggestion that *lof* means 'love' here see on st. 8 above.

5 *með hǫllu keri* 'with slanting bowl'. Neckel-Kuhn assert this simply means the bowl is not full, and so also Ólafur Briem, who explains that the bowl has to be tilted before a draught can be got. CPB 12 renders freely 'with . . . the last drops of my cup', and similarly SG, who think of a bowl being tilted to drain its final dregs. FJ explains in LP 'inclined, i.e. half-full (properly, able to be inclined without spilling)', but it is hard to see how so much can be extracted from the text. DH take the bowl as that of the donor, who is pouring from it into the beaker of his companion. The neatest explanation is that of Holtsmark 2, who thinks of a man sharing his food and drink with a comrade; he has a loaf and a full bowl; the loaf he cuts in half, and the drink he divides by tilting the bowl and pouring to the half-way point, i.e. when the bottom begins to show. Cp. Tristrams saga ch. 46 (ed. Kölbing, 56): *Ok er Tristram hafði við tekit kerinu, þá drakk hann til hálfs, ok þá lét hann meyna drekka þat, sem eptir var í kerinu.*

6 On *félagi* as a word characteristic of the Viking Age see p. 19 above.

53

1-3 CR reads *seva*, which some early editors, and more recently Meissner, take as *sefa*, gen. pl. of *sefi* 'mind' (not otherwise found in pl.); thus Lüning (cited in FJ) rendered 'small sands, small understandings' and explained 'just as grains of sand are small, even so, where the understanding is small, are the souls (*geð*) of men small'. Meissner notes that ὀλιγόψυχος is rendered *grinda-*

fraþjis in Gothic, which he thinks must mean literally 'sand-minded' (OHG *grint* 'sand', ON *grandi* 'sandbank') and takes the genitives as descriptives of an understood *gumnar*: 'of small sands, of small understanding — small are the powers of understanding of many men' ('many' is not accounted for). All this is plainly unsatisfactory; especially in the neighbourhood of *sanda*, we must here have the word *sæva*, gen. pl. of *sær* 'sea' or 'lake'. But the lines remain a *locus desperatus*. The principal attempts at interpretation are:

(1) The genitives are absolute and parallel: where you get small shores, there you also get small lakes, and similarly with men: where there is a man, there is a small understanding (so FJ). Such a use of the gen. would be unique. Wessén 4, 462 thinks the first two lines were proverbial, but admits the syntactic difficulty.

(2) The first gen. is gen. of place (Nygaard 2, §141) and the second is dependent on it (BMÓ): thus, 'On the little shores of little lakes men's minds are small, i.e. provincial'; or both genitives are parallel gen. of place: 'on little shores, on little lakes' etc. (So Läffler 4. *On* lakes seems rather odd; Läffler explains it of fishermen who spend much of their lives on the water.) This has been criticized as anachronistic, and FJ also objects that our poem is concerned with mankind in general, and not merely dwellers in remote districts.

(3) Guðmundur Finnbogason 2, 106 takes the genitives as descriptive of *geð guma*: 'the minds of men are little, of a "small-sand", "small-sea" variety'. This eccentric interpretation is adopted by M. Olsen 7, 31.

(4) H. Pipping 2, 13ff and 4, 182-4 interprets CR *litilla* as *lítil lá* 'little surf' in either or both instances. None of these possibilities gives very plausible sense; plumping finally for emending both, he renders 'Där böljegången är svag vid stränderna, där böljegången är svag på sjöarna, där äro människornas själar små' ('Where the ripples are weak at the shores, where the ripples are weak on the lakes, there men's souls are small'). This is the same notion as (2) and is open to the same objections; further, it is a defect that nothing in the text corresponds to *där*. The emendation was accepted by Kock NN §2405, who however rendered slightly differently: 'Small is the plashing on the shore, small is the plashing on the lake, small are the minds of men'.

(5) Lie 215 takes *litilla* as *lítill á* in both instances, supposed to convey the notion that man is little against the background of the sands, little against the background of the waters. But this would

be more than 'moderately' elliptical, as Lie puts it, and he fails to explain the accusatives (rather than datives) convincingly.

It should be noted that *sær* in the sense 'lake' is evidenced only for East Norse, and is definitely absent from West Norse in literary times, cp. Flat. II 550 *Mjǫrs er svá mikit vatn, at líkara er sjó* and II 327 *þar lá fyrir þeim vatn, er Svíar kalla sjá, er þat ósalt vatn*. But the sense 'lake' appears in Norwegian place-names (Fritzner 2, s.v. *sjár*) and so can hardly be excluded for Hávamál.

6 is also difficult: should we read *hvar* 'everywhere' or *hvár* 'each of two' (agreeing with *ǫld* f.)? And what does *hálf* mean? Reading *hvar*, FJ rendered 'Everywhere men are incomplete, imperfect'; he admitted that *hálfr* does not occur elsewhere in ON in this sense, but asserted in 1888 (FJ 1, 51) that the sense was known in the modern language; this is denied by BMÓ 65, and in his separate edition of 1924 Finnur says only that Blöndal's dictionary provides examples of modern usage which come near it; but this is not really so. The only other way of defending *hvar* is to follow e.g. Heusler 1, 112 and take *hálf* as 'divided into two' (i.e., by implication, the wise and the stupid); but there is no evidence that the word can ever bear this meaning. So it seems better to read *hvár*, as Bugge 2, 250, who explains 'each of the two classes of men is half' i.e. constitutes only a half, which is complemented by the other half. This is followed by BMÓ, who compares *Ek man hér koma með valinkunna menn, en þú haf halfa fyri* Gulaþingslǫg § 266 (NGL I 88), where *halfa* appears to mean 'equally many'. Admittedly, '*class* of men' for *ǫld* lacks exact parallels.

The accumulation of obscurities in this strophe makes it probable that it is corrupt in ways beyond repair.

54

6 *vel mart* normally means 'a good many things', which contradicts 1-3. Kock 2, 107 suggested *vel* might have the force sometimes present in *väl* in modern Swedish: 'just right, not too much nor too little'. But this would be unique in ON, and it is better to follow BMÓ 66 and insert a negative, reading either *era* in 4 (cp. strophe 22) or *vitut* in 6.

55

Singer 12 thinks the sentiment is Biblical, e.g. 'He that increaseth knowledge increaseth sorrow', Ecclesiastes 1.18.

57

4-5 The strophe plainly recommends sociability and points to the ill consequences of solitude; scholars differ however in their interpretation of the second half. Most take *kuðr* (*kunnr*) as having its usual sense 'known', e.g. Bellows: 'man by his speech is known to men'; CPB 7: 'through speech man draws nearer to man'; Wessén 3, 30: 'en man blir känd av en man genom sitt tal'. (For the sentiment cp. Þiðreks saga ch. 121 [ed. Unger, 136]: *af málum verða menn kunnir.*) But with this sense the prepositions are awkward, as was realised by Müllenhoff 257, who emended to *maðr manni verðr af máli kunnr*, followed by FJ 1, 50. But this destroys the parallelism between *brandr af brandi* and *maðr af manni*. The only escape from this dilemma is to follow Kock 2, 27 in taking *kuðr* as 'wise'. This sense is not recorded by the dictionaries for prose, but LP cites three instances from the Edda (not the present passage) with this meaning, and also *kunnr í Kristi greinum* in Pétrsdrápa 12 (Skj. ii 548); Neckel-Kuhn, on the other hand, give *only* the present passage as certainly having the sense 'wise' and assert that 'known' is possible in the other three places. The phrase in Pétrsdrápa, and also the prose compound *fjǫlkunnr* (instead of the more usual *fjǫlkunnigr*) 'learned in magic', suffice to show that *kuðr* could mean 'wise', and this is not only easier syntactically but also provides a crisper contrast with *dœlskr* in the last line. See Hjelmqvist 375-6.

6 *dœlskr* occurs only here in verse, but (as also the noun *dœlska*) a few times in prose, meaning 'foolish'. Modern Norwegian dialects have *dølsk* 'with little to say, ignorant, reserved', *dølska* 'a fool' and *dølskast* 'talk nonsense, fool around'. See Flom 271. *Dul* combines, or wavers between, the senses 'concealment, silence, reserve, proud self-conceit, folly, infatuation' (NN §1779). *Af dul* denotes the *cause* of the man's becoming foolish; the renderings of Bellows ('and the stupid [are known] by their stillness') and Collinder 2 ('en dum känns igen på sin dolskhet') are wrong (not only because they contradict st. 27).

58

This strophe was evidently known to Saxo Grammaticus (*c.* 1200), for what is manifestly a direct rendering of it is placed in the mouth of Ericus disertus in Book V of his Danish History: *Pernox enim et pervigil esse debet alienum appetens culmen. Nemo stertendo victoriam cepit, nec luporum quisquam cubando cadaver invenit.*

(See Martínez-Pizarro for the suggestion that Saxo's account derives from a lost Eiríks þáttr málspaka; if this is correct, the strophe was no doubt quoted there.)

Heusler 1, 112 believed that 4-6 incorporated two pre-existing proverbs, the first in 4-5, the second having some such form as *sjaldan sofandi maðr sigr um getr* (*vegr, hlýtr*). Vápnfirðinga saga ch. 17 (ÍF XI 58) cites *sjaldan vegr sofandi maðr sigr* as a proverb, and this also appears in Flóvents saga ch. 7 (G. Cederschiöld *Fornsögur Suðrlanda* [Lund 1884] 180) and (with *hlýtr* for *vegr*) in Smst. 169. The lines on the wolf find a parallel in the Latin-Danish *Raro lupi lenti prebentur fercula denti. Siällen kommer ligghende wlff lam i monnä* (Låle nr 920); Singer 13 lists numerous other Continental instances, sometimes with different animals, as a fox and a rat.

59

3 *síns* shows that *verka* must be gen. sg. of *verki*, which elsewhere always means 'poem', though *misverk, misverki* 'misdeed' exist side by side. Either we must suppose that the word here = *verk* or we must expel *síns*, which would then allow us to take *verka* as gen. pl. of *verk* (so FJ 1, 52; more hesitantly in his 1924 edition; cp. LP s.v. *verki*).

60

2 Unless we suppose the picture is one of a pile of pieces of bark waiting to be used and which, just like a wood-pile, have to be roofed against the weather, we must take *þakinna* here in an active sense ('bark *for roofing*') rather than in the passive sense usual in the past participle, which this word appears to be. FJ suggests it is an adj. formed directly on *þak* (cp. *gullinn*); an active sense is also present in *lifinn, sofinn, vakinn* (but none of these is from a transitive verb). M. Olsen 7, 33 well compares, from the Norwegian laws, the expressions *taka með stolinni hendi, mjólka stelandi* (v.l. *stolinni*) *hendi* and, from a verse in Gautreks saga (Skj. ii 348), *villtar brautir* 'paths that lead astray'.

6 Cp. *Ár heitir tvau misseri, í misseri eru mál tvau* Rímbegla (Kålund 2, II 7).

The point of the strophe is not very clear; Wessén 3, 31 thinks a parallel strophe has been lost, in which something one does *not* know the measure of would be contrasted.

62

1 *snapa* occurs only here and in Lokasenna 44. It appears to mean something like 'snatch, grab, snuffle for (food)'. The basic notion seems to be that of a short, quick movement (Flom 270, who compares Norwegian dialect *snapp* 'quick'). *Gnapa* is properly 'to project'. Of animals, cp. *gnapir æ grár jór yfir gram dauðum* Brot 7. Here it describes the eagle with head stretched forwards.

3 *aldinn mar* is also in Snorri's Háttatal 67 (Skj. ii 80). The adj. normally means 'old'. Flom 271, however, relates it here to *alda* 'billow' and renders 'billowy', comparing Norwegian dialect *alden* in this sense. Lindquist 1, 132ff and Mezger (independently) render 'high', on the ground that (though this is not certain) it is cognate with Latin *altus*. But 'old' is unexceptionable; FJ compares *en forna fold*.

63

4-6 are normally taken as advice to impart one's secrets to only one intimate (or perhaps to no one at all — see below). But Kock 2, 278 observes that the neg. force of *né* can embrace a preceding as well as a following element, e.g. *skósmiðr né skeptismiðr* 126, *við hleifi . . . né við hornigi* 139 (and similarly in OE). He thinks the notion is 'Don't let just one or two people know — preferably three, and thus the whole world will know' (the same notion, he suggests, appears in st. 28). Such advice would be very out of tune with the watchful and suspicious note of the whole poem. It is true, however, that on the usual view the two halves do not fit well together, and many scholars have denied they can originally have formed a unit (CPB 12 and 461; Wessén 3, 18); Heusler 2, 117-8 makes a new strophe by adding 4-6 to the incomplete st. 65. SG suggest 'Presumably the poet means that a wise man should understand, not only how to speak, but also how to be silent', and von See 3, 40-41 holds that the strophe is advice to exercise one's capacity for question and answer *with discretion*. But it seems more probable that there has been some confusion in the transmission of the text.

Heusler maintains that 4-6 enjoin absolute secrecy: *einn* is the speaker himself. Others take *einn* as denoting one other person, i.e. the speaker's interlocutor (thus Bellows: 'Tell one thy thoughts, but beware of two'; similarly CPB 12), and von See explains that the speaker plus *einn* plus *annarr* constitute the three referred to in 6.

For 6 cp. Málsháttakvæði 3 (Skj. ii 138): *þjóð spyrr allt, þat er þrír menn vitu.* Heusler 1, 113 thinks a pre-existing proverb *þjóð veit, þat er þrír vitu* lies behind the two poems here. Singer 14 quotes Continental parallels (e.g. *Quod tribus est notum, raro solet esse secretum*) and suggests the proverb originated in Germany (though not actually recorded there before the fourteenth century).

64

4-6 cp. Fáfnismál 17: *þá þat finnr, er með fleirum kømr, at engi er einna hvatastr.* FJ thinks this is a borrowing from Hávamál; more likely the two passages were variants in oral tradition. Line 6 is taken for a proverb by Heusler 1, 113 and Wessén 4, 465.

65

Plainly half the strophe has been lost.

66

6 Many early editors took the last word as *lið* 'ale' (e.g. Bugge, CPB 5), and this was defended by BMÓ 67 on the ground that such a sense best fits the context. But this overlooks the occurrence of what is plainly the same expression in Konungs Skuggsiá 46: *En ef konungr heitir þér ok nefnir þér stefnudag, nær þat skal lúkast, þá verðr þar til at standa . . . En þú verðr at leita þíns máls at tómi ef þér sýnist ok vita ef þú hittir í þann lið, er þín vild gangi fram* (spelling normalized). Here we manifestly do not have *lið* n. 'ale'; rather, it must be the word found in the saying *liðar verðr sá at leita, er lítit sax hefir*, which appears in Heiðreks saga (ed. Jón Helgason, 70) and also (if we accept an almost certain emendation) in Vápnfirðinga saga ch. 7 (ÍF XI 41). Rather than assume an otherwise unknown word meaning 'right point, favourable moment' (so Falk 1, 112), it seems best to take it as a metaphorical use of *liðr* 'joint of the body' and to suppose the expression arose from the need to find the joint in dismembering a carcase (see FJ in ANF XIV [1898] 202). Nils Lid points out that, according to a saying widespread in the Norwegian countryside in modern times, a man who could not *treffa leden* in cutting up a carcase had lied that day.

Line 6 (with the final word pronounced *lið*, not *lið*) is known as proverbial in modern Iceland. This may well derive from our poem, though Heusler 1, 113 and Wessén 4, 455 believe the poet incorporated a pre-existing proverb.

67

3 *málungi* i.e. *málum* plus neg. particle *-gi* (A. Noreen §258.1). For other instances with nouns cp. *hornigi* 139 and *þorfgi* Helg. Hj. 39.

The drift of this strophe, and particularly of 4-6, is not clear. FJ offers no special comment, but evidently thinks that, while 1-3 describe meanness, 4-6 exemplify true generosity: a faithful friend will invite you home to consume the second of two hams of which you have already eaten the first. Others think that both halves describe meanness (this entails taking *tryggva* as ironic). SG think the idea is that a mean man will invite you to eat his ham only if the result is the spontaneous doubling of the eaten ham by magic, so that in the end he is left with two. Wennström thinks of the same notion, though for him the doubling is not the result of magic but is a twofold compensation by the guest for what he has eaten (cp. the verb *tvígilda* used of such compensation in the laws). More plausibly, Bo Almqvist has ingeniously suggested to me that the idea is that the 'faithful' friend will invite one home only if a condition which is in fact impossible were to be fulfilled.

68

3 *sólar sýn* is ambiguous: either 'a man's physical ability to see the sun' or 'the appearance of the sun, the fact that the sun appears'. DH (followed by SG, Hannaas 236 and others) prefer the latter, on the ground that the former is embraced in *heilyndi*; but this is hardly conclusive.

6 *án við* is not a (unique) compound preposition, as FJ 1, 54 seems to have thought; the sense is *án at lifa við lǫst*. *Lǫstr* is taken by most interpreters to have its common sense of 'moral failing' (so Bellows: 'a life not stained with sin'). But *lǫstr* can also mean 'a physical defect', as in Heilag. I 584: *sat hann í augnaverk, ok var kominn lǫstr mikill á auga hans annat*, and this appears to fit the context better. (It is unclear why von See 3, 46 should assert that *lifa* seems to rule out this interpretation.)

69

6 *verkum vel* — CPB 7 ('good deeds') and Bellows ('worthy works') are evidently giving *vel* the force of an attributive adj., but this can scarcely be right. DH equate *vel* with a predicative adj., parallel to *sæll*, comparing *illa* in st. 22, and cp. Egils saga ch. 55 (ÍF II 143): *Hann var vel í vexti*. More plausibly, SG explain *vel* as standing for *vel sæll* (so also FJ in his edition; in LP s.v. *vel* he wavers between this and *vel* = *góðr*).

70

1 *lifðum* has an active sense, = *lifanda* 'living'. Only found here.

2 *en sé ólifðum* is an emendation (first proposed by Rasmus Rask in 1818) for CR *oc sęl lifðom* (i.e. *ok sællifðum*), which lacks both alliteration and sense. For the alliteration of the text as emended, cp. *Hvǫtum er betra en sé óhvǫtum* Fáfnismál 31. Other suggestions are *an brendom sé(e)* (Collinder 1, 19), *ok bǫllifðom* (Holthausen 155), *an liðnom séi* (FJ), *ok sé illifðum* (Holtzmann 107), and *ok birglifðum* (M. Olsen 7, 35; but this misses the point of the strophe, which is plainly that *any* sort of life is preferable to death).

3 may incorporate a pre-existing proverb; cp. Málsháttakvæði 4 (Skj. ii 139): *jafnan fagnar kvikr maðr kú*.

4-6 There are two problems here: is the fire a cremation pyre, or a fire consuming the house and property of the rich man, or the domestic fire on the hearth; and, second, is *dauðr* an adjective or a noun?

FJ took the fire for a cremation pyre, and rendered in his 1924 edition: 'I have seen the pyre blaze up in front of a rich man; he himself lay dead outside his door'. (He seems to have found *fyrir* troublesome: in 1888 [FJ 1, 54] he took it as 'destined for', and in LP s.v., B3 as 'for the use of'.) But if the pyre is already alight, the corpse should be on it, not lying on the ground. This difficulty is avoided by understanding the fire as that on the hearth, and rendering 'I saw the fire blaze up for a rich man, but he was lying dead outside the door'. (For this use of *fyrir* cp. Cl-Vig s.v. with dat. A3; it cannot mean 'in the house of', as seems to be implied by Collinder 2, 47 and von See 3, 43.) This gives full force to *en*. Kock 2, 108 also took the fire in this way, and thought the idea was that a living, rich man can see the fire blaze up in front of him, while a dead man lies outside in cold and darkness. But this makes *auðgum* pointless. Another well-established use of *fyrir* with the

dat. is 'to the disadvantage of' (Cl-Vig s.v. with dat. C III), evidently the sense implied by the translation in CPB 8 and 216 (where it is treated as a detached fragment): 'I saw fire consume the rich man's dwelling, and himself lying dead before his door'.
All these interpretations treat *dauðr* as an adj. The normal ON word for 'death' is *dauði*, and FJ denied that *dauðr* could be a noun. But the compound *manndauðr* occurs (beside *manndauði*); the phrase *til dauðs* is found in both old and modern Icelandic (see Fritzner 2 s.v. *dauðr* m., Blöndal s.v. *dauður* m.); modern Norwegian has *daud* as well as *daude* as nouns, suggesting that Old Norwegian too had the strong as well as the weak form; and in 1945 a runic inscription on a crucifix of *c*. 1240 came to light in Ringerike, reading *ek þolde harþan dauþ* (NIYR II 102ff.). Note too *døþer* m., frequent in Old Swedish. We need not hesitate, then, to take *dauðr* here as a noun, and render (with BMÓ 69-71) 'I saw the fire blazing (on the hearth) in front of the rich man; but (unknown to him) death was outside the door'. This is not only by far the most natural way of understanding a fire which blazes *fyrir* somebody (like the fire which *brann* . . . *fyr Vǫlundi* in Vǫlundarkviða 9) but also enables us to link the last line with the expression *dauði er fyrir durum*, which occurs in Maríu saga (ed. C. R. Unger [Christiania 1871] 279) and in *Islendzk Æventyri* (ed. H. Gering, Halle 1882-3) I 210.

71

4-5 The reference to cremation here, as in 81 below and (according to some interpretations) in 70 above, points to a non-Icelandic origin for these lines, since there is neither literary nor archaeological evidence that cremation was ever practised in Iceland; see p. 13 above. Heusler 1, 113 and Wessén 4, 468 take these two lines as a pre-existing proverb, which Heusler suggests was the kernel round which the rest of the strophe was constructed.

72

For the sentiment Kuhn 1, 69 compares Egill Skallagrímsson's words about his dead son in Sonatorrek 12: *mitt afl mest um studdi* and the similar use by Hávarðr ísfirðingr of *aflstuðill* of his dead son (Skj. i 35 and 179).

1 *Sonr er betri* — i.e. better than no son, cp. *bú er betra* 36-7 above. It is not that the comparative is simply equivalent here to

the positive (as Nygaard 2, §58 suggests) but that that with which comparison is made is too obvious to need stating.

3 *genginn* 'departed', i.e. 'dead'; only here, but *framgenginn* is found several times in this sense.

4 *bautarsteinar* occurs only here in poetry, but there are several references in Kings' Sagas to the erection of *bautasteinar* (spelled thus) as memorial stones or gravestones in Norway in the heathen period. Snorri states in the Preface to Heimskringla that *in fyrsta ǫld er kǫlluð brunaǫld; þá skyldi brenna alla dauða menn ok reisa eptir bautasteina. En síðan, er Freyr hafði heygðr verit at Uppsǫlum, þá gerðu margir hǫfðingjar eigi síðr hauga en bautasteina til minningar um frændr sína* (ÍF XXVI 4). In Ynglinga saga ch. 8 he says that Óðinn prescribed cremation as the rule in Sweden *en eptir gǫfga menn skyldi haug gera til minningar, en eptir alla þá menn, er nǫkkut mannsmót var at, skyldi reisa bautasteina; ok helzk sjá siðr lengi síðan* (ÍF XXVI 20, and cp. 29 for Vanlandi's *bautasteinar* on the banks of the River Skúta). Of Egill ullserkr, who fell in battle *c*. 953, Snorri writes (ÍF XXVI 182) that tall *bautasteinar* stand beside his mound, but the corresponding passage in Fagrskinna (ed. FJ [København 1902-3] 34) reads *þar stendr ok bautaðarsteinn hár sem Egill fell*; this form of the word is unique, and complicates attempts to determine the etymology, for, while it is possible that the usual *bauta(r)steinn* is a contraction of this longer form, this cannot be regarded as certain. Some have wanted to connect the first element with the rare *bauta* 'to beat', to give the sense 'stone beaten into the earth'; others have called attention to *bautuðr*, a poetic *heiti* for 'ox', conjectured to mean primarily 'gorer, stabber', and have thus deduced a sense 'phallic stone'; see M. Olsen *Hedenske Kultminder i norske Stedsnavne* I (VSHF 1914, No. 4) 253.

The word has been revived by modern Scandinavian archaeologists to denote a stone without inscription, from prehistoric times, set up on end in the earth. Such stones, up to four or five metres in height, are common in Norway and Sweden, less so in Denmark; they are found both singly and in groups, sometimes on open ground, sometimes at the centre or the edge of mounds or cairns. They occur from the Bronze Age, down through the Iron Age, until the Conversion. Those on open ground are often, but not always, conjoined with simple cremation graves. See further the entry *Bautastein* in KLNM, especially on the archaeological aspects.

5 *standa brautu nær*: cp. the runic verse inscriptions at Ryda in

Uppland (UR nr 838) *Hér mun standa steinn nær brautu* and at Tjuvstigen in Södermanland (SR nr 34) *Styrlaugr ok Hólmr steina reistu at brœðr sína brautu næsta* (spelling normalised). See Jansson 145.

6 *niðr*: 'kinsman'.

73

This and 74 are widely regarded by editors as interpolated: they contain much obscurity, and interrupt the sequence of regular *ljóðaháttr* strophes (73 is in *málaháttr*, and either 74/3 or 74/4 appears to be supernumerary).

1 FJ takes *herjar* as gen. sg.: 'Two (men) are of the same host' (but nevertheless one may inflict death on the other, as, for instance, tongue may inflict death on the head; so be watchful, even against your comrade-in-arms). Very little of this, however, is actually in the text. BMÓ gives the same general sense, though with unnecessary, and impossible, complications. CPB 16 inserts a neg. to read *Tveir rot eins herjar*, and renders 'Two are never on one side', adding the cryptic note (CPB 462) 'somehow wrong'.

At Vafþr. 41 *eins herjar* in AM 748 I 4to (cf. p. 2 above) is certainly an error for *einherjar*, and Müllenhoff 258 suggested the same emendation here, taking the line to mean 'Two are sole fighters (duellists)', i.e. a duel consists of two persons — a remark, one might think, too obvious to be worth making. Sturtevant 3, 32 also reads *einherjar* (apparently without realising it is an emendation); he concedes that elsewhere this word in the pl. always refers to the dead warriors in Valhǫll, 'but here the word is evidently used as a generic term for *warrior*'. He renders 'Warriors are two', supposed to mean 'It takes two to make a quarrel'. This is unconvincing.

It is far better to keep to CR and take *herjar* as nom. pl. (as SG and others) and translate 'Two are the destroyers of one', i.e. two men are superior to one man. For this sense of *herr* cp. the verb *herja*, and *herr alls viðar* as a kenning for 'fire' in Helreið Brynhildar 10. The line then has close parallels in various languages: MHG *zwêne sint eines her*, Danish *To ere een Mands Herre*, medieval Latin *duo sunt exercitus uni* (from the twelfth-century Ysengrimus); see Heusler 1, 114 and Singer 149-50, who thinks the proverb may have travelled to the North during the Viking Age. On this interpretation the line is a warning against rashly taking on overwhelming odds; it has no close connection with the rest of the strophe, which seems to consist of three gnomes, independent, but united by their common message of watchfulness and prudence.

2 For the sentiment 'careless words can bring about one's death' cp. 29/4-6. Reichborn-Kjennerud 3 quotes various foreign parallels, e.g. from Germany *Die Zunge gefährdet den Kopf*. The phrase *tunga huwdhbani* occurs in the Old Swedish laws, in the fragment known as Hednalagen, 'the Heathen Law' (SGL III 275, note 100).

74

4-7 are plainly concerned with the fickleness of the weather, but the drift of 1-3 is obscure; FJ virtually gives up. At one time (FJ 1, 55) he proposed to read *trúirat* with the neg. suffix — 'he who does not trust his food, i.e. that it will last out, is glad of nightfall, for then he can go to sleep without eating. Food is like yardarms: short' — but later he abandoned this. BMÓ 75-8 thought that the picture was of a voyage along the Norwegian coast: at nightfall the voyager disembarks to eat — and this is well enough, given that he has brought adequate food — and sleep. The implication is 'Always take enough to eat, for ships go slowly, weather is changeable, and you can never be sure how long the voyage will last'. 'Short are the yardarms of a ship' means (he says) that ships go slowly (because short yardarms imply short sails). For 1-2 we may compare the proverb *sá bíðr hlæjandi húsa, sem matinn hefr í malnum* (Smst. 156). Against BMÓ's view of 3, Falk 5 urges that its substance recurs in Málsháttakvæði 12 (Skj. ii 141):

> Skips láta menn skammar rár.
> Skatna þykkir hugrinn grár.
> Tungan leikr við tanna sár.
> Trauðla er gengt á ís of vár . . .

(The first line of this probably means 'People make the yardarms of a ship short' rather than 'People say that the yardarms of a ship are short'.) These lines seem to have to do with the need for caution: remember how untrustworthy everything is. In Hávamál the next words, *hverf er haustgríma*, also remind one of unreliability. Falk points out that, on coastal voyages in the fjords, narrow and beset by frequent gusts, a short yardarm was an essential precaution. An alternative, not unattractive, suggestion about the line was advanced by Eiríkr Magnússon 3, 334: the underlying notion, he proposed, was that in a shipwreck a drowning man clutches at a floating yardarm, which, being short, affords less support than he would wish. In other words, things are not trustworthy. This fits both Hávamál and Málsháttakvæði well.

Heusler 1, 115 and some others take *rár* as 'nooks' (from [v]*rá*), alleged here to mean the *skipsrúm* in which one had to curl up to sleep cramped (so CPB 16: 'Short are ship's berths'). But what sense would this give? Heusler does not say; Collinder 1, 22 (later abandoned: 2, 221) explains 'There is little room on board ship, so you cannot take very much food', while SG think it is another reason for welcoming night, when one could sleep more comfortably ashore. This leaves the line in Málsháttakvæði obscure. It is not in fact credible that, when *skips* is conjoined with it, *rá* could be other than the word for 'yardarm'.

75

1-2 (for which cp. 27/7-8) are concluded with a semi-colon in many editions, though they make little sense as an independent sentence. Presumably they point forward to 3 (as implied by various translators), so a colon is more appropriate.

3 *af aurum* is an emendation (originated by S. Grundtvig) for the ms *aflavðrom*, which is plainly corrupt. If *af* is the preposition, *lauðrum* (or *lǫðrum*) could not be right even if it made sense, since it lacks alliteration. Gould proposed *af aulðrum* (i.e. *ǫlðrum* 'ale bouts'), which is palaeographically plausible (cp. st. 14, where *aulðr* was first written *auðr*), but then there would be no sense-connection with 4-6. Other suggestions are *af ǫðrum* (e.g. Bugge 1, 51) and *af auði um* (SG, who archaize *um* to *of*). Cp. Sólarljóð 34 (Skj. i 641): *margan hefr auðr apat*.

6 is obscure. If *vár* is gen. of the noun *vá* 'woe, misfortune', *vítka* must be the infinitive of an otherwise unrecorded verb, apparently meaning 'to blame', perhaps related to *víta*, though that rather means 'to punish'. Thus 'One should not blame him for the misfortune'. Grundtvig emended to *vætkis vá*, with *vá* as the verb apparently seen in st. 19.

76

1-2 For the occurrence of these lines in Eyvindr skáldaspillir's Hákonarmál see p. 13 above. There is a close parallel in the OE elegy The Wanderer (of uncertain date), 108: *hēr bið feoh lǣne, hēr bið frēond lǣne* ('Here possessions are transitory, here friend is transitory'), where the addition of 'here' (i.e. 'in this world') conveys a Christian implication absent from Hávamál. The use of *fé* and *frændr* as an alliterating pair doubtless goes back to early Germanic poetry; that there is any more direct connection between The Wanderer and our poem, as suggested by von See 3, 48-9, is highly improbable.

4-6 For the sentiment cp. Sverris saga ch. 47 (ed. Indrebø, 50): *lifir orð lengst eptir hvern*. Similar observations in Classical and in medieval Continental sources are cited by Singer 14-15. Von See 2, 3 sees a Biblical echo in this strophe (Ecclesiastes 3.19); his further suggestion (3, 47) that *orðstírr* had acquired a specifically Christian connotation in Norse is far from satisfactorily borne out by its use elsewhere in verse and is contradicted by its frequent occurrence in prose without any such connotation.

77

6 *dómr*: literally 'judgment' (whether favourable or unfavourable); but, whereas the Norsemen commonly observed that a man's fair fame would be remembered for ever, they very rarely stated that disgrace would never be forgotten (see Kock 2, 28 and 110, though he is over-dogmatic: Hirðskrá art. 29 is a counter-instance). So, in the context, *dómr* is in practice restricted to 'renown', just as, in the gnome quoted in the note on 76, *orð*, though in itself neutral, refers in the context only to fair fame. The substance of 76 and 77 is therefore identical. It is unnecessary to go further, with Kock, and suppose that *dómr* had itself developed the meaning 'honour, glory'; this is indeed well exemplified in OE *dōm* and Gothic *dōms*, but there is no evidence outside the present passage for such a sense in Norse. (For dispute on this point see Kock 1, 175-8 and 2, 27-28 and 108-111, and Åkerblom 1 and 2; also FJ 4, 314.)

78

2 Most editors have seen *Fitjungr* (who occurs nowhere else) as a symbolic name for a prosperous man. LP, following some of the earlier scholars, took it as 'Fatty', as though connected with *feitr*. But the presence of *j* rules this out. In his 1924 edition FJ proposed instead a connection with *fit* (gen. *fitjar*) 'the web or skin of an animal's foot' and rendered the name (with a query) as 'he who owns many cloven-footed beasts'. Falk 4, 54-5, also connecting with *fit*, drew attention to the presence of this element in Scandina-

vian words for shoes made of this skin (ON *fitskór*, Faroese *fitingskógvur*, Norwegian *fetasko, fete, fetling* and, notably, *fitjung*). He supposes that *fitjung* existed already in ON and takes *Fitjungr* as an eponym for the farmer's state, deriving from the type of footwear used by farmers and not (he says, without evidence) by seamen or aristocratic chieftains. But this theory is both far-fetched in itself and also fails to give the sense we need, which is of someone rich or mighty, not merely a typical farmer. Nevertheless, it was adopted by M. Olsen 7, 36, who rejected in its favour his own earlier and far more attractive proposal (2, 63-76) to deduce the name from the homonym *fit* 'water-meadow'. This word, as *Fit*, or plural *Fitjar*, occurs in West Norse as a farm-name, mostly of fairly humble farms; great farms were higher up, not down in the water-meadows. But there is one big exception, Fitjar on the island of Storð in Hǫrðaland, a *stórbú* owned by Haraldr hárfagri. Olsen suggests that the Fitjungar were the once rich owners of this great farm, reduced to beggary when Haraldr seized it (he further suggests that the Icelandic settler Ǫnundr breiðskeggr, grandson of Úlfr fitjumskeggi, was of this family and that this is why he emigrated).

It is very possible, however, that the name has no special significance. Wessén 4, 456-7 (who believes that the strophe was invented to illustrate what he thinks was a pre-existing proverb, *auðr er valtastr vina*) takes *Fitjungr* as a pure fiction created to alliterate with *fullar*. Support for this approach can be found in the similarly arbitrary use of fictional names in the 'exempla' of Sólarljóð (st. 9, 11, 16 and 20 in Skj. i 636ff.).

3 *vánarvǫlr* 'a beggar's staff' (literally 'a staff of hope') also occurs in Norwegian laws (NGL V, s.v.).

80

This obscure and metrically very irregular strophe, with no apparent connection with its context, seems like a detached fragment of the mystical poetry about runes such as we find below in 142-45; note particularly the resemblance between 4-5 and 142/5-6. The reference of the initial *Þat* is unclear; as the strophe stands, it can only point forward to the last line, which Müllenhoff 259 understood as conveying the 'very modest truth' that silence is best; 'mit komisch ironischem pathos' the poet presents this lesson in the 'concluding strophe' of the Gnomic Poem as the fruit of inquiry into the runes, which had been made by the gods and coloured by the *fimbulþulr*, the Great Sage (doubtless Óðinn himself). This entails identifying *þú* and *hann*. Von See 3, 53 avoids this awkwardness by taking *hann* as the *fimbulþulr*: when his listeners inquire into the runes, Óðinn does best by denying them this knowledge and remaining silent. This, says von See, makes a fitting conclusion to the 'first section' of Hávamál, with its emphasis on caution and silence. Somewhat more plausibly, Heusler 2, 122 took the last line as enjoining holy silence during the ritual of runic enquiry; this too necessitates identifying *þú* and *hann*.

3 *reginkunnum*: 'of divine descent' (not 'world-known', as Cl-Vig); only here in literature, but clearly a traditional epithet of runes, cp. *runo fahi raginakudo* on the seventh-century Noleby-Fyrunga stone and *runaʀ þaʀ ræginkundu* on the ninth-century Sparlösa stone, both in Västergötland (nr 63 and nr 119 respectively in VR), and further Brate, ANF XIV (1898) 331ff., Bugge, ANF XV (1899) 144-5, and Jansson 9 and 189. For *-kunnr* in the sense 'descended from' cp. *áskunnr* Atlakviða 27 and (as a ms variant) Fáfnismál 13, also de Vries 5 s.v. *kundr*.

4-5 See on st. 142 below.

81

See p. 23 above for suggestions that the *málaháttr* strophes beginning here might have some connection with the MHG poetic form known as the 'Priamel', and that the suspicion of women which they sporadically express may derive less from Nordic antiquity than from the Christian Middle Ages.

1 For the sentiment cp. Mǫttuls saga (ed. G. Cederschiöld and F.-A. Wulff, LUÅ 1877, 22): *at kveldi er dagr lofandi* and the twelfth-century Ysengrimus III 594: *vespere laudari debet amoena dies*. Singer 150-51, who cites numerous Continental parallels, thinks the notion is of German origin, borrowed by the Norsemen at an early date.

82

1 *í vindi* — so that one can anticipate on which side the tree will fall? (so FJ). Hannaas 236 ingeniously suggests that the line is intended to contrast with what follows: when it is stormy, stay ashore, and then felling trees (or chopping up wood?) is suitable work.

2 *veðri* with *í* understood from the preceding line (cp. DH). For the sense 'good weather' cp. *vesið með oss unz verði / veðr; nú's brim fyr Jaðri* in a verse of Þjóðólfr hvinverski (Skj. i 19).

4 This sounds like a proverb; so Heusler 1, 43, who compares *mǫrg eru konungs eyru* recorded several times (ÍF XXXIV 156, Fms. IV 374, Sturlunga saga ii 110).

83

3 perhaps derives from a pre-existing proverb; cp. Málsháttakvæði 21: *magran skyldi kaupa hest* (Skj. ii 143).

5-6 are rendered in CPB 14 'Fatten thy horse at home and thy hound at thine house' (similarly Bellows). But the phrasing seems to imply a contrast between *heima* and *á búi*, and this is confirmed by several other passages. At Fms. IV 257 Erlingr Skjálgsson says to his nephew Ásbjǫrn, who is paying him a visit, *ǫrorðr muntu vera heima, frændi, er þú ert svá á búi* and at Biskupa sögur I 132 we find *70 eða 80 heimamenn* contrasted with *hundrað manna . . . á búi*, where the latter phrase evidently refers to visitors; in Þorsteins saga hvíta ch. 8 (ÍF XI 19) a *heimagriðungr* confronts a *búigriðungr*, which seems to mean 'a neighbour's bull, a bull from another farm'. Note too *búrakki* in Laxdœla saga ch. 29 (ÍF V 79), perhaps meaning 'a dog from another farm', *búimaðr* in Sturlunga saga i 89 evidently for 'visitor', and the use of *bú(a)hundr* and *búaköttur* in modern Icelandic to denote a stranger dog and cat. (For other instances where *á búi* seems to mean 'visiting' see ÍF V 136 and XIV 303, and FJ 8, 11. See further BMÓ 79-80.) There can therefore be no doubt that *á búi* means 'at somebody else's house', as was already seen by Sveinbjörn Egilsson s.v. *bú* ('in domo aliena'). FJ objected that he knew no example, in ancient or modern times, of a dog's being fostered thus at someone else's farm; he took *bú* here as *útibú* 'a dependent farm', but the parallel passages do not support this. Admittedly, the point of the advice is not very clear; BMÓ suggested that strangers would be less inclined to spoil a dog with overfeeding, such as would render him obese and useless. Or perhaps the idea is that one should look after a horse but keep a dog lean; let him fatten himself, if he can, at another's expense.

84

4 *á hverfanda hvéli* 'on a turning wheel'; very possibly the reference is to a potter's wheel (see Meringer 455). However, in Alvíssmál

14 *hverfanda hvél* is given as a name for the moon, and CPB 483 suggests that this is the sense here too ('women's hearts are shifty as phases of the moon'), a notion recently revived by Kristján Albertsson. But this seems less probable, especially in view of the occurrence of the expression elsewhere, e.g. Grettis saga ch. 42 (ÍF VII 138): *En til Grettis kann ek ekki at leggja, því at mér þykkir á mjǫk hverfanda hjóli* (v.l. *hvéli*) *um hans hagi*. The phrase *á hverfanda hveli* is common in modern Icelandic, to denote something unstable and fickle; Halldór Halldórsson 7-12 thinks it derives from a fusion of the expression in our poem with the medieval notion of the wheel of fortune. This fusion appears already in Flat. I 93: *er með ǿngu móti treystanda á hennar* (fortune's) *hverfanda hvél*.

4-6 (omitting *því at*) are cited in Fóstbrœðra saga ch. 21 (ÍF VI 225); see p. 2 above. The mss of the saga show a few verbal discrepancies: Flateyjarbók has *eru* for *váru*, R reads 5 as *er þeim hjarta skapat*, both add *ok* before *brigð*, and Hauksbók omits *um*.

In this strophe, as in 81 above and 90 below, we meet the concept of the fickle, deceptive woman so much exemplified in medieval Continental proverb lore (cp. Singer 15ff., who derives the sentiments from medieval clerical misogyny).

85

4 *galandi kráku* — for the belief that crows possessed the gift of prophetic utterance see the story of Óláfr kyrri and the crow in Msk. 293-5.

86

2 *fallandi báru* 'a falling billow', perhaps (as Hannaas 237 suggests) with specific reference to a billow breaking on an underwater reef (which is why it is so dangerous), cp. the use of *fall* to denote such reefs, or water breaking on them (Fritzner 2 s.v., 9, and still in modern Norwegian dialect).

89

7 *tryggr* in the sense 'trusting, confident' is very rarely evidenced in ON, but also occurs in Sonatorrek 22 (Skj. i 37) and in the compounds *auðtryggr* and *tortryggr*; also in modern Icelandic in the phrase *vera tryggur um sig* 'believe oneself secure'. It is the

normal sense of modern Norwegian and Swedish *trygg*, Danish *tryg*.

90

1 *friðr* clearly means 'love' here, as also probably in Skírnismál 19 and possibly in 51 above. This is the original sense of the word, cp. *frjá* 'to woo', *friðill* 'wooer' and *friðla* (> *frilla*) 'mistress'.

3 *óbryddum* — ice-spikes for horses are mentioned only here, but are evidenced from archaeology (e.g. in the Gokstad ship burial from the late ninth century). See Hannaas 238.

8 *stjórnlausu* sc. *skipi*.

9-10 The scene is plainly Norwegian, not Icelandic. *Páfjall* only here, but well known as *tå(e)fjell* in modern Norwegian dialect. The point of the lines is that reindeer can be caught only on skis, which cannot be used in a thaw. See Hannaas 239.

92

6 The verb *fría* or *frjá* (= Gothic *frijōn* rendering ἀγαπᾶν and φιλεῖν) is obsolescent in ON; it is found, apart from the present passage, twice in the Edda (Sigsk. 8 and Lokasenna 19, both somewhat obscure) and once in Málsháttakvæði 5 (Skj. ii 139); it does not occur in prose. Sturtevant 4 argues that in Norse its sense appears to have developed from 'love' to 'woo, caress, fondle'.

94

1 *Eyvitar* is gen. sg. of the same word as appears in the dat. in 28.

2 *er* appears superfluous; similar examples (all at the opening of the second half of a *ljóðaháttr* 'long line') are in Alvíssmál 7: *sáttir þínar er ek vill snemma hafa*, and in Grímnismál 50, Hárb. 25, Helg. Hj. 16 and 22, and Fjǫlsvinnsmál 50. No very satisfactory explanation has been adduced; cp. Fritzner 2, s.v. *er* 8, and SG *Wörterbuch* s.v. *es* I A 1; the latter explain it as an anaphoric particle resuming a preceding element in a simple sentence. M. Nygaard 'Kan oldn. *er* være particula expletiva?' ANF XII (1896) 117-28 implausibly proposes that *er* in the present passage is an explanatory conjunction, giving the reason for 93/1-3 (with 93/4-6 as a parenthesis).

95

3 *hann* must refer to the man who owns the *hugr*; it cannot be the *hugr* itself, for then it is impossible to give sense to *sefa*. Suggestions that *sefi* could mean either 'beloved person' (LP) or 'breast' (Kock 2, 29, cp. FJ 4, 319) lack any foundation. So render 'He is alone with his thoughts'; *sér* is dat. of the refl. pronoun (not a verb, as SG take it).

6 *una sér* is normally used absolutely 'to be content'; its combination with a dat. object is however also found in Hallfreðar saga ch. 11 (ÍF VIII 196): *Hallfreðr . . . undi sér engu eptir fall Óláfs konungs*, and for another instance see Bárðar saga Snæfellsáss (ed. G. Vigfússon, 1860) 13.

96

The story told in 96-102 is not otherwise known; Billingr occurs twice elsewhere as the name of a dwarf. The *ek* of the story is shown by 98 to be Óðinn. For discussion of the sequence of events see Nordal 2.

Most editors interpret 96 as describing a tryst at which the girl has failed to turn up. This entails taking *munr* as 'beloved person', for which cp. *munr Foglhildar* as a kenning for Jǫrmunrekkr in Ragnarsdrápa 6 (Skj. i 2) and possibly *at muni gráta* Baldrs Draumar 12 (so LP). Nordal, however, suggests that the waiting in the reeds comes *after* the events described in 97-8, and takes *munr* as 'satisfaction of my desire'.

97

1 Since the story is unknown elsewhere, it is not possible to say whether 'daughter' or 'wife' of Billingr is meant, for both senses of *mær* are well attested (LP). But the use of *lǫstr* 98 and *flærðir* 102 makes the latter somewhat more likely.

98

3 *mæla man* — apparently 'to win a woman through speech' (see Fritzner 2, s.v. *mæla* v. [lt] 4), but exact parallels are lacking.

5 *einir viti* — we would expect *ein vitim*; FJ emends accordingly.

99

3 *vísum vilja frá* — generally taken closely with the preceding line to mean 'out of my senses' ('I was distraught with love' CPB 21);

FJ says *vili* here is more or less *forstand* ('understanding, reason'). No parallel, however, can be adduced. Kock 2, 279-80 plausibly proposes that *vili* means 'what one desires, joy' (cp. Sigsk. 9); thus, 'I turned back . . . from certain delight'. FJ's objection that this would require *af* instead of *frá* is baseless, but it is trne that line 2 seems a little feeble when left thus isolated.

100

5 *bornum viði* — it is unclear what this is. Some take it to refer to the same thing as *brennandum ljósum*, i.e. torches (so Collinder 2: 'med brinnande ljus och burna facklor', Bellows: 'with burning lights and waving brands'). M. Olsen 7, 38-40 accepts this, quoting modern accounts of how blazing logs were used on Norwegian farms to frighten off bears. (He suggests this is possibly alluded to also in a line in Bjarkamál extant in Saxo's Latin rendering: *igne ursos arcere licet*.) Olsen, however, takes *bornum* to mean '(previously) carried in (and now lying ready for use)'. CPB 463 proposes to read *bronnom viði*, rendered 'burning torches', and similarly Lindquist 3, 253, who postulates metathesis. But the past participle of *brenna* cannot mean 'burning'. FJ thinks it unlikely that the same thing would be mentioned twice, and takes *viðr* as 'timber' which has been 'brought together' as a barricade.

6 *vílstígr* 'path of misery'; the word also occurs in Sverris saga ch. 18 (ed. G. Indrebø, 20). This must be the right reading; Neckel-Kuhn print *vilstígr*, glossed 'freudenspfad, weg zum genuss', but this does not fit the context. *Vitaðr* 'appointed, laid down'.

101

5 *góðu* is of course ironic, as probably in the similar phrases in 102 and 108 and perhaps in 130; cp. Wahlgren.

6 *beðjum á*: not 'tied to her bed' (CPB 21); just as in 97, this expression means on, or in, the bed (as emphasized by Gering 1). The implication of these lines is no doubt that Óðinn is being offensively invited to sate his lust, not on the girl whom he expected to find awaiting him, but on the bitch who has replaced her.

102

6 *flærðir* means 'treachery, deceit', which, as Nordal observes, fits best if we suppose Billingr was the woman's *husband*. Neckel-

Kuhn try to evade the implications of this word by rendering 'falschheit, hier aber etwa: leichtfertigkeit', and cp. NN §21, which renders 'lättsinne' (i.e. wantonness). But this is not what the word means.

103

6 *opt skal góðs geta.* CPB 11 renders 'A good man is in every one's mouth', and FJ and SG similarly take *góðs* as masculine. More probably, though, it is neuter; so e.g. Neckel-Kuhn (*Wörterbuch* 74): 'gutes soll man oft zur sprache bringen'. But certainty is unattainable.

7 *fimbulfambi*: 'great idiot'. *Fimbul-* (only in Eddaic poetry and Snorri's Edda, FJ 9, 70) is prefixed to nouns as an intensifier, cp. 140 and 142, and de Vries 5.

104

For the story of Óðinn's theft of the mead of poetry from the giant Suttungr by seducing the giant's daughter Gunnlǫð, see Snorri's Prose Edda (Skáldskaparmál ch. 5-6) and cp. st. 13-14 above. Richert 9ff. suggests that 104-10 imply a version where Óðinn arrives in Suttungr's halls as a seemingly respectable wooer and goes through a marriage ceremony with Gunnlǫð; see also the discussion by A. G. van Hamel 'The Mastering of the Mead' in *Studia Germanica tillägnade E. A. Kock* (Lund 1934) 76-85, esp. 78-80.

105

7 *síns ins svára sefa* 'her troubled mind'. *Svárr* (only found in poetry) seems to mean primarily 'heavy' (cp. German *schwer*) and evidently implies 'melancholy' here, as in Skírnismál 29. It is true that with this sense the line is strictly illogical, for which reason FJ expelled it; others avoid the illogicality by such renderings as 'her steadfast love' (CPB 22) or 'her strong affection' (Cl-Vig 607), but it is doubtful whether the words can bear this meaning.

106

1 *Rata munn* — Snorri relates that Óðinn won access to Suttungr's dwelling by turning himself into a snake and using the gimlet Rati to bore a passage through the rock.

2 *létumk* is explained by SG and LP 362 as = *lét mér*. But it could well be *létum* with *-k* (from *ek*) suffixed. For such forms of the first person sg. see on 108 and 112.

107

1 *litar* has not been satisfactorily explained. As it stands, it must be gen. sg. of *litr* 'colour, hue, complexion, outward appearance'. Möbius 413 and BMÓ 81-2 think the reference is to Óðinn's transformation into a snake, but whether *litr* can be stretched to mean 'bodily shape' is doubtful; FJ denies it. (This also causes difficulty with *keypts*, for the change can hardly be called a *kaup*; BMÓ speculates that *kaupa* could mean the same as *skipta* 'exchange, win in exchange'.) Richert 10-11, followed by SG, takes *litar* as 'a poetic circumlocution for Gunnlǫð' and connects *keypts* with expressions like *kaupa sér konu*, *brúðkaup* (for he thinks a wedding took place); he renders *litar* as *skönheten* 'the beauty', but this too lacks parallels. Bugge 2, 251 interprets as *hlítar*, which he takes with the second *vel* (the phrase *hlítar vel* 'tolerably well' occurs in prose); he then has to interpret *velkeypts* as gen. sg. n. used substantivally: 'the well-purchased' (i.e. the mead). This is clearly impossible. Others suppose *litar* somehow conceals a word referring to the mead: some early editors read *líðar* (but the genitive of *líð* 'ale' is in fact *líðs*), and Konráð Gíslason (in *Njála* II 406), followed by FJ, emends to *hlutar* 'share, winning'. CPB 22, reading *vél-keyptz litar*, renders 'the fraud-bought mead', without explaining the last word. In all probability the line is corrupt beyond redemption.

4 *Óðrerir* is, in Snorri's account, one of the three vessels in which the sacred mead is stored by Suttungr, and this is evidently also the sense it has in 140 below. Here it would seem rather to denote the mead itself; probably this was the original sense of the word, and its application to the vessel containing it is secondary, for it appears to be compounded from *óðr* 'soul; poetry' and **hrœrir*, agent noun from *hrœra* 'to stir up' (so BMÓ 82, cp. de Vries 4 §390 and Lindroth 176; FJ prefers to connect the second element with the root seen in *rísa*, but the sense would be the same): thus, 'stirrer-up of the soul (or, of poetry)'.

6 The reading of CR *á alda vés jarðar* must be corrupt, for an acc. is required after *á*, and a *ljóðaháttr* 'full line' may not end in a trochaic disyllable (see on 31 above). Editors usually emend to *jaðar* 'rim'. But what is 'the rim of the sacred place of men'? Bugge

1, 56 equates it to Miðgarðr without explanation (though in Snorri's account it is in fact Ásgarðr to which Óðinn brings the mead) and similarly CPB 22 and 466: 'the skirts of the city of men', i.e. the edge of the inhabited world. Another interpretation takes *alda vé* as Valhǫll, either by postulating that in Óðinn's mouth 'men' could allude to his warrior hosts (BMÓ 83-4) or by taking *alda* as from an adjective **aldr* 'ancient' otherwise evidenced only in compounds like *aldjǫtunn* (Neckel 358ff.; similarly M. Olsen 7, 42, who however emends to *aldna*); the *jaðarr* of Valhǫll is then either the fence around it (Neckel) or the land surrounding it (i.e. Ásgarðr). FJ takes *jaðarr* in its secondary sense 'protector, prince' and reads *á alda vé jaðars* 'to the sacred place of the lord of men (i.e. Óðinn)', that is, 'to Ásgarðr'; this would however really require the word-order *á vé alda jaðars* (so SG). As the variety of interpretations suggests, the line is intractable; Bugge's solution is as plausible as any, but no real decision is possible.

108

6 *lǫgðumk arm yfir* is explained by SG as = *lagði arm yfir mik*; for this form of the verb see A. Noreen §465.3. But it could also be first person sg. ('whom I laid my arm over'), which is apparently how Noreen himself takes it, §534 Anm. 3. Evidence for the existence, in both present and past tenses, of a first person sg. form in *-om* (*-um*), with *-k* sometimes suffixed, is adduced by Jón Thorkelsson ANF VIII (1892) 34-51 and by E.Wadstein *ibid*. 86-7, who cites as parallels to *lǫgðumk* the forms *ec bióþomc* 'I offer' and *ec comomc* 'I came' from the Norwegian Homily Book, *ec ætlomk* 'I intend' from the Legendary Saga of St Óláfr and *hengdom ic* 'I hung' from *Diplomatarium Norvegicum* I 600. It is noteworthy that these instances are all Norwegian. Jón and Wadstein explain these forms in the same way: the *-c* (*-k*) is the pronoun *ek* and the *-m* is the same *-m* as in *em* 'am' and which is found more widely in Old Saxon and OHG (*habêm, gâm, stâm* etc.). Falk AFDA XVIII (1892) 192-94 explains differently: in the middle the first sg. and first pl. coincide in form, both being < *omc*; the difference in sense between active and middle is often slight; this may have encouraged the pl. form in the active to intrude itself into the sg. by analogy. See further on *ráðumk* 112, and cp. Noreen §531 Anm. 2.

109

1 *Ins hindra dags* 'the next day'; only here in literature, but found as *hindardags* in Norwegian laws (NGL I 23), and also in Swedish laws, where *hindradagher* regularly has the sense 'day after a wedding'. Richert 11-12 holds that this is the sense in the present passage too.

3-5 On *Hávi* as a name for Óðinn see pp. 36-7 above. From Snorri's account we learn that *Bǫlverkr* is the name under which Óðinn disguised himself while in quest of the mead. But Snorri has nothing corresponding to the substance of this strophe, and it is unclear whether line 3 means 'to ask Hávi for advice' or 'to enquire about Hávi's situation'. Are we meant to understand that the frost-giants do not realise that Hávi and Bǫlverkr are identical?

110

Baugeið — not referred to in Snorri's account. The swearing of oaths on rings is spoken of quite frequently in ON sources: Lndn. 313-5 states that a ring was to lie on the altar of every 'chief temple', to be worn by the *goði* at assemblies where he presided; every man who had legal duties to discharge at the assembly *skyldi áðr eið vinna at þeim baugi*, and cp. similar allusions in Eyrbyggja saga ch. 4 and Víga-Glúms saga ch. 25 (ÍF IV 8 and IX 86). Atlakviða 30 speaks of oaths sworn *at hringi Ullar* and the Anglo-Saxon Chronicle s.a. 876 describes how the Danish host in England swore oaths to King Alfred *on þǣm hālgan bēage*. For a general survey of the topic see Francis P. Magoun Jr 'On the Old-Germanic Altar- or Oath-Ring (*Stallahringr*)' APhS XX (1949) 277-93.

111

On this obscure and much-debated strophe see p. 26 above and Hollander 2, 282-7.

2 *þulr* seems to mean something like 'sage' or perhaps 'seer'. The word recurs in 134, where Loddfáfnir is exhorted not to laugh at a 'hoary *þulr*', since the old often speak wisely, and in 80 and 142 the runes are said to have been coloured by *fimbulþulr*, the mighty *þulr* (presumably Óðinn); the association with age also appears in the other two occurrences in the Edda: *inn hára þul*, referring to Reginn, in Fáfnismál 34 and *inn gamli þulr*, used of Vafþrúðnir, in Vafþr. 9. In other poems the word is applied once to the legendary hero Starkaðr, once to the 'wizard poet' Þorleifr

jarlsskáld, and once by the poet Rǫgnvaldr kali to himself; it does not occur in prose, but an early ninth-century Danish runic inscription from Snoldelev commemorates one Gunnvaldr, son of Hróaldr, *þulr* at Salhaugar (now Salløv), as though this were a recognized public office. The OE cognate *þyle* is used to gloss *orator* and also, it seems, *scurra* and *histrio* (see PMLA 77 [1962] 2), and *þelcræft* (evidently for **þylcræft*) glosses *rethorica*, and in Beowulf Unferth, a courtier of the Danish king Hrothgar, at whose feet he sits, is called *Hróþgāres þyle*. The Norse verb *þylja*, which is doubtless derived from the noun, sometimes appears to mean 'chant, proclaim', as in the present passage, and sometimes 'mumble to oneself' (especially of the mumbling of spells, hidden wisdom etc.), cp. st. 17 above; there is also a noun *þula* 'poetic catalogue, rigmarole'. There has been much speculation as to the original function of the *þulr*: most probably he was some kind of publicly acknowledged wise man, repository of ancient lore and credited with prophetic insight, but since the concept was evidently essentially prehistoric and already obsolescent at the time of our oldest records, certainty is impossible. For further discussion see E. Noreen 2, 19-26, W. H. Vogt 'Der frühgermanische Kultredner' APhS II (1928) 250-63, Axel Olrik 'At sidde på Höj' *Danske Studier* 1909, 1-10, and H. M. and N. K. Chadwick *The Growth of Literature* I (Cambridge 1932) 618-21.

3 *Urðar brunni at* — editors differ as to whether this should be taken with what precedes or with what follows, but since the strophe as a whole is involved in so much obscurity it seems risky to break the regular pattern of *ljóðaháttr* by placing a stop after the first 'long line' (i.e. at the end of line 2); the only parallel would be 69, but there a break occurs at the end of line 3 as well. The *Urðar brunnr* is stated in Vǫluspá 19 to lie beneath the evergreen ash Yggdrasill, and Snorri says in the Prose Edda (Gylfaginning ch. 15) that *þriðja rót asksins stendr á himni, ok undir þeiri rót er brunnr sá, er mjǫk er heilagr, er heitir Urðarbrunnr. Þar eigu guðin dómstað sinn*. In a fragment of a Christian poem the tenth-century skald Eilífr Goðrúnarson speaks of Christ as having his station *sunnr at Urðar brunni* (Skj. i 144), evidently a Christian appropriation of the concept of the Well of Fate as the seat of wisdom.

112

1 *Ráðumk* 'I advise'; not a refl. form (for 'advise' is always *ráða*,

not *ráðask*) but a first person sg. in -*um* with -*k* from *ek* suffixed; cp. on *létumk* 106 and *lǫgðumk* 108, and note *hétomk* beside *ek hét* 'I was called' in Grímnismál 46-54; *heita* is never refl. in this sense (cp. SG *Wörterbuch* 421/40-48). *Loddfáfnir* is not mentioned outside Hávamál, and the etymology of the name is mysterious. The first element has often been connected with *loddari* 'trickster', but this word occurs only in latish texts and is probably a loan from West Germanic (cp. OE *loddere*, MLG *Lodder*, German *Lotter*), in which case it would hardly be found in Hávamál. For a speculative discussion of the problem see Sturtevant 5, 488-9.

114

3 *þings né þjóðans máls* — Fritzner 1 suggested that this was a corruption (by Icelanders ignorant of a Norwegian technical term) of *þings né þjóðarmáls*. The phrase *á þingi eðr þjóðarmáli* (or in the pl.) is found in three fifteenth-century Norwegian documents, where *þjóðarmál* appears to mean much the same as *þing*; for this sense of *mál* cp. OHG (Latinized) *mallus* in Lex Salica, *malloberg* = *lǫgberg*. Fritzner compares the set phrase *á þingi eða þjóðstefnu*. (Seip 96-7 supports Fritzner by pointing out that the corruption would be palaeographically natural.) It is, however, hazardous to emend on the basis of fifteenth-century records, and CR makes reasonable sense, whether we take *þjóðans mál* to mean 'the king's speech' or 'the king's business'.

118

1 *Ofarla* 'high up', mostly rendered by editors 'sharply' or the like, as though metaphorical; but this lacks parallels. FJ, more literally, explains 'in the head', implying a mortal wound, a sense present in *ofarliga* in Ǫlkofra þáttr ch. 3 and Njáls saga ch 142 (ÍF XI 93 and XII 392). Kock NN §§804 and 2984A reads *ofárla*, referring to premature death.

119

5-6 occur also in st. 44, and 8-9 also (virtually) in Grímnismál 17.

120

7 *líknargaldr* 'healing charms' (only here). What precisely is referred to is unclear; SG explain as 'the art of making yourself loved' (cp. on 123). FJ suggests the compound means in effect no more than *líkn* 'benevolence', but *-galdr* does not appear elsewhere as an empty suffix.

123

6 *líknfastan at lofi* is somewhat unclear. *Líknfastr*, which is found only here, is generally explained by editors as 'assured of favour', i.e. popular, beloved, though, as Lindquist 2, 11 remarks, 'popularity' seems a curiously extended sense for *líkn*, which normally means 'solace, comfort, mercy'. But cp. st. 8 above, where *lof* and *líkn* are also conjoined. There seems in fact no acceptable alternative to understanding the line as 'assured of favour in respect of praise', i.e. 'generally liked and praised'.

124

1 *Sifjum* 'kinship', here, uniquely, in a metaphorical sense.

5 *brigðum* is dat. sg. m. of the adj. *brigðr* 'false, deceitful'. The dat. is usually explained (FJ, SG) as due to attraction to an understood *manni*. Kock's proposals to emend (NN §§1421C, 3395) are uncalled for, since the construction occurs elsewhere: *gott er vammalausum vera* Sólarljóð 30, *illt er veillyndum at vera* Hugsvinnsmál 127 (Skj. i 640 and ii 207).

125

6 *þér* is dat. of comparison with *verra*. The word order is awkward: Bugge and Jón Helgason emend *þér við* to *við þér*.

126

5-6 For *né* negativing the preceding as well as the succeeding element cp. *við hleifi . . . né við hornigi* in 139 below.

8-9 For the variation from indicative to subj. in two co-ordinated conditional clauses cp. 30 above. The present instance differs, however, in that *ef* does not appear. For similar omission of *ef* in conditional sentences in the indicative cp. *gestr em ek Gjúka*

Grípisspá 14 and other instances cited in DH. The usage is particularly common in the laws.

127

6 It is uncertain whether *þ* (with abbreviation mark) in CR should be expanded to *þér* (FJ, Ólafur Briem) or *þat* (Neckel-Kuhn, Jón Helgason); Bugge put *þér* in his text but altered to *þat* in the appendix. With *þat*, we must take the sense to be 'When you see evil, call it evil — don't extenuate it for reasons of weakness or cowardice'. Those who prefer *þér* differ somewhat among themselves as to the drift of the passage: BMÓ renders 'Wherever you observe wickedness (in a man), regard it as prejudicial to yourself (even if it is actually directed against someone else)'; FJ takes *bǫl* rather as 'misfortune': thus, 'Wherever you see a misfortune, regard it as your own' (so also Einar Ól. Sveinsson 2, 310-11). This strikes a note of (Christian?) altruism which sorts ill with the last line; Nordal 3, 191 (also reading *þér*) explains the passage as an incitement to be perpetually alert against encroachments on one's interests: do not be slow to act, but flare up and take vengeance immediately.

128

7 For *geta at* with dat. 'to be pleased with, to rejoice in' cp. Grettis saga ch. 64 (ÍF VII 210): *eigi læt ek mér at einu getit*. This idiom is now obsolete in Icelandic, and was evidently not understood by the copyists of some of the late paper mss, who substituted *þín* for *þér* (giving, of course, a different meaning).

129

7 *gjalti* (dat.) is a loanword from early Irish *geilt* (now *gealt*) 'one who goes mad from terror; a panic-stricken fugitive from battle; a crazy person living in the woods and supposed to be endowed with the power of levitation; a lunatic' (DIL). This is the earliest occurrence in Norse of this word, and its only appearance in poetry; in prose it is found a number of times, in the phrase *verða at gjalti*, of persons who flee away overcome by hysterical fright — in some instances, just as in the present strophe, from battle. For example, in Eyrbyggja saga ch. 18 (ÍF IV 37-8) a man called Nagli (who, significantly, has arrived from the Hebrides) is so aghast at an outbreak of violence and the brandishing of weapons that he *hljóp umfram ok í fjallit upp ok varð at gjalti*, and was only with difficulty restrained from hurling himself over a precipice. For other instances, see Fritzner 2, s.v. *gjalti* and the full discussion in Einar Ól. Sveinsson 1. In early Irish legend the most celebrated example is the tale of Suibne geilt, who *looked up* (cp. line 5) at the start of the Battle of Magh Rátha and fled hysterically, to live as a solitary madman in the wilderness (a motif also found in some of the Norse occurrences). That the phenomenon was native to Ireland was well known to the Norwegian author of the manual of court etiquette Konungs Skuggsiá, who gives an elaborate description of it in his account of the 'Wonders of Ireland': see Kuno Meyer in *Folk Lore* V (1894) 311-12, reprinted in *Ériu* IV (1908) 11-12, and J. I. Young in *Études Celtiques* 3 (1938) 23, and for a general discussion of the whole phenomenon, N. K. Chadwick in *Scottish Gaelic Studies* V (1942) 106-53.

9 *þik* — the ms *þitt* is kept by many editors, to mean something like 'you and yours'; the nearest parallel is *sitt bjó sannvinr rétta . . . til betra* in a thirteenth-century verse of Ámundi Árnason (Skj. ii 59).

130
The last line may have been a pre-existing proverb: it has a very general sense and is not closely attached in meaning to what goes before.

131
6 *eigi ofvaran*: 'not too cautious', because then, FJ explains, you may be led into cowardice. CPB 463 suggests reading *eigi óvaran*.

132
7 *gangandi* 'tramp'. The alliterating phrase occurs elsewhere: *ala gest ok ganganda með góðan hug til guðs þakka* in an old Norwegian homily (*Gammel Norsk Homiliebog*, ed. C. R. Unger [Christiania 1864] 123) and cp. examples from Old Danish cited by Fritzner 2 s.v. *gangandi*.

134
5 On the *þulr* see on st. 111.
   7 See Introduction p. 27.

8 For *skarpr* in the sense 'shrunk, withered' cp. its application to *fiskr, skreið, skinnstakkr*, and note the related *skorpa* 'to be shrivelled', *skorpinn*, 'shrivelled'. For *belgr* meaning 'person' (or possibly 'mouth' as e.g. SG take it) cp. Hamðismál 26: *opt ór þeim belg bǫll ráð koma*, and note the proverb in Gull-Þóris saga ch. 18 (ed. Kålund, 39): *hafa skal góð ráð, þó at ór refs belg komi*.

10-12 *þeim er* evidently refers back to *belg*, but the meaning of these last three lines is very obscure. The last word in 10 is surely *hám*, dat. pl. of *há* 'skin' (not found elsewhere in ON, but known in modern Icelandic) rather than dat. sg. of *hamr* (as some nineteenth-century editors thought), which means '(temporarily adopted) shape, form'. The final word in the strophe appears to be *vílmǫgum*, dat. pl. of *vílmǫgr* 'wretch' (literally 'son of misery'), which is listed among names for cowards and wretches in Snorra Edda I 532 and II 610 and in a *þula* printed at Skj. i 663, and also occurs twice elsewhere in poetry. FJ thinks the lines describe the 'withered bag' (i.e. the old man) wandering around among other old men, depicted as 'skins' (*hám* and *skrám*) and 'wretches'. But the three verbs all mean 'dangle, swing to and fro' and cannot give the required sense. Since the three verbs are all more or less synonymous, and *hám* and *skrám* are also near-synonyms, some editors have naturally tried to make *vílmǫgum* too synonymous with the other substantives: Wisén 110-21 achieved this by emending *hám* to *hámum*, dat. pl. of a supposed **hám* 'wretch' (cp. Swedish dialect *håm* 'wretch, clown') and by taking *skrám* to be from a supposed **skrái* cognate with Swedish dialect *skråe* 'miserable fellow'. This obliged him to take the verbs in the same sense as FJ. Eiríkr Magnússon 2 and 5 read the last word as *vilmǫgum* from a supposed **vilmagi* (*vil* 'bowels, tripes' + *magi* 'stomach'), but this still leaves the meaning of the whole passage deeply obscure. Rolf Pipping 2, 4, followed by Hummelstedt, suggests the *þulr* is a magician hanging up in a tree, like a shaman or like Óðinn in 138, to acquire mystical knowledge; the 'skins' are the bodies of sacrificed men and animals. (This is compatible with either interpretation of the last word.) This is the only interpretation which makes sense, but it is undeniably highly speculative.

135

5 *geya* — for the transitive use of the verb *geyja* in the sense 'revile' cp. the verse of Hjalti Skeggjason quoted in Ari's Íslendingabók and beginnking *vilk eigi goð geyja* (ÍF I 15). The imperative is *gey*,

and the final -*a* here must be the negative suffix; I therefore print *geya*, though CR, and editors generally, write *geyia*.

6 *hrekir* — CR has *hrǫkir*, and, since *ǫ* is commonly employed there for *æ*, Nygaard 1, I 5 and Neckel-Kuhn interpret this as *hrækir*, from *hrækja* 'to spit'. But this does not seem to go well with *á grind*. Bugge 1 and FJ understand the ms as *hrekir*, from *hrekja* 'to drive away'. This gives excellent sense, but it should be regarded as an emendation since (as Bugge p.x admits) *ǫ* is not found elsewhere in CR for *e*. Another possibility, giving the same sense, is *hrøkkvir* (so BMÓ 85, DH); this too is an emendation, since the *v* cannot be dispensed with. (Björn K. Þórólfsson, *Um íslenskar orðmyndir á 14. og 15. öld* [Reykjavík 1925] 60, cites forms of *hǫggva* with loss of *v* in later medieval mss, and Anthony Faulkes points out to me that the Prose Edda Utrecht ms, written *c.* 1600 but from an old exemplar, has *stocir* for *støkkvir* and *hògaz* for *hǫggvask* at FJ 9, 19/2 and 44/25 respectively. It remains questionable whether we can reckon on such a loss in a ms as old as CR.)

For variation between the true imperative and the subj. used in imperative sense cp. *þú ráð nemir ok ríð heim síðan* Fáfnismál 20, and see Nygaard 2, §183.

136

1 *tré* can surely only refer to the beam (*loka, slagbrandr*) raised to admit a guest: you need a stout beam on a door (or possibly, as M. Olsen 7, 48 prefers, on an outer gate, *grind*) which is going to let in everybody. This sounds like advice against over-generosity, but there is no denying that this causes difficulty in that it contradicts both the general note of Norse etiquette and the immediate surroundings of 1-3; for 4-6 cannot satisfactorily be interpreted to mean anything other than 'Give a ring', i.e. a gift (to anyone who comes).

But attempts to find alternative interpretations are uniformly unconvincing. BMÓ 85 thinks *tré* means 'cudgel' — you would need a strong cudgel if it is to swing on everyone's head. This removes the contradiction, but *ríða* cannot be used with the simple dat. (*at* is needed), and *at upploki* is left somewhat unattached on this rendering. Others take *baugr* as used uniquely for a door-ring (*hurðarhringr*): Gering (in SG) thinks this was a device to make the door extra-secure, Falk 8, 223-5 supposes it was a door-knocker to ensure the visitor really was heard instead of going away frustrated and cursing. But *gef* cannot mean 'affix'. Hugo Pipping 3 and 5 thought *baugr* could mean 'anus', so that 4 would mean 'Stick your bum out at him' (in order, says Pipping, to nullify the 'evil eye' of the frustrated beggar). But the evidence for *baugr* in this sense is not strong (see however M. Clunies-Ross in *Medieval Scandinavia* 6 [1973] 80ff.)

5 *þat* is hardly 'the failure to give' (BMÓ); more probably it means 'people, visitors', cp. *rekkar þat þóttusk* 49.

137

On this strophe see especially the articles by Reichborn-Kjennerud (R-K) and Cederschiöld in the Bibliography, and BMÓ 89-93.

5 *ǫl* — probably the reference is not to mere excess in drinking, but to ale poisoned by bearded darnel, *lolium temulentum*, ON *skjaðak* (cp. Marstrander).

6 *jarðar megin* is also referred to, as one of the ingredients in Grímhildr's drugged potion, in Guðrúnarkviða II 21 (CR there actually has *urðar magni* [dat.] but this is doubtless corrupt for *jarðar magni*, which appears in the paraphrase of the lines in Vǫlsunga saga [ed. R. G. Finch, London 1965, 62] and, as *jarðar megni*, in what seems to be a borrowing from that poem in Hyndluljóð 38 and 43). There may well be a specific connection with the so-called *terra sigillata*, cakes of earth rich in iron oxide, stamped with the image of Diana or Christ, exported from Lemnos and recommended (e.g. by Pliny and Galen) as a remedy against poison. This is referred to in the Old Icelandic Medical Miscellany (Kålund 1, 381): *jǫrð sú, er á innsigli er lǫgð ok manns líkneski er á, hon er góð við orms biti ok annarra flugorma, ok ef manni er gefinn ólyfjansdrykkr, þá drekki af þessari jǫrðunni; þat hrindr eitri út, en mann sakar ekki* (cp. BMÓ 89). There may also be a connection with the more general belief in the earth's holy and curative properties (cp. *heil sjá in fjǫlnýta fold* Sigrdr. 4). Lines 7 and 15 perhaps allude to notions that sicknesses can be transferred to the earth through symbolic acts. (FJ queries whether *terra sigillata* was known in the North so early, and thinks the picture is one of over-indulgence in alcohol and consequent vomiting on the earth.)

8 *eldr* — Cederschiöld suggests this refers to need-fire, carried from farm to farm in times of pestilence, a practice widespread in early modern times in Scandinavia, Germany and Gaelic Scotland. R-K thinks the reference is more comprehensive and includes an

allusion to the use of glowing iron for cauterisation, cleaning of dirty wounds etc. (but, as FJ points out, *eldr* can scarcely mean 'glowing iron'), and also to fumigation for expelling evil spirits; he compares the Sunnmøre proverb *eld er råd mot trollskap*.

9 *abbindi* occurs elsewhere in ON only in the late fourteenth-century AM 194 8vo (Kålund 2, I 68-9): *Tak oxa gall ok ríð um endaþarms rauf, þá mun batna við abbindi*. However, R-K 5, 161 draws attention to *åbende* in a list of diseases preserved in a modern Norwegian work on black magic (the list dating, he thinks, from the early sixteenth century), and in the late eighteenth-century *Registr yfir íslenzk sjúkdómanöfn* by Sveinn Pálsson we find *afbendi er þegar manni finnst sér vera sífellt mál að ganga þarfinda sinna, en lítið eitt verður ágengt*. The word doubtless denotes tenesmus, and is probably borrowed from OE *gebind* in the sense *tenacitas ventris, tentigo* which it bears in the Leiden Glossary. This is a symptom of dysentery, against which oak bark and bast are a well-known traditional remedy.

10 *ax* 'ear of corn'. Cederschiöld thought this was senseless and proposed to read *øx* 'axe', with a reference to the custom (known in later Scandinavian folk-tradition) of setting an axe above the door as a protection against sorcery. But this is unnecessary, and also rash in view of the mention of *ax óskorit* as a constituent of Grímhildr's potion in Guðrúnarkviða II 22. R-K shows that there is much evidence from later times in Scandinavia (and elsewhere) of the use of ears of corn to ward off trolls, magic etc.; he cites (R-K 4) a custom from Bodin, in north Norway, of affixing eight ears of corn, arranged in a cross, on the door of the cowshed at Christmas-time *til hjelp mot hustroll og anna utyske*; ears of corn were also used as supposed remedies for sties, toothache, and other afflictions often believed to emanate from wizards and trolls.

11 *hǫll við hýrógi* is not satisfactorily explained. The last word, if not corrupt, can only mean 'household strife'. It cannot be said that 'hall' gives any reasonable sense here, though it is taken thus by Sveinbjörn Egilsson, FJ and others ('Dispute between members of the household does not come outside the house, is short-lived'). The ms has *haʋll*, which could equally well be read as *haull* 'hernia', but this gives no sense either. The sign *aʋ* can also be read as *ø*; we might suppose then that we have here a word **høll* (or, better, **høllr* m.) 'elder-tree', cognate with Swedish and Norwegian *hyll*, Danish *hyld* (all originally masculine). This tree is not native to Iceland, and no name for it is certainly known in ON (either or both of the tree-names *hallarr* and *yllir*, Skj. i 673, may possibly

be connected, cp. de Vries 5, s.vv.; the latter means 'elder' in modern Icelandic). The elder has played a prominent part in folk-medicine since classical antiquity; but how is it a remedy for domestic strife? R-K suggests the idea is that this is the 'household tree', residence of domestic spirits who ward off strife and sickness from the home. (M. Olsen 7, 51 emends to *hasl* 'hazel' and thinks of a hazel-rod as an implement of domestic chastisement.)

12 *heiptum* — for this word in a rather similar connection cp. Sigrdr. 12: *málrúnar skaltu kunna, ef þú vilt at manngi þér heiptum gjaldi harm*. R-K thinks the 'hatreds' referred to are the workings of the evil eye, against which moon-shaped amulets were employed in classical antiquity. The moon in fact plays a very small part in Germanic pagan religion, cp. de Vries 4, §197.

13 *beiti* is otherwise recorded in ON, once as a *heiti* for 'ship' (plainly irrelevant here) and also as a rare by-form of *beit* 'pasturage'. Some scholars take it in this sense here, e.g. Fritzner 2, s.v., who explains, with a query, 'When the cattle come out to the pasture, they escape from diseases caused by lice and other pests' (so also DH). But this scarcely makes sense, and the strophe appears to be concerned with the diseases of men, not of animals. Other suggestions are: (a) 'beet'; Latin *beta* was borrowed into West Germanic languages at an early date, as OE *bete*, OHG *bieza*, MLG *bete*, and BMÓ 93 proposed that it had also been borrowed into ON and appeared here. Pliny mentions beet as a remedy for snakebite. But its use is unknown in Nordic folk-medicine, and the plant itself does not seem to have reached the North until a far later date. (b) 'alum'; Cederschiöld referred to Germanic verbs meaning 'to tan, to apply chemical liquid in tanning or dyeing', as Swedish *beta*, German *beizen*, Norwegian dialect *beita* etc., the basic sense being 'cause (the acids) to bite'. There is a corresponding noun denoting the liquid itself: Swedish *beta*, Old Danish *bed* etc., and the suggestion is that *beiti* here is the ON form of this word; since alum was commonly used for this purpose in the Middle Ages and has also been employed since antiquity as a remedy for, among other things, wounds (*þat hreinsar augu . . . ok lætr ill sár eigi vaxa*, Kålund 1, 386), Cederschiöld proposed the sense 'alum' for this passage. (c) 'bait' or, more precisely, 'earth-worm' (R-K); elsewhere in ON 'bait' is *beita* f., but *beite* is known as a masculine noun in Norwegian, and in southern Norwegian dialect means 'earth-worm' rather than bait in general. The worm has been employed since ancient times as a remedy for wounds of various sorts and rashes (Pliny XXX 106,

115). The Old English Leechdoms (ed. Cockayne II 329) recommend worms for dog-bites, and R-K adduces much evidence of their use in Nordic folk-medicine. This interpretation of *beiti* is clearly the most plausible.

14 *við bǫlvi rúnar* — for the therapeutic use of runes cp. the references to *bjargrúnar, brimrúnar* and *limrúnar* in Sigrdr. 9-11. R-K takes *bǫl* as bodily injury or disease, but such a sense is unparalleled; 'misfortune' or 'evil' is a better rendering.

15 Heusler 1, 46 takes this line as a proverb.

138

On the content of this and the following strophes see pp. 29-34.

2 *vindga* — an adj. *vindugr* (evidently 'wind-blown' here) is otherwise known only in modern Icelandic, but there is nothing suspect about it; the elaborate objections of Eiríkr Magnússon 4, 27-40 are over-nice. SG compare *sǫndugr* from *sandr*. A compound *vingameiðr* ('windy tree'?) appears three times in scaldic verse, but there is no need to print a compound form here.

7-9 bear a strong resemblance to Fjǫlsvinnsmál 20: *Mímameiðr hann heitir / en þat manngi veit / af hverjum rótum renn*; some scholars (e.g. FJ, SG) hold that they are borrowed thence. *Hvers* should perhaps be emended to *hverjum*, for as it stands it is obseure; FJ thinks *trés* is to be understood (which would be, as he says, 'completely illogical'), SG understand *kyns*.

139

If this strophe is taken to be in *ljóðaháttr*, the last line lacks alliteration, and BMÓ therefore emended *þatan* (so CR) to *ofan*. But the strophe is in fact clearly in *fornyrðislag*.

1 *sældu* — *seldo* in CR can stand for *seldu* 'gave' (which makes no sense), *sældu* 'blessed' or *sœldu* 'refreshed', either of which is defensible. It is needless to emend to *heldu* 'maintained' (Holthausen 156) or *sǫddu* 'sated' (Gering in SG).

140

3 *Bestla* was Óðinn's mother. For speculations on the etymology of the name see A. M. Sturtevant PMLA 67 (1952) 1156f. Her father's name is given as *Bǫlþorn* (sic) in Snorri's Prose Edda. Who his son (i.e. Óðinn's uncle) was is not recorded.

6 *ausinn Óðreri* is difficult. *Ausa* commonly means 'sprinkle', with the dat. of that which is sprinkled (e.g. *ausa barn vatni*). We might therefore take *ausinn* here as nom. to agree with *ek*, and *Óðreri* as referring to the mead itself (as apparently in 107). Thus DH, who are then obliged to explain *ausinn* as 'moistened (internally)'. This seems implausible, but the only alternative is to take *ausinn* as acc. modifying *drykk*, giving the sense 'ladled from (the vessel) Óðrerir' (so FJ). Such an ablatival construction with *ausa* cannot be paralleled.

141

2 It is probable that, as well as the adj. *fróðr* 'wise', ON possessed a homophone meaning 'fruitful, fertile', cp. *inn fróði* as the title of Freyr in Skírnismál 1 and 2, and Swedish *frodig* 'luxuriant, rich', *frodlem* 'penis' etc. Such a sense would fit the context excellently here. See de Vries 5, s.v. *Fróði*, Turville-Petre 1, 321, E. Hellquist *Svensk Etymologisk Ordbok* (Third Edition, Lund 1948) s.v. *frodas*, and A. Noreen *Ynglingatal* (Kungl. Vitt. Hist. och Antik. Akad. Handlingar 28, 2, Stockholm 1925) 213.

142

5-6 are almost identical with 80/4-5.

fáði 'coloured'. References to 'colouring' runes also occur in 144 and 157, and this same verb appears in a number of Scandinavian runic inscriptions from the early period, e.g. the Einang stone (Norway, *c.* 400) has [*ek Go*]*dagastiʀ runo faihido* 'I, Godagast, coloured the runes', the Rök stone (Sweden, *c.* 800) has *uarin faþi*, and similarly *auaiʀ faþi* on two early ninth-century inscriptions from Denmark. (But in some of the inscriptions the context suggests that *fá* may already have come to be used sometimes merely to mean 'carve' or 'cut', as in later Icelandic, cp. Blöndal s.v. and Jansson 166.) Guðrúnarkviða II 22 speaks of *hvers kyns stafir* (evidently runes) as *ristnir ok roðnir* 'carved and reddened', and one of the stones at Överselö (Sweden) states *Hér skal standa steinar þessir, rúnum roðnir, reisti Guðlaug* (spelling normalised). The verb *steina* 'to paint' is also found in runic inscriptions in the same connection, e.g. from Gerstaberg (Sweden): *Ásbjǫrn rísti ok Úlfr steindi*. Traces of colour still survive on some Swedish stones. For discussion and further instances see de Vries 5, s.v. *fá* 2,

Jansson 162-8, and H. Arntz *Handbuch der Runenkunde* (Second Edition, Halle-Saale 1944) 285-6.

fimbulþulr 'the mighty sage'. Only here and in 80 above. Doubtless a name for Óðinn, cp. *Fimbultýr* Vsp. 60.

ginnregin 'mighty gods', a compound found several times elsewhere. The element *ginn-* seems to have intensive force: it occurs also in the expression *ginnheilǫg goð* in Lokasenna 11 and Vsp. 6 etc., and is probably to be identified with the first element in the early seventh-century runic Danish *ginoronoR, ginArunAR* on the Stentoften and Björketorp stones respectively; see DR 653-4 and Moltke 147, n. 28 for references. The intensifying prefix *gjøn-* in modern Norwegian dialect perhaps derives from *ginn-*.

7 *Hroptr* (or *Hróptr*?) is widely evidenced as a name for Óðinn. The etymology is obscure and disputed, nor is the problem made any simpler by the occurrence of *Hroptatýr* (as in 160) as another Óðinn-name. Its governing of the gen. *rǫgna* has sometimes been thought to present a puzzle, which some editors have sought to resolve by printing *hroptr* as a common noun (though the meaning of such a noun is purely speculative). Most probably the phrase simply means 'Hroptr among the gods', cp. *Yggjungr ása* Vsp. 28 and, in OE, *Bēowulf Scyldinga* (so Bugge 1, 395 and 2, 253, cp. NN §805B). For a (somewhat divergent) discussion of the phrase see also Vogt. The expression *rúnar . . . reist . . . Hroptr* occurs also in Sigrdr. 13.

143

2-3 *Dáinn* and *Dvalinn* are mentioned together in Grímnismál 33 (and thence in Snorri's Prose Edda) as two of the four harts who nibble the twigs of Yggdrasill. Dvalinn is widely recorded as a dwarf-name (e.g. Vsp. 11); Dáinn also occurs a number of times as the name of a dwarf (e.g. Hyndluljóð 7) and once, in a *þula*, as a name for a fox, but nowhere as an elf-name.

4 *Ásviðr* is not recorded elsewhere.

144

rísta 'cut', *ráða* 'interpret' and *fá* 'colour' clearly have 'runes' as the object to be understood, and possibly *freista* 'make trial of' does too.

7 The force of *senda* is unclear. Falk 1, 111-12 suggests it might mean 'to sacrifice', on the basis of Beowulf 599-600, which states

that the monster Grendel *lust wigeð, swefeð ond sendeþ* 'executes his pleasure. slays and "sends"', where *sendeþ* must mean something like 'kills' (if the text is sound; some editors emend). Cp. *ósent* in 145. and see Liberman for a full. rather speculative, discussion.

145

3 is evidently proverbial. cp. *sér æ gjǫf til gjalda* Gísla saga ch. 15 (ÍF VI 52), *sér gjǫf til gjalda* Viktors saga ok Blávus (ed. Jónas Kristjánsson. Reykjavík 1964) 20.

6 *Þundr* is a common name for Óðinn.

7 *fyr þjóða rǫk* seems to mean 'before the creation of peoples', though *aldar rǫk* Vafþr. 39 certainly means 'the end of mankind, doomsday'. *Rǫk* covers a wide semantic field, from 'basis, reason, origin' to 'course of events. history' and thence to 'destiny. final doom'.

8-9 The reference of these lines is obscure; possibly they relate to the events described in 139.

146

St. 146-63 are generally referred to as the Ljóðatal (Catalogue of Spells), a name first given by Müllenhoff; there is no indication in CR that the scribe regarded them as a separate section. Snorri plainly knew these verses, for portions of Ynglinga saga ch. 6-7 (in Heimskringla) are manifestly based on them; he understood the *ek* of the verses as Óðinn. unquestionably rightly.

148

3 *hapt* 'fetter'. apparently here metaphorical.

6 *velir* is pl. of *vǫlr* 'stick, club'. Bugge 1, 62 and 2, 253 interpreted *veler* in CR as *vélir*, pl. of *vél* (such a form is found, though the normal pl. is *vélar*). But, as CPB 468 points out, this breaks the metrical rule which Bugge himself later proclaimed (Bugge 3, cp. on st. 31 above). Ynglinga saga ch. 6 states *Óðinn kunni svá gera, at í orrostu urðu óvinir hans blindir eða daufir eða óttafullir, en vápn þeira bitu eigi heldr en vendir*; the last word suggests that Snorri was reading *velir*, but at the same time the whole phrase seems to imply that his text was somewhat different from ours. For this reason SG proposed *bítat vápn heldr en velir*. But that Snorri's

text was different does not entail that it was necessarily better, and *vǫlr* is used elsewhere of a weapon, at any rate in the compound *vígvǫlr*.

149

3 *bóglimum* — many editors read *boglimum*, with the first element meaning 'curved' or 'flexible'. But elsewhere in ON this notion is conveyed by *bjúg-*, as in *bjúglimir* in Tindr Hallkelsson (Skj. i 136), and compounds in *bog-* are related to *bogi* 'bow', cp. BMÓ 4, 3-4. It appears from 4-7 that the word implies 'arms and legs'; *bógr* means 'shoulder', but the OHG cognate *buog* could mean 'hip' as well, and BMÓ suggests that the Norse word too originally possessed this double sense. The word also occurs in Grógaldr 10, a strophe fairly plainly derivative from the present passage.

150

2 *af fári* 'with hostile intent, maliciously'. (Bellows' 'from afar' is a strange error.)

3 *fólki* in the dat. seems to require the sense 'battle' rather than 'people'. (Neckel emended to *fólk*; the phrase *í fólk vaða* occurs in Haraldskvæði and Darraðarljóð, Skj. i 25 and 390.)

151

This strophe appears to refer to the carving of malignant runes on a piece of wood, as in the story in Grettis saga ch. 79, where an old woman carves such runes on a *rótartré* (ÍF VII 249).

3 CR *rás* is problematic. Skírnismál 32 (which also has to do with magic) speaks of *hrás viðar* (gen.) 'sappy wood', and this phrase is also found occasionally in prose. But if we read *hrás* there is no alliteration. It will not do to emend to *hrótum*, as proposed by BMÓ 94, since his belief that there existed a noun *hrót* 'root' is false (the kenning *hjarta hrót* Skj. i 104 means 'heart's roof', i.e. breast). As *rót* is usually held by etymologists to descend from a prehistoric *vrót* (though the East Norse forms, which show no *v-*, present a difficulty) FJ read *á vrótum hrás viðar*; but an attributive adj. preceding its noun ought to bear the alliteration. H. Pipping 2, 19, observing that a *sappy* piece of wood is hardly suitable for carving, suggested *á rótum (v)rás viðar*, postulating an adjective *(v)rár* 'gnarled, crooked', cp. Swedish dialect *vrå* 'cross-

grained, stubborn' and Middle English *wrāh* 'peevish, crabbed' (OED s.v. *wraw* a.). The safest emendation, and a very small one, is to read *rás* as *rams* 'strong' (so, independently, Holtausen 156, Lindquist 3, 262 and M. Olsen 7, 56).

152

2 This line alliterates only if *sé* is taken as the alliterating word; most editors have been properly reluctant to believe that the verb could take precedence in this way (especially as *sé* does not alliterate in 150, 155 or 157), though Bugge 1, 395 and BMÓ 94 suggest, not very plausibly, that this might be acceptable if *loga* is taken as beginning line 3. But none of the proposals to replace *hávan* by a word on *s*- is very attractive: among them are *sofǫndum* (Bugge 1, 62; so also, with further changes, CPB 26), *sjálfan* (M. Olsen 1 and 3, 303), *sviðinn* (Gering in HG), *síðan* (NN §2303, comparing *síd* 'wide' of a hall in OE), *slunginn* or *sveipinn* (Sijmons in SG, with *loga* as dat. of the noun), and *sjávanr* (H. Pipping 2, 23, supposed to mean 'without any water', to agree with *ek*). Olsen's is perhaps the best of these, though it gives rather feeble sense.

155

On this much-discussed strophe see in particular Läffler 2, 33-48 and 3, B. M. Ólsen 3, E. Noreen 3, and Strömbäck 1, 168-82 and 2, 18-22.

2 *túnriða* only occurs here in ON, but the cognate *zunriten* occurs once in MHG in a list of demonic beings against whom protection is sought (printed in ZFDA, N.F.29 [1896-7] 337, cp. 347). The Norse word clearly refers to the same class of creature as *kveldriða, myrkriða, trollriða* 'witch, trollwoman' (the occurrences of these words are listed in BMÓ 3, 72-3). That these are shape-changers is implied by Postola sögur (ed. C. R. Unger, Christiania 1874) 914: *kveldriður eða hamhleypur . . . fara yfir stór hǫf ríðandi hvǫlum eða selum, fuglum eða dýrum*, cp. the reference to *hamr* in 6 below. BMÓ understood *tún*- as 'house, farm-building' and supposed that the *túnriður* sat astride the ridge of the roof, drumming with their heels, like Glámr in Grettis saga and Þórólfr bægifótr in Eyrbyggja saga (so also SG). But it is only ghosts who do this, and *tún*, though it can mean 'the entire farm-complex, the yard with the surrounding buildings', never means simply 'house'

or 'building'. FJ therefore saw the *túnriður* as beings riding in the air above the farmsteads. Most likely, however, *tún-* means 'fence' here, as in German *Zaun* and modern Swedish dialect *tun*, and alludes to the proclivity of witches to sit astride fences, as mentioned in the Older Västergötland Law, Rb. 5, 5 (ed. Wessén [1954] 29), which states that it is a gross libel (*vkuæþins orþ*) to address the following words to a woman: *Iak sa at þu ret a quigrindu löshareþ ok i trols ham, þa alt var iamrift nat ok dagher* 'I saw that you rode on a *kvígrind* with hair dishevelled, in the shape of a troll, when night and day were equal'. *Kvígrind*, which is also recorded in seventeenth-century Norwegian, must mean 'one of the hurdles composing a sheep- or cattle-fold' (see E. Noreen 3, 57-8).

5-7 CR *þeir villir* is best emended to *þær villar*, since it refers to the feminine *túnriður*. Some editors defend the ms as *constructio ad sensum*, arguing that the concept embraces males as well as females; at any rate, NGL II 308 and 326 has *sa er kallar nokorn mann trollridu* and, more cogently, *ef karlum æda konom værdr þat kænt, at þau se trol æda fordædor æda ridi manni eda bufe . . . þa skal hann eda hona flytia a sio ut* (NGL II 385).

This strophe clearly refers to the well-evidenced Norse belief that a person's soul (*hugr*) could in certain circumstances depart temporarily from his body and range abroad by itself (Fritzner 2, s.v. *hugr* 3), sometimes taking on a new physical shape (*hamr*), while the owner's body lay in a trance. (See for example Ynglinga saga ch. 7, where Óðinn is said to possess this gift: *Óðinn skipti hǫmum. Lá þá búkrinn sem sofinn eða dauðr, en hamr var þá fugl eða dýr, fiskr eða ormr ok fór á einni svipstund á fjarlæg lǫnd*.) But the syntax and exact purport of 5-7 are obscure and have given rise to numerous interpretations, all highly problematic. Läffler, who followed CR in keeping *heim hama* and *heim huga* as four separate words, took the *túnriður* as persons bewitched against their will, whom the helpful Óðinn is able to release 'so that these straying ones go to the home of their (true, human) shapes, the home of their (true, human) souls'; here, *hama* and *huga* depend on *heim*, which is taken as acc. sg. of the substantive and direct object of *fara*. But this interpretation accords ill with the apotropaic character of most of Ljóðatal, and *þeir villir* (as he reads) cannot function as the subject (the adj. would have to be weak); further, Läffler's view implies that the shape-shifter possesses not only two *hamir* but also two *hugir*, which is contrary to all our other sources. Strömbäck avoids these difficulties by accepting that the spell is apotropaic and that *villir* is predicative; he emphasizes that the full-line pairs in *galdralag* tend to show similarity or identity of meaning (e.g. *kaldan straum kili, kaldan sjá kili* or *manna glaum mani, manna nyt mani*), so that *hamr* and *hugr* must be more or less synonymous, both referring to the 'unattached soul', the 'shape' moving at large through the air while the body lies inert 'at home'. This gives a rendering much the same as Läffler's ('. . . so that they go astray, to the home of their shapes, the home of their souls') but escapes the difficulty of postulating two *hugir* in one being.

However, this use of *heimr* with the gen. to denote 'where something truly belongs' is unparalleled and suspect, and since *villr* is frequently used with the gen. (*villr vega* 47, *dœgra villr* etc.), it is hard to believe that *hama* and *huga* do not here depend on *villar* (which on Strömbäck's interpretation is left awkwardly otiose). Thus one might render '. . . so that they go home, astray from their (assumed) shapes, their (ill) intentions (?)' (cp. BMÓ). But this is a very doubtful rendering of *huga*, and *heim* is most awkwardly placed; it is therefore probably better to read *heimhama* and *heimhuga* as compounds: '. . . so that they go astray from (i.e. can never find their way back to) their home-shapes (i.e. their original shapes lying at home) and their *heimhuga*'. This last word is difficult; it can hardly mean 'their home-souls' (so M. Olsen NIÆR 2, 629) since this once more implies the false view that these beings had two souls each, and LP's 'desire or ability to go home' is far-fetched; FJ's later view (in his edition of 1924) that 7 simply repeats the sense of 6 in a loose and careless way is more attractive. (CPB 27 and SG cut the knot by emending to *heimhaga* 'home pastures, homesteads', which gives good sense.) Some support for this general approach can be found in Egils saga ch. 57 (ÍF II 171): *Sný ek þessu níði á landvættir þær, er land þetta byggva, svá at allar fari þær villar vega, engi hendi né hitti sitt inni, fyrr en þær reka Eirík konung ok Gunnhildi ór landi.*

156

4 This line has often been compared to Tacitus' description (Germania, ch. 3) of the *barritus*, the concerted 'battle-roar' with which Germanic warriors inflamed their own courage and terrified the enemy as they drew up for the contest. According to Tacitus, they placed their shields to their mouths to impart a fuller and deeper note (*obiectis ad os scutis, quo plenior et gravior vox repercussu*

intumescat). The word *randóp* ('shield-cry') may occur in a verse of Þórðr Kolbeinsson (ÍF III 193) but the text is uncertain (cp. Skj. i 209). Berserks are commonly described in the sagas as howling and biting the edges of their shields, e.g. Egils saga ch. 64 (ÍF II 202): *þá kom á hann berserksgangr, tók hann þá at grenja illiliga ok beit í skjǫld sinn*, and see other instances cited by Falk 2, 154. Cp. B. M. Ólsen ANF XVIII (1901) 196-8.

157

On the connection between Óðinn and hanging see pp. 31-2.

158

The pagan Norsemen are depicted as 'baptizing' new-born infants in a good many passages in the sagas, e.g. Egils saga ch. 31, Laxdœla saga ch. 25 (ÍF II 80 and V 71) and further references in Cl-Vig and Fritzner 2 s.v. *ausa* (*vatni*), which is the regular expression (not elsewhere with *verpa* as here). Konrad Maurer *Ueber die Wasserweihe des germanischen Heidenthumes* (Abh. der bayer. Akad. der Wissenschaften XV, München 1880), noting the absence of satisfactory evidence for this practice in Germanic heathendom outside Scandinavia, attributed the custom to Christian influence, a view that has been widely followed; cp. however de Vries 4 §137. Walter Baetke *Christliches Lehngut in der Sagareligion* (Berichte über die Verh. der Sächs. Akad. der Wissenschaften zu Leipzig, Phil.-Hist. Kl. 98, 6, Berlin 1952) 25-6 suggests that the pagan Norsemen did not in historical fact practise baptism and that these passages are misrepresentations by christianizing saga-writers; this obliges him to suppose, implausibly, that the present strophe is 'a late addition'.

159

Unlike the other strophes, this does not appear to refer to knowledge of a spell.

3 *fyrir* governs *liði*.

6 *ósnotr* elsewhere in the poem alliterates on the vowel, but there is a number of instances in the Edda where the negative prefix *ó-* is ignored in the alliteration: see on 70/2 above, and cp. *óleiðastan lifa* Skírnismál 19, *ógott um gala* Lokasenna 31. Some

Commentary 143

have thought *snotr* would make better sense, but emendation is not called for.

160

1 Apart from the problematic 152, this is the only strophe in Ljóðatal where the numeral does not alliterate. Some editors therefore suspect corruption; H. Pipping 2, 24 substitutes *flutti* for *gól* in 2, which, he suggests, has entered from 4.

2 *Þjóðreyrir* is not mentioned elsewhere.

3 *Dellingr* appears in lists of dwarf-names in a *þula* (Skj. i. 672) and in Fjölsvinnsmál 34, and is said in Vafþr. 25 to be the father of Day (*Dagr*). The phrase *fyr Dellings durum* occurs in a formula which opens four of the riddles of Gestumblindi (in Heiðreks saga). The name has been thought to mean 'bright one', cp. early Irish *dellrad* 'sheen, brilliance'.

6 *Hroptatýr* is well evidenced as a name for Óðinn, cp. *Hroptr* 142.

162

3 The adjective *manungr* occurs only here; it appears to mean 'maiden-young', i.e. in the prime of maidenhood, cp. *jóðungr* Sigsk. 36 and OE *cildgeong*.

5 The sudden reappearance of Loddfáfnir here is strange, and it may well be that 4-9 properly belong to Loddfáfnismál.

163

7-8 i.e. Óðinn's wife Frigg.

9 Óðinn in fact had no sister.

The notion that Óðinn has a great secret which he will communicate to none (save his wife) has often reminded readers of the unanswerable riddle posed by the disguised Óðinn in Vafþr. 54 and in Heiðreks saga (Skj. ii 246): 'What did Óðinn say in Baldr's ear before he mounted the pyre?'; the query exposes the questioner's identity, since only Óðinn knows the answer.

BIBLIOGRAPHY AND ABBREVIATIONS

AFDA   *Anzeiger für deutsches Altertum und deutsche Literatur* (bound with ZFDA)
ANF   *Arkiv för nordisk filologi*
ANOH   *Aarbøger for nordisk Oldkyndighed og Historie*
APhS   *Acta Philologica Scandinavica*
Beck, Heinrich   'Hávamál' *Kindlers Literatur Lexikon* III (Zürich 1967) col. 1514-6
Bellows, Henry Adams   *The Poetic Edda* translated from the Icelandic (New York 1923)
Beyschlag, Siegfried
    1. Review of Ivar Lindquist 'Die Urgestalt der Hávamál' *Deutsche Literaturzeitung* 79 (1958) col. 635-40.
    2. 'Zur Gestalt der Hávamál. Zu einer Studie Klaus von Sees' ZFDA 103 (1974) 1-19
Biskupa Sögur gefnar út af hinu íslenzka Bókmentafèlagi. I-II (Kaupmannahöfn 1858-78)
Blöndal, Sigfús   *Islandsk-Dansk Ordbog* (Reykjavík 1920-4)
BMÓ   Ólsen, Björn Magnússon. Unless otherwise stated, references are to ANF XXXI (1915) 52-95
de Boor, Helmut   Review of Klaus von See 'Die Gestalt der Hávamál' PBB (Tübingen) 95 (1973) 366-76
Boyer, Régis   *La Vie Religieuse en Islande (1116-1264)* Thèse présentée devant la Faculté des Lettres et Sciences Humaines de Paris le 11 Juin 1970 (Lille 1972)
Brate, Erik   *Sämunds Edda* översatt från isländskan (Stockholm 1913)
Briem, Ólafur (ed.)   *Eddukvæði* (Reykjavík 1968)
Brix, Hans   'Noter til Hávamál' *Edda* 58 (1958) 100-5
Brot   *Brot af Sigurðarkviðu* in *Edda*
Bruhn, Karl   'Mysteriös utbildning och undervisning i Norden under hednatiden' *Festskrift tillägnad B. Rud. Hall* (Nåssjö 1946) 32-62
Bugge, Sophus
    1. *Norrœn Fornkvæði ... almindelig kaldet Sæmundar Edda hins Fróða* (Christiania 1867)
    2. 'Efterslæt til min udgave af Sæmundar Edda' ANOH (1869) 243-76
    3. [Remarks on ON metrics] in L. V. A. Wimmer (ed.) *Beretning om Forhandlingerne på Det første nordiske Filologmøde* (København 1879) 140-6

4. *Studier over de nordiske Gude- og Heltesagns Oprindelse* Förste Række (Christiania 1881-9)
Cederschiöld, W. 'Läkeråden i Hávamál 137' ANF XXVI (1910) 294-300
Chadwick, H. M. *The Cult of Othin* (London 1899)
Clarke, D. E. Martin *The Hávamál, with selections from other poems of the Edda* (Cambridge 1923)
Cl-Vig *An Icelandic-English Dictionary* by Richard Cleasby and Gudbrand Vigfusson, Second edition (Oxford 1957)
Collinder, Björn
1. 'Eddica' *Nordisk tidsskrift for filologi* Fjerde Række, 10 (1921) 15-47
2. *Den Poetiska Eddan* i översättning (Stockholm 1957)
CPB *Corpus Poeticum Boreale* ed. Gudbrand Vigfusson and F. York Powell. 2 vols. (Oxford 1883). References are to vol. I.
Curtius, E. R. *European Literature and the Latin Middle Ages* Translated from the German by Willard R. Trask (London 1953)
Detter, F. 'Hárr' PBB XVIII (1894) 202-3
DH *Sæmundar Edda* ed. F. Detter and R. Heinzel. 2 vols. (Leipzig 1903)
DIL (*Contributions to*) *A Dictionary of the Irish Language* Royal Irish Academy (Dublin 1913-76)
DR *Danmarks Runeindskrifter. Text* ed. Lis Jacobsen and Erik Moltke (København 1942)
Dronke, Ursula 'Óminnis hegri' in *Fest. Holm-Olsen* 53-60
Edda The Poetic Edda is cited according to the enumeration (but not the orthography) in Neckel-Kuhn
Einar Ól. Sveinsson
1. 'Vísa í Hávamálum og írsk saga' *Skírnir* CXXVI (1952) 168-77
2. *Íslenzkar Bókmenntir í Fornöld* I (Reykjavík 1962)
Eiríkr Magnússon
1. [on st. 2 and 3] PCPhS IX (1884) 21-31
2. [on st. 4, 8, 13, 19 and 134] PCPhS XVI (1887) 5-18
3. 'Anmærkninger til I "Fornyrðadrápa" og til II "Islandsk Ordsprogsamling" Kbhvn. 1886' ANOH (1888) 323-48
4. *Odin's Horse Yggdrasill* (London 1895)
5. 'Vilmǫgum or vílmǫgum?' ANF XV (1899) 319-20
6. [on st. 129] *Saga-Book of the Viking Club* V (1908) 399-400
7. [on st. 53] *Year-Book of the Viking Club* I (1909) 69-70 (= PCPhS LXXXII [1909] 1-2)

Elmevik, Lennart 'Glömskans häger. Till tolkningen av en Hávamál-strof' *Scripta Islandica* 19 (1968) 39-45

Eriksson, Manne
1. 'Torp och villa' NB 31 (1943-4) 72-100
2. 'Tallen på torpet' SL (1958) 83-103
3. 'Tallen och det farliga torpet' SL (1967) 28-50

Falk, Hjalmar
1. 'Oldnorske ordforklaringer' ANF V (1889) 111-24
2. *Altnordische Waffenkunde* VSHF 1914, No. 6 (Kristiania 1914)
3. (ed.) *Sólarljóð* VSHF 1914, No. 7 (Kristiania 1914)
4. 'Litt om sagatidens sko' MM (1917) 51-63
5. 'Hávamál strofe 74' MM (1922) 173-5
6. *Odensheite* VSHF 1924, No. 10 (Kristiania 1924)
7. 'De nordiske hovedguders utviklingshistorie' ANF XLIII (1927) 34-44
8. 'Nogen Edda-studier' *Studier tillägnade Axel Kock* (=ANF Tilläggsband, Lund 1929) 223-31

Faulkes, Anthony *Two Versions of Snorra Edda* II. *Edda Islandorum* (Reykjavík 1977)

Fest. Genzmer *Edda, Skalden, Saga. Festschrift zum 70. Geburtstag von Felix Genzmer* ed. Hermann Schneider (Heidelberg 1952)

Fest. Holm-Olsen *Festskrift til Ludvig Holm-Olsen* (Øvre Ervik 1984)

Finnur Jónsson
1. 'Leiðrjettingar á ýmsum stöðum í Sæmundar-Eddu' ANF IV (1888) 26-58
2. Review of H. Gering *Glossar zu den Liedern der Edda* ANF XIV (1898) 195-204
3. *Den oldnorske og oldislandske Litteraturs Historie* I Second edition (København 1920)
4. 'Eddatolkning. Nogle modbemærkninger' ANF XXXVII (1921) 313-27
5. *Norsk-Islandske Kultur- og Sprogforhold i 9. og 10. Årh.* Det kgl. Danske Videnskabernes Selskab. Historisk-filologiske Meddelelser III, 2 (København 1921)
6. *Hávamál* Tolket af Finnur Jónsson (København 1924)
7. *De Gamle Eddadigte* udgivne og tolkede af Finnur Jónsson (København 1932)
8. (ed.) *Saga Óláfs Tryggvasonar af Oddr Snorrason Munk* (København 1932)

9. (ed.) *Edda Snorra Sturlusonar* (København 1931)
FJ Finnur Jónsson. Unless otherwise stated, references are to his edition of *Hávamál* (København 1924)
Flat *Flateyjarbók* 3 vols. (Kristiania 1860-8)
Fleck, Jere 'Óðinn's Self-Sacrifice : A New Interpretation' *Scandinavian Studies* 43 (1971) 119-42 and 385-413
Flom, G. T. 'A Group of Words from *Hávamál I* in the Light of Modern Norwegian and Icelandic Dialects' *Publications of the Society for the Advancement of Scandinavian Study* I (1911-14) 251-73
Fms. *Fornmannasögur* 12 vols. (Kaupmannahöfn 1825-37)
Foerste, W. 'Zur Geschichte des Wortes Dorf' *Studium Generale* 16 (1963) 422-33
von Friesen, Otto 'Om några fornvestnordiska vers. II. Till Hávamál str.1' ANF XVIII (1902) 72-5
Fritzner, Johan
   1. 'Þing eðr þjóðarmál. Hávamál 114' ANF I (1883) 22-32
   2. *Ordbog over Det gamle norske Sprog* Second edition. 3 vols. (Kristiania 1883-96)
Gering, Hugo
   1. 'Zu Hǫvamǫl str.100 [101]' *Zeitschrift für deutsche Philologie* XXXIV (1902) 133-4
   2. (ed.) *Hugsvinnsmál* (Kiel 1907)
Gould, Chester N. '*Hávamál*, Stanza 75' *Modern Philology* XXIV (1927) 385-8
Gras, E. J. '*Hávamál*' *Neophilologus* 15 (1930) 131-5
Guðmundur Finnbogason
   1. 'Lífsskoðun Hávamála og Aristoteles' *Skírnir* CIII (1929) 84-102
   2. 'Nokkrar athugasemdir við Hávamál' *Skírnir* CIII (1929) 103-8
Guðni Jónsson (ed.) *Eddukvæði. Eddulyklar*. 3 vols. (Akureyri 1954)
Gutenbrunner, Siegfried 'Versteckte Eddagedichte. II Eine Sprichwortreihe' *Fest. Genzmer* 83-6
Hagman, Nore 'Kring några motiv i Hávamál' ANF LXXII (1957) 13-24
Halldór Halldórsson *Örlög orðanna* (Akureyri 1958)
van Hamel, A. G. 'Óðinn Hanging on the Tree' APhS VII (1932-3) 260-88
Hannaas, Torleiv 'Til Hávamál' *Festskrift til Finnur Jónsson* (København 1928) 229-39

Hárb.   *Hárbarðsljóð* in *Edda*
Harris, Joseph   'Satire and the Heroic Life: Two Studies' in *Oral Traditional Literature: A Festschrift for Albert Bates Lord* ed. John Miles Foley (Columbus, Ohio 1981) 322-40
Heggstad, Leiv   'Ymist or syntaksen i Sæbyggjemaalet' MM (1916) 159-66
Heilag.   *Heilagra manna sǿgur* ed. C. R. Unger. 2 vols. (Christiania 1877)
Helg. Hj.   *Helgakviða Hjǫrvarðssonar* in *Edda*
Hermann Pálsson   *Áhrif Hugsvinnsmála á aðrar fornbókmenntir* Studia Islandica 43 (Reykjavík 1985)
Heusler, Andreas
   1. 'Sprichwörter in den eddischen Sittengedichten' *Zeitschrift des Vereins für Volkskunde* XXV (1915) 108-15 and XXVI (1916) 42-57 (= A. H., *Kleine Schriften* II [Berlin 1969] 292-313)
   2. 'Die zwei altnordischen Sittengedichte der Havamal nach ihrer Strophenfolge' *Sitzungsberichte der königl. preussischen Akademie der Wissenschaften* (1917) 105-35 (= A.H., *Kleine Schriften* II [Berlin 1969] 195-222)
HG   *Die Lieder der älteren Edda* herausgegeben von Karl Hildebrand. Zweite, völlig umgearbeitete, Auflage von Hugo Gering (Paderborn 1904)
Hirðskrá   ed. R. Meissner (Weimar 1938)
Hjelmqvist, Theodor   Review of DH. ANF XXII (1906) 371-9
Hkr.   *Heimskringla* ed. Bjarni Aðalbjarnarson. 3 vols. ÍF XXVI-XXVIII (Reykjavík 1941-51)
von Hofsten, Nils   *Eddadikternas djur och växter* Skrifter utgivna av kungl. Gustav Adolfs Akademien 30 (Uppsala 1957)
Hollander, Lee M.
   1. 'Hávamál strofe 81' MM (1922) 175-7
   2. 'Two Eddic Cruxes' *Germanic Review* 7 (1932) 280-7
Holm, Gösta   'Ordet fvn. (h)neisa, f., sv. nesa' in *Fest. Holm-Olsen* 152-61
Holthausen, Ferdinand   'Zu den Eddaliedern' ZFDA LXXX (1944) 155-6
Holtsmark, Anne
   1. 'To Eddasteder' *Arv* 13 (1957) 21-30
   2. 'Til Hávamál str. 52' MM (1959) 1
   3. 'Hávamál' KLNM VI (1961) col. 256-9
   4. 'Kattar Sonr' SBVS XVI (1962-5) 144-55
Holtzmann, Adolf   *Die aeltere Edda übersetzt und erklärt* (Leipzig 1875)

Hummelstedt, Eskil   'Norr. vilmógum Hávamál 134' SNF XXXIX (1949) 25-7
Hunke, Waltraud   'Odins Geburt' *Fest. Genzmer* 68-71
ÍF   *Íslenzk Fornrit* (Reykjavík 1933—)
Jansson, Sven B. F.   *Runinskrifter i Sverige* Tredje upplagan (Värnamo 1985)
Jón Helgason
  1. *Norrøn Litteraturhistorie* (København 1934)
  2. 'Norges og Islands Digtning' in *Litteraturhistorie. B. Norge og Island* ed. Sigurður Nordal. Nordisk Kultur VIII:B (Stockholm etc. 1953)
  3. (ed.) *Eddadigte* I. *Vǫluspá Hávamál* 2. ændrede udgave. Nordisk Filologi. Tekster og Lærebøger til Universitetsbrug (København etc. 1955)
Kauffmann, Friedrich   'Odin am Galgen' PBB XV (1891) 195-207
KLNM   *Kulturhistoriskt lexikon för nordisk medeltid* 22 vols. (Malmö etc. 1956-78)
Knudsen, Gunnar   'Bornholmske Torp-Navne' NB 33 (1946) 24-33
Kock, Ernst A.
  1. 'Domen över död man' ANF XXXIII (1917) 175-8
  2. 'Bidrag till eddatolkningen' ANF XXXV (1919) 22-9, XXXVII (1921) 105-35 and XXXVIII (1922) 269-94
  3. *Fornjermansk forskning* LUÅ N.F. Avd.1, Bd 18, Nr 1 (1922)
  4. *Notationes Norrænæ* LUÅ (1923-44)
Konunga Sögur   ed. Guðni Jónsson. 3 vols. (Reykjavík 1957)
Konungs Skuggsiá   ed. Ludvig Holm-Olsen. 2. reviderte opplag. Norrøne tekster nr. 1 (Oslo 1983)
Kristján Albertsson   'Hverfanda hvel' *Skírnir* CLI (1977) 57-8
Kuhn, Hans
  1. 'Die Rangordnung der Daseinswerte im alten Sittengedicht der Edda' *Zeitschrift für deutsche Bildung* 15 (1939) 62-71 (= H. K., *Kleine Schriften* II [Berlin 1971] 266-76)
  2. Review of Hermann Schneider 'Eine Uredda' AFDA 64 (1950) 71-82 (= H. K., *Kleine Schriften* II [Berlin 1971] 18-29)
  3. Review of Ivar Lindquist 'Die Urgestalt der Hávamál' AFDA 72 (1960) 15-23 (= H. K., *Kleine Schriften* II [Berlin 1971] 37-45)

Kühnhold, Christa 'Zwei Miszellen zur altisländischen Dichtung' ZFDA 107 (1978) 179-83
Kålund, Kristian
 1. (ed.) *Den islandske lægebog* Kgl. Danske Vidensk. Selsk. Skrifter, 6. Række, historisk og filosofisk Afd. VI. 4 (København 1907)
 2. (ed., in part with N. Beckman) *Alfræði Íslenzk* I-III. Samfund til Udgivelse af Gammel Nordisk Litteratur 37, 41, 45 (København 1908-18)
Köhne, Roland
 1. Review of Klaus von See 'Die Gestalt der Hávamál' *Skandinavistik* 2 (1972) 128-31
 2. 'Zur Mittelalterlichkeit der eddischen Spruchdichtung' PBB (Tübingen) 105 (1983) 380-417
Liberman, Anatoly 'Germanic *sendan* "To Make a Sacrifice"' *Journal of English and Germanic Philology* 77 (1978) 473-88
Lid, Nils 'At hitta í lið. Til Hávamál 66, 6' MM (1925) 18-24
Lie, Hallvard 'Noen gamle tvistemål i Hávamál' in *Fest. Holm-Olsen* 215-20
Lindblad, Gustaf *Studier i Codex Regius av Äldre Eddan* Lundastudier i nordisk språkvetenskap 10 (Lund 1954)
Lindquist, Ivar
 1. 'Till två små dikter i Havamal' *Ver Sacrum* (Göteborg 1917) 126-35
 2. 'Ordstudier och tolkningar i Havamal' SNF IX:1 (1917) 1-17
 3. *Die Urgestalt der Hávamál* Lundastudier i nordisk språkvetenskap 11 (= LUÅ, N.F. Avd.1, Bd 52 Nr 1. Lund 1956)
Lindroth, Hjalmar 'Boðn, Són och Óðrœrir' MM (1915) 174-7
Lndn. *Landnámabók*, cited from Jakob Benediktsson (ed.) *Íslendingabók, Landnámabók* ÍF I (Reykjavík 1968)
LP *Lexicon Poeticum Antiquæ Linguæ Septentrionalis* Oprindelig forfattet af Sveinbjörn Egilsson. Forøget og påny udgivet ... 2. udgave ved Finnur Jónsson (København 1931)
LUÅ *Lunds Universitets Årsskrift*
Låle *Östnordiska och latinska medeltidsordspråk*, Peder Låles ordspråk och en motsvarande svensk samling, utgivna för 'Samfund til Udgivelse af Gammel Nordisk Litteratur' av Axel Kock och Carl af Petersens. 2 vols. (København 1889-94)

Läffler, L.Fr.
1. 'Det evigt grönskande trädet' *Festskrift til H. F. Feilberg* (published as the 1911 volume of MM, *Danske Studier* and SL) 617-96
2. 'Om några underarter av ljóðaháttr' [Part 2] SNF V:5 (1914)
3. 'Till Hávamáls strof 155' ANF XXXII (1916) 83-113
4. 'Hávamál 53:1-3' ANF XXXII (1916) 316-21

Marstrander, Carl   'Skjæks øl' *Festskrift til Amund B. Larsen* (Kristiania 1924) 186-9

Martínez-Pizarro, J.   'An *Eiríks Þáttr Málspaka*? Some Conjectures on the Source of Saxo's Ericus Disertus' in *Saxo Grammaticus: A Medieval Author between Norse and Latin Culture* ed. Karsten Friis-Jensen (Copenhagen 1981) 105-19

Matras, Christian   'Et færøsk ordsprog og en strofe i Hávamál' MM (1938) 151-2

Meissner, R.   'Litilla Sanda Litilla Sęva' ZFDA LXXV (1938) 83-6

Meringer, R.   'Wörter und Sachen IV' *Indogermanische Forschungen* XIX (1906) 401-57

Mezger, Fritz   'á aldinn mar' ANF L (1934) 271-2

MHG   Middle High German
MLG   Middle Low German
MM   Maal og minne

Mogk, Eugen
1. 'Das zweite Liederbuch des Cod. Reg. der Eddalieder' *Zeitschrift für deutsche Philologie* XVII (1885) 293-313
2. 'Eine Hǫvamǫlvísa in der Niála' PBB XIV (1889) 94

Moltke, Erik   *Runes and their Origin. Denmark and Elsewhere* (Copenhagen 1985)

Msk.   *Morkinskinna* ed. Finnur Jónsson (København 1932)
Müllenhoff, K.   *Deutsche Altertumskunde* V (Berlin 1891)
Möbius, Thd.   [critical remarks on *Hávamál* in Bugge's edition] *Zeitschrift für deutsche Philologie* I (1869) 412-14

NB   *Namn och bygd*
Neckel, G.   'Zu den Eddaliedern' ANF XLIII (1926-7) 358-73
Neckel-Kuhn   *Edda: Die Lieder des Codex Regius nebst verwandten Denkmälern* herausgegeben von Gustav Neckel. Dritte [*recte* Vierte], umgearbeitete Auflage von Hans Kuhn. I Text. II Kurzes Wörterbuch (Heidelberg 1962-8)

NGL   *Norges Gamle Love* indtil 1387 ed. R. Keyser, P. A. Munch, etc. 5 vols. (Christiania 1846-95)

NIYR   *Norges Innskrifter med de yngre Runer* ed. Magnus Olsen and Aslak Liestøl (Oslo 1941—).
NIÆR   *Norges Indskrifter med de ældre Runer* ed. Sophus Bugge and Magnus Olsen. 4 vols. (Christiania 1891-1924)
Njála   udgivet efter gamle Håndskrifter af det kongelige nordiske Oldskrift-Selskab. 2 vols. (København 1875-89)
NN   *Notationes Norrœnæ*. See under Kock.
Nordal, Sigurður
    1. 'Átrúnaður Egils Skallagrímssonar' *Skírnir* XCVIII (1924) 145-65 (= S.N., *Áfangar. Annað Bindi: Svipir* [Reykjavík 1944] 103-28)
    2. 'Billings mær' *Bidrag till nordisk filologi tillägnade Emil Olson* (Lund etc. 1936) 288-95
    3. *Íslenzk Menning* I (Reykjavík 1942)
Nordenstreng, Rolf   'Ett förslag till texträttelse i Hávamál' ANF XXV (1909) 190-1
Noreen, Adolf   *Altisländische und Altnorwegische Grammatik* Fourth edition (Halle 1923)
Noreen, Erik
    1. *Några anteckningar om ljóðaháttr och i detta versmått avfattade dikter* UUÅ (1915)
    2. 'Eddastudier' *Språkvetenskapliga Sällskapets i Uppsala Förhandlingar* (1919-21) 1-44 (= UUÅ 1921)
    3. 'Om ordet *häxa*' *Språkvetenskapliga Sällskapets i Uppsala Förhandlingar* (1922-4) 53-61 (=UUÅ 1924)
Nygaard, M.
    1. 'Eddasprogets Syntax' I-II, in *Inbydelseskrift til den offentlige Examen i Kristiansands Kathedralskole* 1865 and 1867.
    2. *Norrøn Syntax* (Kristiania 1905)
Næs, Olav   *Hávamál 1-78. Kommentar og Metrikk* Det Kongelige Norske Videnskabers Selskab. Skrifter no. 5—1979 (Trondheim etc. 1979)
OE   Old English
OED   *The Oxford English Dictionary* ed. J. A. H. Murray and others (Oxford 1888-1933)
OHG   Old High German
Ohrt, F.
    1. 'Odin paa Træet' APhS IV (1929-30) 273-86
    2. 'Eddica og Magica' APhS IX (1934-5) 161-76
Olsen, Magnus
    1. 'Til Hávamál strofe 152' ANF XXIII (1907) 189-90

2. *Stedsnavne-studier* (Kristiania 1912)
3. 'Cruces Eddicæ' ANF XXXIX (1923) 303-20
4. "Haldit maðr á keri" MM (1926) 103-9 (= M.O., *Norrøne Studier* [Oslo 1938] 158-65)
5. 'Hávamál 33' *Festskrift til Hjalmar Falk* (Oslo 1927) 202-4 (= M.O., *Norrøne Studier* [Oslo 1938] 166-8)
6. 'Fra Hávamál til Krákumál' *Festskrift til Halvdan Koht* (Oslo 1933) 93-102 (= M.O., *Norrøne Studier* [Oslo 1938] 234-44)
7. *Edda- og Skaldekvad* V *Hávamál* Avhandlinger utgitt av Det Norske Videnskaps-Akademi i Oslo. II. Hist.-Filos. Klasse. Ny Serie. No. 3 (Oslo 1962)
8. "Bú er betra" MM (1918) 60-8 (= M.O., *Norrøne Studier* [Oslo 1938] 169-77)

Ólsen, Björn Magnússon
1. 'Smá bidrag til tolkningen af Eddasangene' ANF IX (1893) 223-35
2. 'Til Eddakvadene. II. Til Hávamál' ANF XXXI (1915) 52-95
3. 'Hávamál v. 155' ANF XXXII (1916) 71-83
4. 'Um nokkra staði í Svipdagsmálum' ANF XXXIII (1917) 1-21

Olson, Emil   'En syntaktisk anmärkning till Hávamál 1:1-4' *Studier tillegnade Esaias Tegnér* (Lund 1918) 538-41

ON   Old Norse

Paasche, Fredrik   *Norges og Islands Litteratur* (= *Norsk Litteraturhistorie* ed. Francis Bull and others, I) Ny utgave ved Anne Holtsmark (Oslo 1957)

Page, R. I.   Review of Klaus von See 'Die Gestalt der Hávamál' *Scandinavica* 13 (1974) 61-3

PBB   *Beiträge zur Geschichte der deutschen Sprache und Literatur* begründet von Wilhelm Braune, Hermann Paul, Eduard Sievers

PCPhS   *Proceedings of the Cambridge Philological Society*

Pipping, Hugo
1. 'Zur Lesung und Deutung von Hǫvamǫl 39' *Neuphilologische Mitteilungen* 29 (1928) 83-6
2. 'Eddastudier III' SNF XVIII:4 (1928) 1-25
3. 'Hávamál 136' *Studies in Honor of Hermann Collitz* (Baltimore 1930) 155-8
4. 'Några anteckningar om galdralag' APhS IX (1934-35) 177-84

5. 'Nya stöd för gamla åsikter' ANF LVIII (1944) 40-1
Pipping, Rolf
    1. 'Fsv. ora' SNF VIII:2 (1917)
    2. 'Oden i galgen' SNF XVIII:2 (1928)
    3. 'Hávamál 21 och ett par ställen hos Seneca' APhS XX (1949) 371-5
PMLA   Publications of the Modern Language Association of America
Raknes, Ola   [on st.2] MM (1918) 47-8
Reichardt, Konstantin   'Odin am galgen' *Wächter und Hüter: Festschrift für Hermann J. Weigand* (New Haven 1957) 15-28
Reichborn-Kjennerud, I.
    1. 'Lægerådene i den eldre Edda' MM (1923) 1-57
    2. 'Eddatidens medisin' ANF XL (1924) 103-48
    3. 'Tunga er hǫfuðs bani' MM (1933) 69
    4. 'Eldr við sóttum — Ax við fjǫlkyngi' MM (1934) 149
    5. 'Tillegg til de norrøne ordbøker II' MM (1946) 161-6
Richert, M. B.   *Försök till belysning af mörkare och oförstådda ställen i den poetiska eddan* UUÅ (1877)
Rooth, Erik   'Furan på fjällhyllan. Ett diskussionsinlägg' SL (1966) 3-23
SBVS   *Saga-Book of the Viking Society*
Schneider, Hermann   *Eine Uredda* (Halle 1948)
von See, Klaus
    1. 'Sonatorrek und Hávamál' ZFDA XCIX (1970) 26-33
    2. 'Disticha Catonis und Hávamál' PBB (Tübingen) XCIV (1972) 1-18
    3. *Die Gestalt der Hávamál* (Frankfurt/Main 1972)
    4. 'Probleme der altnordischen Spruchdichtung' ZFDA CIV (1975) 91-118
Seip, D. A.   'Om et norsk skriftlig grunnlag for Edda-diktningen eller deler av den' MM (1957) 81-195
SG   *Die Lieder der Edda* herausgegeben von B. Sijmons und Hugo Gering. Text, Einleitung, Wörterbuch, Kommentar. 4 vols. in 5 (Halle 1888-1931). Unless otherwise stated, references are to the commentary on *Hávamál*.
SGL   *Samling af Sweriges Gamla Lagar* ed. H. S. Collin and C. J. Schlyter. 12 vols. and Glossary (Stockholm and Lund 1827-77)
Sigrdr.   *Sigrdrífumál* in *Edda*
Sigsk.   *Sigurðarkviða in skamma* in *Edda*

Singer, Samuel   *Sprichwörter des Mittelalters* I (Bern 1944)
Skj.   *Den norsk-islandske Skjaldedigtning* B. Rettet tekst ed. Finnur Jónsson. 2 vols. (København 1912-15)
Skulerud, Olai   'Nye oplysningar om norsk ordforråd' *Studier tillägnade Axel Kock* (= ANF Tilläggsband, Lund 1929) 541-72
SL   *Svenska landsmål och svenskt folkliv*
SmR   *Smålands Runinskrifter* I. Text ed. Ragnar Kinander (Stockholm 1935-61)
Smst.   *Småstykker 1-16* udgivne af Samfund til Udgivelse af Gammel Nordisk Litteratur (København 1884-91)
Smyser, H. M.   'Ibn Fadlan's Account of the Rūs, with Some Commentary and Some Allusions to *Beowulf*' *Medieval and Linguistic Studies in Honor of Francis Peabody Magoun, Jr.* ed. J. B. Bessinger and Robert P. Creed (London 1965) 92-119
SNF   *Studier i nordisk filologi*
Snorra Edda   *Edda Snorra Sturlusonar* 3 vols. [The 'Arnamagnæan' edition] (Hafniæ 1848-87)
Sperber, H.   'Zu Hávamál 84' PBB XXXVII (1912) 149
SR   *Södermanlands Runinskrifter* I. Text ed. Erik Brate and Elias Wessén (Stockholm 1924-36)
Stefán Karlsson   'Þorp' *Gripla* III (1979) 115-23
Stock. Homil.   *Homiliu-Bók. Isländska Homilier efter en Handskrift från tolfte århundradet, utgifna af D:r Theodor Wisén* (Lund 1872)
Ström, Folke   *Den döendes makt och Odin i trädet* Göteborgs Högskolas Årsskrift LIII (1947)
Strömbäck, Dag
   1. *Sejd. Textstudier i nordisk religionshistoria* Nordiska Texter och Undersökningar 5 (Stockholm etc. 1935)
   2. 'The Concept of the Soul in Nordic Tradition' *Arv* 31 (1975) 5-22
Sturlunga saga   ed. Jón Jóhannesson, Magnús Finnbogason and Kristján Eldjárn. 2 vols. (Reykjavík 1946)
Sturtevant, Albert Morley
   1. 'The Old Norse Hávamál in Modern Norwegian Folk Song' *Journal of English and Germanic Philology* 9 (1910) 340-55
   2. 'The Relation of Loddfáfnir to Odin in the Hávamál' *Journal of English and Germanic Philology* 10 (1911) 42-55

3. 'Notes on the Poetic Edda' *Scandinavian Studies and Notes* 9 (1926-7) 31-6
4. 'A Note on the Semantic Development of Old Norse *fría:frjá* < Gothic *frijōn* "to love"' *Scandinavian Studies and Notes* 16 (1940-1) 194-6
5. 'Etymologies of Old Norse Proper Names used as Poetic Designations' *Modern Language Notes* 64 (1949) 486-90
6. 'Certain Old Norse Proper Names in the Eddas' *PMLA* 67 (1952) 1145-62

Sveinbjörn Egilsson *Lexicon Poeticum Antiquæ Linguæ Septentrionalis* (Hafniæ 1860)

Torp, Alf *Gamalnorsk Ordavleiding* Nyutgåva . . . av Gösta Holm. Studier utg. av Kungl. Humanistiska Vetenskapssamfundet i Lund. Scripta Minora, 1973-4: 2 (Lund 1974)

Turville-Petre, E.O.G.
1. 'The Cult of Freyr in the Evening of Paganism' *Proceedings of the Leeds Philosophical and Literary Society, Literary and Historical Section* III (1935) 317-33
2. *Myth and Religion of the North* (London 1964)

UR *Upplands Runinskrifter* Tredje delen. I. *Text* ed. Elias Wessén and Sven B. F. Jansson (Stockholm 1949-51)

UUÅ *Uppsala Universitets Årsskrift*

Vafþr. *Vafþrúðnismál* in *Edda*

Valtýr Guðmundsson *Privatboligen på Island i sagatiden* (København 1889)

Vesper, Ekkehart 'Das Menschenbild der älteren Hávamál' *PBB* (Halle) LXXIX Sonderband (1957) 13-31

Vogt, W. H. 'Hroptr Rǫgna' *ZFDA* LXII (1925) 41-8

VR *Västergötlands Runinskrifter* I. *Text* ed. Hugo Jungner and Elisabeth Svärdström (Stockholm 1958-70)

de Vries, Jan
1. 'Odin am Baume' *Studia Germanica tillägnade E. A. Kock* (Lund 1934) 392-5
2. 'Om Eddaens Visdomsdigtning' *ANF* L (1934) 1-59
3. *De Skaldenkenningen met mythologischen Inhoud* (Haarlem 1934)
4. *Altgermanische Religionsgeschichte* 2 vols. Second edition (Berlin 1956-7)
5. *Altnordisches Etymologisches Wörterbuch* (Leiden 1961)
6. *Altnordische Literaturgeschichte* I. Second edition (Berlin 1964)

VSHF   *Videnskapsselskapets Skrifter.* II. *Hist-filos. Klasse* (Kristiania)
Vsp.   *Vǫluspá* in *Edda*
Wahlgren, Erik   'Góð Kona' *Scandinavian Studies and Notes* 16 (1940-41) 185-93
Wennström, Torsten   'Några Edda-ställen' *ANF* LV (1940) 276-83
Wessén, Elias
1. 'Den isländska eddadiktningen. Dess uppteckning och redigering' *Saga och sed* (1946) 1-31
2. 'Det fattiga hemmet och det ensamma trädet. Till tolkningen av ett par strofer i Havamal' *Svio-Estonica* 14 (1958) 19-24
3. *Havamal. Några stilfrågor* Filologiskt Arkiv 8 Kungl. Vitterhets Historie och Antikvitets Akademien (Stockholm 1959)
4. 'Ordspråk och lärodikt. Några stilformer i Havamal' *Septentrionalia et Orientalia. Studia Bernhardo Karlgren Dedicata* (= Kungl. Vitterhets Historie och Antikvitets Akademiens Handlingar 91, Stockholm 1959)

Wilson, Joseph   Review of Klaus von See 'Die Gestalt der Hávamál' *Scandinavian Studies* 46 (1974) 175-9

Wimmer, Ludvig F. A. and Finnur Jónsson (ed.)   *Håndskriftet Nr. 2365 4to gl. kgl. Samling på det store kongelige bibliothek i København (Codex regius af den ældre Edda) i fototypisk og diplomatisk gengivelse* (København 1891)

Wisén, Theodor   *Emendationer och exegeser till norröna dikter* IV (Lund 1891)

ZFDA   *Zeitschrift für deutsches Altertum und deutsche Literatur*

Åkerblom, Axel
1. 'Bidrag till diskussionen om str. 77 i Havamal' *ANF* XXXIV (1918) 171-3
2. 'Dómr um dauðan hvern. (Háv. str. 77)' *ANF* XXXVI (1920) 62-5

HÁVAMÁL

EDITED BY DAVID A. H. EVANS

GLOSSARY AND INDEX

COMPILED BY ANTHONY FAULKES

VIKING SOCIETY
FOR NORTHERN RESEARCH
UNIVERSITY COLLEGE LONDON

PREFACE

Apart from ordinary personal pronouns all words in the *Hávamál* text issued by the Viking Society in 1986 are glossed and all proper names entered in the following list. Except where curtailed by "etc.", references given to the occurrence of a word may be taken to be complete. The appearance of "n" after a reference means that there is comment on the word in the notes of the edition.

I owe warm thanks to Mr Paul Bibire, Cambridge, for typing in my text and preparing the disk from which the Glossary has been set.

Anthony Faulkes

ABBREVIATIONS

a.	adjective	*neg.*	negative
abs(ol).	absolute(ly)	*nom.*	nominative
acc.	accusative	*num.*	numeral
adv.	adverb(ial)	*obj.*	object
art.	article	*OE*	Old English
aux.	auxiliary	*ord.*	ordinal
comp.	comparative	*o-self*	oneself
conj.	conjunction	*p.*	past
dat.	dative	*pers.*	person
def.	definite	*pl.*	plural
e-m	einhverjum	*poss.*	possessive
e-n	einhvern	*pp.*	past participle
e-s	einhvers	*prep.*	preposition(al)
e-t	eitthvat	*pres. (p.)*	present participle
e-u	einhverju	*pret. pres.*	preterite-present
f.	feminine	*pron.*	pronoun
gen.	genitive	*rel.*	relative
imp.	imperative	*sg.*	singular
impers.	impersonal	*s-one*	someone
indecl.	indeclinable	*s-thing*	something
inf.	infinitive	*subj.*	subjunctive
interrog.	interrogative	*subst.*	substantive
intrans.	intransitive	*sup.*	superlative
irreg.	irregular	*sv.*	strong verb
m.	masculine	*trans.*	transitive
md.	middle voice	*vb(s).*	verb(s)
n.	neuter	*wv.*	weak verb

Glossary 1

-**a** *neg. suffix* used with vbs. 11/5 12/1 22/6 27/7 30/2 31/4 35/2 38/2 52/2 75/1 124/6 150/4 158/6; combined with suffixed 1st pers. pron. 39/1 150/5 152/5; with preceding *ne* 135/5. Cf. **-at, -t**.

á (1) pres. of **eiga** 9/2 25/6 26/3 55/6 59/2 62/6.

á (2) *prep.* (1) with dat. 'on' 1/7 2/5 34/3 38/5 41/3 83/2 84/4 89/2 90/4 116/5 138/7 157/2, postposition 35/6 38/2 50/2 ('in'?) 97/2 101/6 105/2 111/2 138/2 154/5; 'on to' 19/1; 'in' 3/3, postposition 155/3; 'at' 83/6; 'on, in' (activity) 112/6, 154/3; 'on, by using' 151/3; of time, 'in the course of' 74/6,7.

(2) with acc. 'to' 59/3 107/6 135/6; 'on' 82/2, 'into, at' 62/3; 'on to' 136/6, postposition 158/3 (with *þegn*); abstractly: 'to' 111/6, 'into' 102/6, 'upon' 93/4,5 82/5,6 (to be understood also in lines 7 and 8, see **orka**).

(3) as adv. 'in it, about this' 108/1.

abbindi *n.* 'tenesmus, useless straining of the bowels' 137/9.

aðal *n.* 'natural characteristic, distinguishing feature' 103/9.

áðr *conj.* 'before' 1/2.

af *prep.* with dat. 'from, off' 21/3 44/3 45/3 57/1,3,4,6 117/8 123/1 138/9 140/2 141/4,6 149/6,7; 'because of, through' 69/3,4,5,6 75/3 150/2. As adv. 'from her' 130/7.

afglapi *m.* 'fool' 17/1.

afhvarf *n.* 'indirect route, roundabout way' 34/1.

afl *n.* 'strength' 160/4.

aka (ók) *sv.* with dat. 'drive' 90/3 ('as if one were to drive', 'like driving').

akr *m.* (-rs) '(corn)field' 88/1,4.

ala (ól) *sv.* 'nourish, foster' 48/3; pp. *alinn* 'produced, born' 72/2.

ald- see **ǫld**.

aldinn *a.* 'aged, ancient' 62/3 104/1.

aldregi *adv.* 'never' 6/8 76/5 79/5 93/3 115/6 117/6,9 121/6 122/6 123/2 128/6 132/6 134/6.

aldri *adv.* 'never' 77/5.

aldrtregi *m.* 'life-sorrow' 20/3n.

álfr *m.* 'elf' 143/2 159/4 160/5.

allr *a. pron.* 'all, every' 1/1 23/6 24/2 25/2 53/4 100/3 159/5; '(the) whole (of)' 23/2 51/6 99/6 121/10 124/3 138/3 154/6 161/3,5; *þessu ǫllu* '(in) all this' 89/8; *ǫllum* 'for or to everyone' 136/3 153/2; n. 'everything, it all' 17/4 26/2 163/4, with pl. vb. and complement 98/4 (or as adv., 'altogether'), 'anything' 124/4; gen. n. as adv. 'entirely' 69/1.

allþarfr *a.* 'very needful, useful' (*e-m* 'to, for s-one') 164/3 (referring to *mál*).

alskjótr *a*. 'absolutely fast, the very fastest' 89/4 ('a horse at maximum speed'?).
alsnotr *a*. 'completely wise' 55/6.
án *prep*. 'without'; with inf., *án at lifa* 'without living' 68/6.
andskoti *m*. 'opponent, enemy' 148/5.
ann pres. of **unna**.
annarr *pron. a. and ord. num*. 'another (person)' 8/6 9/6 30/2 35/6 45/1 47/5 58/2 65/2 75/5 93/3 94/2 115/5 124/6 131/8; 'a second (person)' 63/5; *þat ... annat* 'this second one' (*ljóð*) 147/1.
api *m*. 'ape, fool' 75/3 122/7.
aptann *m*. 'evening' 98/1.
aptr *adv*. 'back' 14/5 99/1 104/2 139/6 145/9.
ár *adv*. 'early' 58/1 59/1.
árliga *adv*. 'early (in the day)' 33/1.
armr *m*. 'arm' 108/6 163/8.
ársáinn *a*. (*pp*.) 'sown early (in the year)' 88/1.
áss *m*. (pl. **æsir**) 'one of the race of gods associated with Óðinn' 143/1 159/4 160/4.
ást *f*. 'love' 92/3 93/1.
Ásviðr *m*. 143/4.
-at *neg. suffix* with vbs. 10/2 11/2 30/5 50/3 69/1 114/4 133/4 146/2 152/4 158/4; with imp. 112/5 127/7; followed by suffixed 2nd pers. pron. *skalattu* 'you shall not' 113/6 125/6 129/6. Cf. **-a, -t**.
at (1) *prep*. with acc. 'after, in memory of' 72/6.
at (2) *adv*. with comp. *at heldr* 'the more (for that)' 96/6.
at (3) *conj*. 'that' 110/2 138/1, 'so that'? 162/2; correlative with *svá* 39/3,6 89/8 100/2 114/2 133/5,6 149/5 150/5 152/5 155/5 157/6, with *þat* 25/6 27/3,5 64/6 131/10, with *því* 14/5, with *þess* 19/6, with *hitt* 22/6 99/5, with *ifi* 108/2. As rel. particle (?) *einn at* 77/5 ('one thing of such a kind that', 'of one thing that it'). Cf. **því at**.
at (4) *particle* with inf. 1/5 19/6 38/4 41/6 54/5 68/6 95/6 97/6 111/1 114/6 124/5 152/6 153/3 154/3; indicating purpose 44/6 109/3 119/7.
at (5) *prep*. with dat. 'at' 22/3 31/3 32/3 67/3 134/5, 'at' or 'for' 136/3, postposition 111/3,9; 'to' 25/5, postposition 61/2; 'into' 120/6 130/6, 'on to' 149/3; 'along' (postposition) 10/2 11/2n 11/5; 'on, in' (postposition) 49/2; 'in, with' 19/2; 'subject to, the object of' 5/4 30/1 132/5, 'the cause of' 118/5 121/7, see **vera (2), verða, hafa**; 'so as to be' (postposition) 115/7; 'about' 23/3

46/3 80/2 109/5; 'with regard to' (or 'in'?) 6/1n 6/3 57/5 117/7 (or 'from, arising from'?) 123/6, 'with' 116/7 (see **fá (2)**) 128/7; 'as' (postposition) 127/6 (see **kveða**); of time, 'to' 23/5, 'in, at' 81/1; elliptically with gen. 'at (the house of), at s-one's' 14/3 67/5.

átjándi *ord. num.* 'eighteenth' 163/1.
átt 2nd pers. sg. pres. of **eiga**.
átti *ord. num.* 'eighth' 153/1.
auðigr *a.* 'wealthy, rich' 47/4 70/5 75/4.
auðr *m.* 'wealth' 10/4 59/6 78/4.
auga *n.* 'eye' 7/5 82/4.
augabragð *n.* 'wink, sidelong glance'; *verða at augabragði, hafa e-n at augabragði* 'become, make s-one, an object of mockery' 5/4 30/1; 'a twinkling of an eye' (i.e. it lasts no longer) 78/5.
auk *adv.* 'also, again' 98/1.
aurum dat. pl. of **eyrir**.
ausa (jós) *sv.* 'pour, ladle (*e-u* from something)'; pp. 140/6n.
ax *n.* 'ear of corn' 137/10.

báðir *a. pron.* 'both'; n. *bæði* (i.e. 'both men and women') 91/2.
band *n.* 'band, bond' 149/3. Cf. **bǫnd**.
bani *m.* 'death' 15/6; 'cause of death (*e-s* to s-thing)' 73/2.
bára *f.* 'wave' 86/2.
barn *n.* 'child' 15/2 86/8.
barr *n.* 'needles (of a conifer), foliage' 50/3.
baugeiðr *m.* 'ring-oath' 110/1n.
baugr *m.* '(arm-)ring' 136/4.
bautarsteinn *m.* 'memorial stone' 72/4n.
baztr, beztr *a. sup.* 'best' 68/1; n. 27/3; n. as subst. or adv. *hefir hann bazt* 'it will be best for him, he will do best' 80/6; n. as adv. 48/2.
beðmál *n. pl.* 'bed-talk' 86/5.
beðr *m.* 'bed'; in pl. (but referring to only one bed) 97/2 101/6.
beitta (tt) *wv.* 'tack, beat (against the wind)' (the ship in dat.) 90/8 ('or (as if one) should beat').
beiti *m.* 'earth-worm' 137/13n.
belgr *m.* 'skin, (skin-)bag' 134/8n.
bera (bar) *sv.* 'carry' 78/3; with suffixed neg. *-at* 10/2 11/2; 'bring, put, place' 149/2; pp. *borinn* 'carried (up or in)' 100/5n.
berr *a.* 'bare'; n. as adv. (or subst.) 'plainly, openly' (or 'what is plain, open') 91/1.
Bestla *f.* 140/3.

betri *a. comp.* 'better' 10/1 11/1 71/4 72/1; *inn betri* 'the better person' 125/7; n. *betra* 36/1,6 37/1 163/4, with dat., 'better than' 10/4; *betra er* 'it is better (that it should be)' 145/1,4; *betra er e-m* '(it) is better for s-one' 70/1 124/4n.

beztr *a. sup.* see **baztr**.

bíða (beið) *sv.* 'suffer' 15/6; 'endure, last long enough (continue? achieve, manage?)' 41/6.

biðja (bað) *sv.* 'ask, beg (*e-s* for s-thing, *e-m* for s-one, *sér* for o-self)' 37/5; abs. 'pray, invoke' 144/5; 'wish, invoke, call down (s-thing on s-one)' 136/5; *þá er þér bǫls beðit* 'then evil will be called down upon you, s-one will wish you evil' 126/10. With acc. and inf. 'bid s-one do s-thing' 131/5.

bila (að) *wv.* 'flag, give way, fail' 125/7.

Billingr *m.* 97/1.

binda (batt) *sv.* 'bind, tie (up)' 101/6.

bíta (beit) *sv.* 'bite, cut, wound, harm'; *b. e-m ofarla* 'cause a wound high up in s-one' 118/1n; with suffixed neg. *-t* 148/6 (*þeim*: dat. of advantage, 'for them').

bitsótt *f.* 'sickness, illness caused by a bite or sting' 137/13.

bjarga (barg) *sv.* with dat. 'save' 154/3; with suffixed 1st pers. pron., suffixed neg. and additional 1st pers. pron. 152/5 (*honum* = the hall).

bjóða (bauð, boðinn) *sv.* 'invite, offer (*e-m e-t* s-one s-thing) 92/2; impers. passive *myndi mér boðit* 'I would be invited' 67/2.

bjǫrn *m.* 'bear' 86/7.

blanda (að) *wv.* with dat. 'mix; blend, exchange, share?' 44/4; *e-u er blandat* 's-thing is mixed, there is a mixing, combining of (in?) s-thing' 124/1 ('they are blended, i.e. joined, in affinity').

blindr *a.* 'blind'; as subst. 'a blind man, that a man should be blind' 71/4.

blóðugr *a.* 'bloody' 37/4.

blóta (blét) *sv.* 'worship, sacrifice' 144/6.

bogi *m.* 'bow' 85/1 (dat. dependent upon *trúi* 88/2, like all the datives in between).

bóglimar *m. pl.* 'limbs, arms and legs'; *at bóglimum mér* 'on my arms and legs' 149/3n.

borinn pp. of **bera**.

bráðr *a.* 'hasty, impatient' 2/4n; n. as adv. *brátt* 'quickly, soon' 153/6.

brandr *m.* 'piece of firewood' 57/1; *á brǫndum* '(sitting) on a pile of firewood' 2/5n.

braut *f.* 'road, way' 10/2 11/2 34/3 72/5 89/2.

breiðr *a.* 'broad'; n. as adv. 'broadly, extensively' 152/4.
brenna (1) (brann), *pres.* **brenn** or **brennr** *sv.* intrans. 'burn' 51/2 57/2; *b. upp* 'flame up' 70/4; with suffixed neg. *-at* 152/4 ('it will not burn'); pres. p. 85/2 100/4.
brenna (2) (d) *wv.* trans. 'burn, cremate' 71/5 81/2.
bresta (brast) *sv.* 'break'; pres. p. 'breaking' (or 'twanging'? 'breakable'?) 85/1.
brigð *f.* 'changeableness, inconstancy' 84/6.
brigðr *a.* 'changeable, unreliable, deceptive (*e-m* for someone)' 91/3 ('not to be relied upon by women'); *en sé brigðum at vera* 'than it would be for a man to be unreliable (deceptive), than for one to be unreliable' 124/5n.
brjóst *n. pl.* 'breast' 8/6 9/6 84/6.
bróðurbani *m.* 'one's brother's slayer' 89/1.
brók *f.* (*pl.* **brœkr**) 'breeches' 61/4.
brotinn *a.* (pp. of *brjóta*) 'broken' 86/6.
brotna (að) *wv.* intrans. 'break' 89/6.
brúðr *f.* 'bride, wife' 86/5.
brunninn pp. of **brenna (1)**.
brunnr *m.* 'spring, well' 111/3.
bú *n.* 'dwelling, establishment, farm' 36/1 37/1; *á búi* 'at s-one else's house' 83/6n.
búa (bjó) *sv.* 'live, dwell' 34/3 95/2.
bundit pp. of **binda**.
byrðr *f.* 'burden, load' 10/1 11/1.
byrr *m.* '(sailing-)wind' 90/7.
bæði n. of **báðir**.
bœn *f.* 'prayer; begging' 36/6.
bœta (tt) *wv.* 'put right, cure, settle, repair' 153/6.
bǫl *n.* 'evil, trouble, misfortune, harm' 126/10 137/14; 'mischief, malice' 127/5,6.
Bǫlverkr *m.* 109/5.
Bǫlþórr *m.* a giant 140/3.
bǫnd *n. pl.* = the gods 109/6.
bǫrkr *m.* 'bark (of tree)' 50/3.

dagr *m.* 'day' 74/6 81/1 82/4; acc. *fimm daga* 'for five days' 51/3; gen. of a point in time 109/1n.
Dáinn *m.* 143/2.
dauðr (1) *m.* 'death' 70/6n.
dauðr (2) *a.* 'dead'; as subst. 'a dead person' 77/6.
daufr *a.* 'deaf'; as subst. 'a deaf person' 71/3.

Dellingr m. 160/3.
deyfa (ð) wv. 'dull, (make) blunt' 148/4.
deyja (dó) sv. 'die' 76/1,2,3,5 77/1,2,3,5.
dómr m. 'judgement, reputation' 77/6.
drekka (drakk) sv. 'drink' 12/5 83/1 137/5; subj. (optative) 'let him drink' 19/2; pp. *drukkit* 81/6; 'drunk up, finished' 66/4.
drjúgr a. 'lasting, ample, substantial'; n. as adv. 'strongly, without weakening' 79/6.
drykkr m. 'drink' 105/3 140/4.
duga (ð) wv. 'be of use, serve, be successful or adequate' 71/3; *at einugi dugi* 'that he was good for nothing' 133/6.
dul f. 'reserve' or 'folly' 57/6; 'folly' or 'conceit' 79/6.
durum dat. pl. of **dyrr**.
Dvalinn m. 143/3.
dvelja (dvalða) wv. 'delay, hold up'; *mart dvelr e-n* 'many things will be a hindrance for s-one, much will hold one up' 59/4.
dvergr m. 'dwarf' 143/3 160/3.
dyrr f. pl. 'doorway' 70/6 160/3.
dýrr a. 'precious' 105/3 140/5.
dæll a. 'easy (to manage)' 5/3.
dœlskr a. 'foolish' 57/6.
dœma (ð) wv. 'judge; express opinions (*of* about), discuss' 111/7.

eða conj. 'or' 17/3 19/3 etc.; 'or (if)' 67/4 109/7; 'or as if' 90/7,9; 'or who' 163/9; 'or else' 136/5.
ef conj. 'if' 4/5 16/3 etc.; 'whether' 109/6; correlative with *þá* 17/5 30/5 80/6 89/6, with *ok* 151/2.
egg f. 'edge (of weapon)' 148/4.
ei adv. 'not' 39/3.
eiga (á, átta) pret. pres. vb. 'have, possess' 8/5 9/2 25/6 29/5 36/4 44/1 45/1 55/6 59/2 62/6 119/5; *eiga sér* 'have for o-self' 26/3.
eigi (1) subj. of **eiga**, sg. 36/4, sg. or pl. 29/5n.
eigi (2) adv. 'not' 114/2 131/6.
eignask (að) wv. md. 'gain possession of (for o-self)' 79/2.
eik f. 'oak' 137/9.
einn a., num. and pron. (n. **eitt**) (1) 'one' 89/6, 'one person' 63/4 124/3 163/5, 'one thing' 77/4, 'one of them' (sc. *ljóð*) 146/4, sc. *lær* 67/6; 'the same' 35/3; *eins* 'of one man' 73/1; *einna* with sup. = 'of all' 64/6; 'a certain' 101/4 118/2.
(2) 'only, alone' 18/1 52/1 95/1, 'nothing but' 124/6; *þeiri einni* 'to that (female) person only, alone' (with *kennik*) 163/7; *einn sér*,

einn saman 'on one's own, all alone' 47/2 95/3, *einir saman* 'they only (only the two people concerned) between themselves' 98/5.

einnhverr *pron. a.* 'someone' 121/10.

einnættr *a.* 'one night old' 86/3.

einugi dat. sg. n. of **engi**, 'for not one thing, for nothing' 133/6.

ekki *pron.* n. of **engi**, 'nothing' 5/5 27/5; 'none, not any' (?) 97/5.

eldr *m.* 'fire' 3/1 68/1 70/4 83/1 137/8; dat. of comparison 'than fire' 51/1.

elli *f.* 'old age' 16/4.

ellipti *ord. num.* 'eleventh' 156/1.

en *conj.* 'but' 16/4 21/4 etc.; 'and' 7/5 42/6 74/7 etc.; 'and yet' 32/3; after comp. 'than' 6/9 36/6 40/6 70/2 95/6 124/5, 'than that' 10/3 11/3,6 71/5 145/2,5; *heldr en* 'rather than, instead of' 151/6.

endrgefandi *m.* (*pl.* **-endr**) 'one who gives again, repeated giver' 41/4.

endrþaga *f.* 'silence in return, reciprocated silence' 4/6n.

engi *pron. a.* (cf. **øngr, ekki, einugi**) 'no, not any' 16/5 19/5 43/5 61/5 88/2 93/2; 'no one' 27/4 56/5 64/6.

enn *adv.* 'further, in addition' 46/1; 'again', i.e. 'back' 101/2 108/2.

eptir *prep.* with acc. 'after' 72/3; as adv. 105/5 see **hafa**.

er (1) *rel. particle* and *conj.* (1) 'who, which' 40/2 62/5 142/5; *sá er, sá ... er, þann er, þeir ... er, því er, hinn (...) er* etc. 8/2 18/2 22/5 etc.; *þeirar er* 'who' or 'whom' 108/6, *þeim ... er* 'about which' 138/8, *þat (...) er* 'what' 8/5 95/2, 'which' 136/2 160/2, *þeiri einni er* 'to that one alone who' 163/8; *hveim er* 'for whoever' 76/6; *þá ... hverr er* 'then ... whoever, whenever anyone' 124/2.

(2) 'when' 17/2 24/6 27/2 etc.; *þá er* 'when' 6/4 125/8; correlative with *þá* 23/5 25/5 51/5 64/5 96/2 101/2 102/5 etc.; *opt ... er* 20/5; *þar ... er* 'where' 145/9; *færa ... er fleira* 'the less ... the more' 12/5; 'when' or 'if' ('which'?) 163/5; 'when, although (that which?), it being the case that' 93/5.

(3) pleonastic 94/2n.

er (2) pres. of **vera** (2); *era, erat* = *er* + neg. suffix *-a, -at* 'is not' 12/1 22/6 30/5 69/1 124/6 133/4 ('there is no man'); *erusk* = *eru* + suffixed reflexive pron. 'are to each other' 32/2 41/5.

eta (**át**) *sv.* 'eat' 121/8 151/6; 'cause by eating (*sér* to o-self)' 20/3; pp. *etit* 67/6.

ey *adv.* 'for ever' 16/2 35/3; 'always' 70/3 145/3.

eyra *n.* 'ear' 7/4 ('with his ears').

eyrarúna *f.* 'confidante, close friend, lover (*e-m* of s-one)' 115/7 ('to be your lover').

eyrir *m.* (pl. **aurar**) 'ounce' (unit of weight or value); in pl. 'money, wealth' 75/3.

eyvit *f.* 'nothing'; dat. *eyvitu* ... *því er* 'nothing of what' 28/4; gen. *eyvitar* ... *þess er* 'for nothing that' 94/1.

fá (1) (ð) *wv.* 'colour' 80/5 142/5 144/3; with suffixed 1st pers. pron. *í rúnum fák* 'I apply colour in (engraved) runes' 157/5.

fá (2) (fekk) *sv.* 'get, obtain' with acc. 6/8 130/7, 'receive' 117/9, 'gain, win' 92/3, abs. 92/6; pp. *fengit* 40/2; with gen. 'take' 33/2; *fá e-m e-s* 'provide s-thing for s-one' 106/2, 'bring, cause s-one s-thing' 20/4; *fá sér e-s* 'get o-self s-thing' 52/6; *fá á e-n* 'affect s-one, get a hold over s-one' 93/4,5. Md. imp. with suffixed 2nd pers. pron. *fásktu at e-u* 'provide yourself with s-thing' 116/7.

faðir *m.* (gen. **fǫður**) 'father' 140/3.

faðmr *m.* 'embrace'; *í faðmi e-m* 'in s-one's embrace' 113/6.

fagr *a.* 'fair, beautiful, pleasant'; n. as subst. or adv. 45/4 92/1 130/8; sup. 54/5 91/4.

falla (fell) *sv.* 'fall' 139/6 158/4; pres. p. 86/2.

far *n.* 'vessel, ship' 154/3.

fár (1) *n.* 'mischief, malice' 24/5n 150/2n.

fár (2) *a.* 'few'; acc. pl. m. *fá* 25/6 59/2 62/6; in sg. 'not many, i.e. none at all' 159/6; n. as subst. *fátt* 'little, few things' 103/8 104/3, gen. *fás* 107/3; dat. sg. n. *fá* 'little' 33/6 ('can't ask about anything much'). Cf. **færa**.

fara (fór) *sv.* 'go, travel' 3/6 (pp.) 44/6 47/2 114/6 116/6 155/5 156/5; imp. with suffixed 2nd pers. pron. 119/7; pp. with direct object 'travelled over' 18/3; pp. *farinn* 'gone' or 'overtaken, caught up with' 34/6n.

fastr *a.* 'firm'; (of a promise) 130/9.

fé *n.*,'property, wealth' 58/3 69/5 79/3; 'possessions, riches, money' 92/2; 'cattle' 76/1 77/1; gen. sg. *féar* 39/4 (gen. of respect) 40/1.

feginn *a.* 'happy, pleased (*e-u* with s-thing), glad of, welcoming to' 74/1 128/5 ('do not rejoice in').

fegrst sup. n. of **fagr**.

feita (tt) *wv.* 'fatten' 83/5.

félagi *m.* 'comrade' 52/6.

fengit pp. of **fá (2)**.

fet *n.* 'step, pace'; dat. of extent 'by a foot's pace' 38/3.

Glossary

fiðr = finnr, pres. of **finna**.
fimbulfambi *m.* 'great booby' 103/7.
fimbulljóð *n.* 'mighty song, spell or incantation' 140/1.
fimbulþulr *m.* 'mighty sage' 80/5 142/5n.
fimm *num.* 'five' 51/3 74/6.
fimmti *ord. num.* 'fifth' 150/1.
fimmtándi *ord. num.* 'fifteenth' 160/1.
finna (fann) *sv.* 'find, notice, discover' 24/4 25/4 47/5 64/4 101/4 142/1; with suffixed 1st pers. pron. and suffixed neg. 'I have not found' 39/1; with acc. and inf. *finna e-n sofa* 'find s-one sleeping' 97/2; 'meet, visit, seek out' (object understood) 44/6 119/7.
firar *m. pl.* 'people' 26/6.
firði dat. of **fjǫrðr**.
firna *wv.* 'reproach, blame, condemn, find fault (*e-n e-s* with s-one for s-thing)' 93/1 94/1.
firr *adv. comp.* 'farther away' 34/6.
firrask (ð) *wv. md.* 'hold back from, avoid, reject, go (get) away from (*e-n* s-one)' 162/2.
Fitjungr *m.* 78/2.
Fjalarr *m.* 14/3.
fjall *n.* 'mountain' 3/6 116/5.
fjándi *m.* 'enemy' 127/7.
fjórði *ord. num.* 'fourth' 149/1.
fjórtándi *ord. num.* 'fourteenth' 159/1.
fjǫðr *f.* 'feather' 13/4.
fjǫlð *f.* 'multitude'; as obj. of *fara* 'a great deal' 18/3; acc. as adv. 'in numerous ways, of numerous kinds' 74/5.
fjǫlkunnigr *a.* 'skilled in magic' 113/5.
fjǫlkynngi *f.* 'magic, witchcraft' 137/10.
fjǫr *n.* 'life' 58/3.
fjǫrðr *m.* 'fjord'; dat. *firði* 116/5.
fjǫrlag *n.* 'death' 118/5.
fjǫtra (að) *wv.* 'fetter (*e-u* in or by s-thing)' 13/5.
fjǫturr *m.* 'fetter' 149/6.
flár *a.* 'treacherous, false, deceitful, cunning'; n. *flátt* as subst. or adv. 45/5 90/2, sup. 91/5.
fláráðr *a.* 'deceitfully intentioned, deceitfully planning or counselling' 118/4.
flaumslit *n. pl.* 'breaking of happy relationship (*e-m* with s-one)' 121/7.
fleinn *m.* 'shaft, spear' 86/1 150/3.
fleiri *a. comp.* 'more (in number)'; n. as subst. 12/5.

flet *n*. 'boards (of a hall, i.e. the wooden platform or 'benches' used for seating)' 1/7; pl. *á fletjum* i.e. 'in the hall or house' 35/6.

fljóð *n*. 'woman' 79/3 92/3 102/6.

fljúga (fló) *sv*. 'fly'; pres. p. 86/1; with neg. suffix *-a* 150/4.

flóð *n*. 'flood' 137/15 (perhaps referring to the sea, or to a disease, 'the flux').

flot *n*. 'the state of being afloat'; *á floti* 'afloat' 154/3 ('when it is afloat').

flótti *m*. 'flight' 31/2n.

flærð *f*. 'deceit, treachery'; in pl. 102/6.

fold *f*. '(flat) land, field' 137/15 ('earth'?).

fólk *n*. 'host, army of men fighting, battle' 150/3 158/5.

forðum *adv*. 'once (upon a time), formerly, long ago' 47/1.

formælandi *m*. (*pl*. **-endr**) 'supporter, advocate, speaker on one's behalf' 25/6 62/6.

fótr *m*. 'leg' 89/6; *mér af fótum* 'from my legs' 149/6.

frá *prep*. with dat. (postposition) 'from' 99/3 110/5 (see **svíkja**) 156/7.

fram *adv*. 'forward' 1/2; 'on' 79/6; comp. *framarr* 'farther on' (with dat. 'than his weapons', i.e. he should not leave his weapons behind) 38/3.

frami *m*. 'advancement, benefit, profit' 104/5; 'luck' 2/6n; ?'courage, ability, growth, success, fame'? 160/5.

fregna (frá) *sv*. 'ask, enquire' 28/2 63/1; *f. e-n e-s* 'ask s-one about s-thing' 109/3; *f. at e-u* 'ask about s-thing' 33/6; pp. *freginn* 30/5 ('is not questioned').

freista (st) *wv*. 'try, make trial of' (with gen.) 2/6 144/4 (abs.), 'put to the test' 26/6.

fría *wv*. 'woo' 92/6.

friðr *m*. 'peace, truce, quarter' 16/5 127/7; 'affection, friendship' 51/3; 'love' 90/1n.

fróðr (1) *a*. 'wise, well-informed' 14/3 28/1 30/4 31/1; as subst., dat. sg. 'to a wise person' 107/3, partitive gen. 7/6 63/2.

fróðr (2) *a*. 'fruitful, fertile' 141/2n.

frægr *a*. 'famous' 140/2.

frændi *m*. (*pl*. **frændr**) 'kinsman, relative' 69/4 76/2 77/2.

frævask (að) *wv*. *md*. 'produce seed, be (become) fruitful, fertile' 141/1.

frœkn *a*. 'brave, bold, valiant' 48/1 64/5.

fugl *m*. 'bird' 13/4.

fullr *a*. 'full' (perhaps predicative; *fyr* 'for') 78/1 (i.e. 'I saw their pens were full').

fuui *m.* 'flame' 57/3.
fylgja (lgð) *wv.* with dat. 'accompany, be in (a person), be a characteristic (of s-one)' 133/5 ('that there is no fault in him'); 'go with, be part of, belong to' ('constitute, comprise'?) 163/6.
fyr *prep.* (1) with dat., 'before, in front of' 70/6 160/3; 'in the face of' 158/6; 'in the presence of' or 'for the benefit of' 143/2; 'for (the benefit of), in the possession of' 78/2 (see **fullr**).
(2) with acc., of time, 'before' 145/7.
fyrðar *m. pl.* 'men' 149/2 159/2; partitive gen. (with *þeim*: 'for those (kind of) people') 54/4.
fyrir (1) *prep.* with dat. (postposition) 'in front of, before' 70/5n; 'in the presence of' 159/3 (with *liði*); 'in the presence of' or 'for (the benefit of)' 143/3,4.
(2) *adv.* 'before, already (when s-one arrives)' 1/7 133/2; 'in advance' 56/5; *nýsask fyrir* = *nýsa fyrir sér* ('ahead of, in front of, around o-self') 7/6.
fyrri *a. comp.* 'former, earlier'; *vera fyrri at e-u* 'be the first to do s-thing, initiate s-thing' 121/7.
færa comp. n. of **fár (2)** as subst., 'less' 12/4.
fǫgnuðr *m.* 'entertainment, pleasant treatment' 130/7.

gá (ð) *wv.* with gen. 'attend to, pay attention to' 114/2.
gagnhollr *a.* 'totally (or mutually) well-disposed, loyal, friendly' 32/2.
gagnvegr *m.* 'direct route' 34/5.
gala (gól) *sv.* 'chant, intone, sing' 149/4 ('I chant such a spell') 152/6 156/4 160/2; pres. p. 'screeching, croaking' 85/4; 'invoke, call up, conjure up' 29/6; *g. e-t e-m* 'produce (increase) s-thing in s-one by incantation' 160/4.
galdr *m.* (**rs**) 'incantation, charm, spell' 152/6.
galli *m.* 'defect, fault, flaw' 133/5.
gamall *a.* 'old'; pl. as subst. *gamlir* 'old men' 134/7.
gaman *n.* 'pleasure, entertainment' 47/6; *mannskis g.* 'the pleasure of anyone's company' 114/5; 'sexual pleasure' 99/6 161/3 ('the pleasure of her love').
gamanrúnar *f. pl.* 'pleasant private intercourse, relationship (*e-m* with s-one)' 120/6 130/6 ('secret love'?).
ganga (gekk) *sv.* 'go' 19/6 38/3 59/3 109/2; 'go on, leave' 35/1; 'walk, walk away' 149/5 157/6; with acc. object 'pass through' ('before one passes on or forward through') 1/2n; 'turn out' 40/6; *g. af* 'leave' 21/3; *g. fram í* 'advance into', i.e. 'increase in' 79/6; *g. um* (= *ganga yfir*?) 'befall, be experienced by' 94/3,

'befall' or 'be current about' (or 'among'?) 28/6n. Pres. p. *gangandi* 'wanderer, traveller' 132/7; pp. *genginn* 'departed, dead' (i.e. 'after his father's death') 72/3.

garðr *m.* 'courtyard, premises' 13/6; pl. 108/3 ('dwelling places').

gátt *f.* 'door-opening'; pl. 1/1.

geð *n.* 'disposition' 6/3 18/4; 'mind' 44/4 53/3; 'mind, wits, sense' 13/3 14/6 17/6n; 'mind', i.e. 'inclination' 12/6 20/2, 'frame of mind, intention' 46/3; 'inclination, heart' 99/6 161/3.

gefa (gaf) *sv.* 'give' 16/4,6 49/2 52/2 105/1 138/5; imp. 136/4, with neg. suffix -*at* 'do not give' 127/7; pp. 'given in marriage' 81/4.

gefandi *m.* (*pres. p.*) (pl. -**endr**) 'giver, host' 2/1.

geirr *m.* 'spear' 16/6 38/6 138/4.

geit *f.* (*pl.* **geitr**) '(she-) goat' 36/4.

gel(r) pres. of **gala**.

gestr *m.* 'guest' 2/2 7/1 31/3 32/6 35/2 103/2 132/7 135/5.

geta (gat) *sv.* (1) 'get, obtain' 17/5 44/3 45/3 58/5 65/3 70/3 104/3 140/4; 'get possession of' 112/4 etc. (or 'if you are able, i.e. to profit by it'?) 162/7; 'receive' 123/3; *ef getr* 'if he can get it' 130/10; *g. sér e-t* 'get s-thing for o-self' 4/5 8/2 76/6; *g. e-m vel* 'provide for (treat) s-one well, be a cause of good to s-one' 135/7; impers. *getr e-m at e-u* 'one is pleased with s-thing, rejoices in s-thing' 128/7; with inf. 'manage to, be lucky enough to' 79/2.

(2) with gen. 'speak of, talk about' 103/6.

geyja (gó) *sv.* 'bark at, sneer at, insult'; imp. with neg. suffix -*a* 135/5.

-gi *neg. suffix* (cf. **-ki**) 67/3 139/2.

gildi *n.* 'return, repayment' 145/3.

gína (gein) *sv.* 'open the mouth'; pres. p. 85/3.

ginnregin *n. pl.* 'mighty powers' 80/4 142/6.

gjalda (galt) *sv.* 'give back, pay' (*við e-u* 'in return for s-thing') 42/3 45/6.

gjalti *dat. sg.* 'a panic-stricken person, madman' 129/7n.

gjǫf *f.* 'gift' 42/3 44/5 46/6 48/6 145/3.

gjǫfull *a.* 'liberal (*e-s* of s-thing)' 39/5.

gjǫld *n. pl.* 'repayment, requital, return (*e-s* for s-thing)' 46/6 65/3 117/10.

glaðr *a.* 'merry, happy' 15/4 103/1 (with *skal vera*); n. *glatt* 55/5.

glama *wv.* 'talk noisily' 31/6n.

gleðja (gladda) *wv.* 'gladden'; md. 'make each other glad (*e-u* with, by means of, i.e. by giving each other s-thing)' 41/2.

glíkr *a.* 'like, similar to' 129/7; 'corresponding to, in accordance with (*e-u* s-thing)' 46/6.

glissa (t) *wv*. 'mock, sneer' 31/5.
gløggr *a*. 'careful, close, niggardly'; as subst., 'a niggardly person' 48/6.
gnaga (að) *wv*. 'gnaw' 106/3.
gnapa (ð) *wv*. 'reach, stretch forward' 62/1.
góðr *a*. (*n*. **gott**) 'good' 4/4 34/4 101/5 102/1 108/5 120/5 123/4 130/5 133/4 134/7; 'kind' 117/10; *g. e-m* 'beneficial to s-one' 12/1,2 112/4 etc. (i.e. *ráð* n. pl.) 162/7 (i.e. *ljóð*); *g. e-s* 'liberal of s-thing' 39/2 ('hospitable'); acc. m. as subst. 'a good one' 61/7 (*hest*) 76/6 (*orðstír*); n. as subst. 'goodness, what is good, s-thing good' 44/3 45/3 103/6n 128/7 130/10, 'kindness' 123/3.
gól p. of **gala**.
gráðugr *a*. 'greedy' 20/1.
gramr *a*. (used as subst.) 'hostile person, enemy' 31/6.
gras *n*. 'grass, pasture' 21/3, 'vegetation' 119/9.
grey *n*. 'female dog' 101/4.
grind *f*. (*pl*. **grindr**) '(cattle- or sheep-) pen' 78/1; '(barred) gate' 135/6.
grjót *n*. 'fragmented rock, (compacted) stones' 106/3.
grunr *m*. 'suspicion'; *e-m er g. at e-u* 's-one is suspicious about s-thing' 46/3.
grœta (tt) *wv*. 'make weep'; pp. 110/6 ('caused G. to be made to weep').
gullinn *a*. 'golden' 105/2.
gumi *m*. 'man' 12/6 13/3 (pl. ?) 14/6 17/6 28/6 (pl. ?) 38/6 (dat.) 53/3 (gen. sg. or pl.) 72/3 94/3 103/1 157/6; nom. pl. *gumnar* 32/1, gen. pl. *gumna* 15/5 18/5 129/8.
Gunnlǫð *f*. 13/6 105/1 108/4 110/6.
gætinn *a*. 'wary, careful' 6/3.
gǫrla *adv*. 'exactly, for certain, quite' 31/4.
gǫrva *adv*. 'fully, carefully' 102/2.
gǫrvallr *a*. 'absolutely all' 146/7.
gøra, gørva (rð) *wv*. 'make' 80/4 94/5 123/5 142/6; 'do, act' 114/1.

há *f*. 'hide, skin' 134/10.
háð *n*. 'scorn, mockery'; *hafa e-n at háði* 'treat s-one with scorn, hold s-one up to derision' 132/5.
háðung *f*. 'insult, disgrace, humiliation' 102/7.
hafa (ð) *wv*. 'have' 49/5 68/5; 'gain possession of' 58/3 99/5 102/9 161/3; 'keep, hold' 64/3; pres. subj. with neg. suffix -*t* 'do not

have' 61/7; with suffixed 1st pers. pron. 96/6; 'get' or 'behave' 80/6 ('he will do best'); as aux. with pp. 3/6 9/5 18/3 40/2,5 107/2 110/2, forming pluperfect 67/6 109/7; *h. e-n at e-u* 'hold s-one up to s-thing, make s-one the object of s-thing' 30/2 132/6 (imp. with 2nd pers. pron. suffixed); *h. eptir* 'keep, retain possession of' 105/5. Md. *hafask vel* 'do (feel) well, thrive, flourish' 141/3.
halda (helt) *sv.* 'hold (*á e-u* on to s-thing)'; subj. (optative) with neg. suffix 'let (a man) not hold' 19/1.
haldandi *m.* (*pl.* **-endr**) 'controller, keeper' 29/5.
hálfbrunninn *a.* (*pp*). 'half-burnt' 89/3.
hálfr *a.* 'half' 52/4 53/6n 59/6 ('wealth half belongs to, is half in the power of').
háll *a.* 'slippery' 90/4.
hallr *a.* 'sloping, slanting, inclined' 52/5n.
halr *m.* 'man, person' 20/1 49/6 102/3 118/2 129/9 151/4 158/6; 'a free man' 36/3 37/3 (complement).
haltr *a.* 'lame'; as subst., 'a lame man' 71/1, 'when one is lame' 90/9.
handarvanr *a.* 'lacking hand or arm, one-armed'; as subst., 71/2.
hanga (hekk) *sv.* 'hang' (intrans.) 138/1; pres. *hangir* 134/10; p. subj. 'might hang' 67/4.
hapt *n.* 'fetter, restraint, curb' 148/3n; 'bond, shackle' 149/7.
hár *a.* 'high'; dat. sg. n. *hávu* 119/9, acc. sg. m. *hávan* (with *sal*) 152/2.
hárr *a.* 'grey-haired' 134/5.
hatr *n.* 'hatred' 153/4.
haustgríma *f.* 'autumn night' 74/4.
Hávi *m.* 'the high one, High = Óðinn' 109/3,4 111/9,10 164/1,2.
heðinn *m.* 'fur cloak or coat' 73/3.
heill *a.* 'whole, unharmed, healthy, safe' 156/6,7,8; 'sincere, unreserved, genuine' 105/6; *illa h.* 'in bad health' 69/2. In greeting, 'hail to', 'blessed be', 'good wishes to' 2/1 164/5,6,8.
heilla (að) *wv.* 'bewitch, put a spell on'; subj. 129/9.
heilyndi *n.* 'health' 68/4.
heim *adv.* 'home' 21/2 (vb. of motion understood); 'to s-one's house' 67/2.
heima *adv.* 'at home' 5/3 36/3 37/3 83/5 103/1.
helmhamr *m.* 'home shape, proper shape' 155/6n.
heimhugr *m.* 'home thought, proper thought' 155/7n (i.e. 'they are confused').
heimisgarðar *m. pl.* 'courtyards of a house, homestead(s), premises' 6/5.

heimskr *a.* 'foolish' 20/6 94/4 (predicative, 'makes into fools'); as subst. 93/5.
heimta (mt) *wv.* 'claim'; *h. aptr* 'recover possession of' or 'take back home' 14/5.
heipt *f.* 'fury, hatred'; gen. pl. 151/5; dat. pl. 'with, for, in case of hatreds' 137/12.
heiptmǫgr *m.* 'person of hatred, enemy' 148/3.
heita (hét) *sv.* (1) 'be called' 13/1 103/7 146/4 (usually after the name); pp. (*vera* understood) 63/3.
(2) *h. e-u* 'promise s-thing' 130/8 ('promise fair', 'make fair promises').
heitr *a.* 'hot'; comp. with dat. 'hotter than' 51/1.
heldr *adv. comp.* (*conj.*) '(but) rather, instead' 6/3; *h. en* 'rather than, instead of' 151/6; *in heldr* 'either (any more than them)' 61/6; *at heldr* 'the more (in spite of that)' 96/6.
henda (nd) *wv.* '(try to) get (catch) hold of' 90/9.
hér *adv.* 'here' 67/1.
herr *m.* (*pl.* **herjar**) 'harrier, destroyer' 73/1.
hestr *m.* 'horse' 61/6 83/5 89/4.
heyra (ð) *wv.* 'hear'; with inf. 'hear (s-one, people) doing s-thing, hear s-thing being done' 111/7,11.
hildingr *m.* 'warrior' or 'prince' 153/5.
hildr *f.* 'battle' 156/6,7.
hindri *a. comp.* 'following' 109/1.
hinn *pron.* 'that one (in contrast)'; *hinn (...) er* 'that one (...) who' 8/1 27/8 75/1; n. *hitt* 'this on the other hand' 99/4.
hitta (tt) *wv.* 'hit' 66/6.
hittki = *hitt* (n. of **hinn**) 'that on the contrary' + neg. suffix *-gi*, 'not'; *h. ... at* 22/4, *h. ... þótt* 24/4, *h. ... hvat* 26/4.
hjálp *f.* 'help, salvation' 146/4.
hjálpa (halp) *sv.* 'help, save (*e-m við e-u* s-one from, against s-thing)' 146/5.
hjarta *n.* 'heart' 37/4 55/4 95/2 96/4 121/8; pl. 84/5.
hjǫrð *f.* 'herd, flock' 21/1 71/2.
hjǫrr *m.* 'sword' 158/6.
hlátr *m.* (*dat.* **hlátri**) '(scornful) laughter' 42/4 132/5.
hleifr *m.* 'loaf' 52/4 139/1.
hlíf *f.* 'protection' 82/6.
hljóð *n.* 'hearing' 7/3n (dat. 'with his hearing').
hlýða (dd) *wv.* 'listen (*á e-t* to s-thing, *e-u* with s-thing)' 7/4 111/6 164/8.
hlýja *wv.* with dat. 'protect'; 3rd pers. sg. with suffixed neg. 50/3.

hlæja (hló) *sv.* 'laugh (*at e-u, e-m* at s-thing, s-one)' 22/3; imp. with suffixed 2nd pers. pron. 134/6; *h. við e-m* 'smile at s-one, laugh pleasantly with s-one' 46/4.
hlœgi *n.* 'laughter, ridicule' 20/4.
hníga (hné) *sv.* 'sink down'; 'fall (in battle)' 158/6 (with neg. suffix).
hóf *n.* 'moderation, due amount'; *at hófi* 'in accordance with what is proper' 19/2n; *í hófi* 'within bounds' 64/3.
hold *n.* 'flesh' 96/4.
horn *n.* '(drinking) horn'; dat. with neg. suffix *-gi* 'no, any horn' 139/2.
horskr *a.* 'wise, sensible' 63/3 91/6 96/5 102/8; as subst., 'a wise person, man' 6/4 20/5 (pl.) 93/4 94/4.
hotvetna *pron. n.* 'everything whatever, all kinds of things' 48/5. Cf. **hvívetna**.
hraðmæltr *a.* 'fast in speech, fast talking' 29/4.
hreinn *m.* 'reindeer' 90/10.
hrekja (hrakða) *wv.* 'drive away' 135/6 (optative).
hrímþurs *m.* 'frost-giant' 109/2.
hringleginn *a.* (*pp.*) 'lying in a ring, coiled' 86/4.
hrís *n.* 'brushwood' 119/8.
Hroptatýr *m.* 160/6n.
Hroptr *m.* 142/7n.
hross *n.* 'horse' 71/1.
hrœsinn *a.* 'boastful (*at e-u* about or in s-thing)' 6/2n.
hrørna (að) *wv.* 'wither, decay' 50/1.
hugall *a.* 'thoughtful' 15/1.
hugbrigðr *a.* 'changeable in mind, fickle (*við e-n* towards s-one)' 102/3.
hugr *m.* 'thought, feelings' 91/3 95/1 105/6 117/10 ('opinion'? 'intention'?) 121/10 124/3; acc. pl. *hugi* 91/6 161/4; *mæla um hug* 'speak around (other than, contrary to) what one thinks' 46/5.
hundr *m.* 'dog' 83/6.
hús *n.* 'house' 89/3.
hvaðan *adv.* 'from anywhere, from everywhere' 156/8.
hvar *adv.* 'where' 1/6; 'everywhere'; *hér ok hvar* 'here and there, in various places' 67/1; interrog. 2/3.
hvárr *pron. a.* 'each (of two)' 53/6n; with partitive gen. 88/6.
hvars = *hvar er* 'wherever' 127/5 137/5 153/4.
hvat *pron.* 'what' 26/5; 'everything whatever' 5/3; interrog. '(why or) how' 50/6n 110/3.
hvatr *a.* 'keen, active'; as subst. 59/6, sup. 64/6.

hvé *adv.* 'how' 144/1-8.
hveim *pron. a. dat.* 'for any' 95/5; *h. er* 'for anyone who, for whoever' 76/6.
hvél *n.* 'wheel' 84/4.
hverfa (1) (hvarf) *sv.* 'turn' (intrans.), 'revolve'; pres. p. 'turning' 84/4; '(re)turn' 99/1.
hverfa (2) (ð) *wv.* 'make turn'; *h. hugi e-m* 'turn (change) s-one's thoughts or feelings (or mind?)' 161/4.
hverfr *a.* 'changeable' 74/4.
hverr *pron. a.* (*acc.* **hvern**) (1) 'each, every' 14/6 37/6 73/3; 'every (kind of)' 102/7 136/6; 'each one, each person, everyone' 36/3 37/3 77/6; with partitive gen. 'every' 7/6 15/5 18/5 54/2 55/2 56/2 63/2 64/2; *h. er* 'whoever'; *þá ... h. er* i.e. 'whenever s-one' 124/2.
(2) 'which, what' 18/4 133/3; *hvers* 'of what (kind?)' 138/9n ('from what (kind of) roots'). Cf. **hvat, hveim**.
hvítarmr *a.* 'white-armed' 161/5.
hvívetna *pron. n. dat.* (of **hotvetna**) 'everything whatsoever, all kinds of things' 22/3 23/3.
hyggja (1) *f.* 'understanding, intelligence, intellect' 160/6.
hyggja (2) (hugða) *wv.* 'think'; with suffixed 1st pers. pron. *-k* 111/5; with acc. object *h. flátt* 'think deceitful thoughts' 45/5 90/2 91/5 ('when we are thinking most deceitful thoughts'); with acc. and inf. 24/2 25/2; with *at*-clause 110/2, 'expect, intend' 99/4; *h. at e-u* 'think about, ponder over s-thing' 23/3; pp. *hugat* 'intended (*e-m* for s-one)' 40/5. Md. with inf. *hyggjask munu* 'think that one will' 16/2.
hyggjandi *f.* 'thought, intellect, mind' 6/1n.
hýróg *n.* 'household strife' 137/11.
hæðinn *a.* 'mocking, scornful (*at e-m* of s-one)' 31/3.
hætta (tt) *wv.* 'risk (*e-u til* s-thing for it)' 106/6.
hættr *a.* 'at risk' 88/6.
hǫfuð *n.* 'head'; i.e. 'life' 106/6; *hǫfuðs bani* 'a man's complete destruction' (but in this context perhaps literal) 73/2.
hǫgg *n.* 'blow' 82/7.
hǫggva (hjó) *sv.* 'cut (down)' 82/1.
hǫlðr *m.* 'free farmer; man' 42/5 94/5.
hǫll *f.* 'hall' 137/11n; dat. *hǫllu* 109/4 111/9,10 164/2.
hǫnd *f.* 'hand, arm' 73/4 149/7.

í *prep.* (1) with acc. 'to' 66/2,3; 'into, on to' 66/6; 'into' 79/6 84/6 158/5; 'in (from in)' 73/3; 'to (bring about)' 104/5; (of time) 'at'

37/6. (2) with dat. (of place) 'in' 10/5 13/6 35/3 96/2 104/6 113/6 129/6 150/3 157/5, postposition 8/6 ('dependent on') 109/4 111/10 164/2, 'on' 90/10; (of time) 'in' 26/3·(place?) 82/1 (to be understood also in lines 2 and 3) 90/7; (abstract) 'with, by means of' 52/3, 'in' (manner) 64/3.
iðgjǫld *n. pl.* 'return, recompense (*e-s* for s-thing)' 105/4.
ifi *m.* 'doubt'; *ifi er mér á* 'I am doubtful about it' 108/1.
illa *adv.* 'badly' 69/2 (see **heill**) 126/8; 'not well' 45/2 46/2; 'incompletely, inadequately' 90/6; with dat. 'badly off (in s-thing), having a bad (s-thing)' 22/2 ('with an evil disposition').
illr *a.* 'bad' 9/4 34/2 51/2 105/4 117/5,8 118/3 123/1 133/6; dat. sg. n. as subst. 'with evil' 128/5.
in *adv.* pleonastic with comp. 61/6.
inn (1) *adv.* 'in' 2/2 3/2.
inn (2) (*n.* it) *art.* 'the'; usually with a. and subst. 7/1 14/3 67/5 92/5 96/5 100/2 101/5 102/5,8 104/1 105/3 108/5 117/10 140/2,5 161/2 162/3; with comp. a. and subst. 109/1; with subst. preceding 80/3; with a. used as subst. *it sama* 28/3 76/3 77/3, with comp. a. used as subst. 125/7,8, with ord. num. used as subst. 51/5; combined with another pron. for emphasis *sá inn* with a. and subst. 94/6, *síns ins* with a. and subst. 105/6,7, *þat (...) it* with ord. num. used as subst. 131/9 ('this third thing') 148/1–163/1 ('this third one', i.e. *ljóð* etc.).
innan *adv.* 'from inside' 112/7.
inni *adv.* 'inside' 133/2.
íss *m.* 'ice' 81/5 83/2 86/3 90/4.

jaðarr *m.* 'rim, edge' 107/6n.
jafnspakr *a.* 'equally wise' 53/5.
jarl *m.* 'earl, ruler next in rank to a king' 97/4.
jór *m.* 'horse' 89/5 90/3.
jǫrð *f.* 'earth' 137/6,7.
jǫtunn *m.* 'giant' 104/1 106/5 108/3 143/4 164/4.

-k *1st pers. pron.* suffixed to vbs. 'I' 67/3 96/3 ?106/2n ?108/6n 111/4,5 112/1–137/1 154/6 157/5; pleonastic 13/5 39/1 (+ neg. suffix -*a*) 96/6 108/4 150/6 155/4 163/2; combined with neg. suffix and doubled 150/5 (*stǫðva + ek + a + ek*) 152/5 (*bjarga + ek + a + ek*) after separate *ek*.
kala (kól) *sv.* 'be (become) cold, freeze'; pp. *kalinn á kné* 'with cold knees' 3/3.
kálfr *m.* 'calf' 87/1.

kanna (að) *wv.* 'explore, make trial of, get to know' 102/2 ('if one examines (them, it) carefully').

karl *m.* 'man, male' 91/3.

katli dat. sg. of **ketill**.

kaupa (keypta) *wv.* 'buy, obtain by exchange' 83/3; *kaupir sér e-t í e-u* 'one buys s-thing for o-self with, in exchange for s-thing' 52/3; pp. *keyptr* 'bought' or 'exchanged' 107/1n ('which was a good bargain').

kenna (d) *wv.* 'teach (*e-m* to s-one)'; with suffixed 1st pers. pron. 163/2.

ker *n.* 'goblet, cup, bowl' 19/1 52/5.

ketill *m.* 'kettle'; dat. sg. *katli* 85/8.

-ki (= **-gi**) *neg. suffix* 22/4 24/4 26/4.

kjósa (kaus) *sv.* 'choose (*e-m* for s-one)' 137/6 (imp.).

kné *n.* 'knee' 3/3.

koma (kom) *sv.* (*pres.* **kømr**) 'come' 4/2 6/5 7/2 17/2 20/5 27/2 30/3 33/3 51/5 62/2 64/5 66/2 98/2 100/1 134/9 145/9 156/8 158/5; 'arrive' 133/3; impers. *er yfir kømr* 'when one has got across it' 81/5; *er at e-u kømr* 'when s-thing comes' 23/5 25/5n; pp. 2/2 3/2 101/2 104/2 107/5 108/2 109/6.

kona *f.* (*gen. pl.* **kvenna**) 'woman' 81/2 ('wife'?) 84/3 ('wife'?) 90/1 91/3 101/5 108/5 113/5 118/3 130/5 161/5; 'wife' 115/5 131/8 146/2 163/3.

konungr *m.* 'king' 86/8.

kópa (ð) *wv.* 'stare' 17/1.

koss *m.* 'kiss' 82/8.

kráka *f.* 'crow' 85/4.

kú acc. of **kýr**.

kuðr *a.* 'wise' 57/5n.

kunna (kann, kunna) *pret. pres. vb.* 'know (how to do s-thing)' 28/2 33/6; 'be able to' 103/8; *k. svá* 'be able to do that, have such knowledge or ability' 159/6; 'know, understand' 5/5 21/5 27/5 60/3 146/1 147/1–163/1, with neg. suffix *-at* 146/2; with object understood (*mál*) 164/6; 'know about' 163/5; 'know of, perceive, know (s-thing) to be' 127/5; *k. skil e-s* 'know details of s-thing' 159/5; with *at* and inf. 'know how to, be able to' 152/6.

kveða (kvað) *sv.* 'say' 84/3 134/7; with a., 'say s-thing is s-thing' 12/2 ('as they say it is good'); 'speak, utter, recite, perform' 164/1,5; *k. við* 'say in reply' 26/5; imp. with 2nd pers. pron. suffixed 127/6n (*k. e-t at e-u* 'account s-thing to s-thing, declare s-thing as (to be) s-thing').

kveðja (kvadda) *wv.* 'call (on, to)'; *k. e-n at e-u* 'appeal to s-one

for s-thing, persuade s-one to s-thing' 130/6; *k. e-t e-u* 'invoke s-thing for s-thing' 137/12; *k. e-n e-s* 'call forth s-thing from s-one, provoke s-one to s-thing' 151/5.
kveld *n.* 'evening, nightfall' 81/1.
kvenna gen. pl. of **kona**.
kveykja (kt) *wv.* 'kindle'; md. 'catch fire' 57/3.
kvikr *a.* 'alive'; as subst., 'a living person' 70/3.
kyn *n.* 'kind, origin, nature'; *hvers kyns* 'of what kind (kin?)' 133/3.
kynni *n.* 'visit to an acquaintance' 17/2 30/3 33/3.
kýr *f.* 'cow'; acc. *kú* 70/3.
kyrra (ð) *wv.* 'calm, quieten' 154/4.
kømr pres. of **koma**.

langvinr *a.* 'long-standing friend, old friend' 156/3.
láta (lét) *sv.* (1) with acc. and inf. 'cause, let, make s-one (to) do s-thing' 105/5 ('I left her with'); 'allow' 117/6 (imp. with 2nd pers. pron. suffixed); *létumk fá* 'I caused (Rati's mouth) to provide for me' (md.) or 'I caused (it) to provide' (suffixed 1st pers. pron. *-k*) 106/2n; with acc. understood 130/9 ('let it (the promise) be firm').
(2) with acc. and pp. 'cause s-one to be s-thing' 110/5 ('caused S. to be cheated and G. to be grieved'); with pp. in an impers. expression 128/7 ('let yourself be pleased, take pleasure', see **geta**).
(3) *l. sem* 'behave as though' 33/5.
laun *n. pl.* 'reward, recompense, repayment' 39/6 123/3 (*e-s* for s-thing).
lausung *f.* 'deception, falsehood' 42/6 45/6.
leggja (lagða) *wv.* 'lay'; *lǫgðumk yfir* = *lagði yfir mik* or *lagða ek yfir* 108/6n; pp. *lagit* 'laid, placed' 84/6.
leiða (dd) *wv.* 'lead, take, accompany, conduct' 156/3.
leiðask (dd) *wv. md.* 'hate, take a dislike to' 130/10.
leiðr *a.* 'loathed, hateful, unwelcome' 39/6; as subst., 'a hated, unwelcome person' 35/4 40/4 66/6.
leika (lék) *sv.* 'play, move to and fro, dance' 155/3; 'deceive, outwit, make a fool of (you)' 131/10.
leikr *m.* 'play, game' 86/7.
leita (að) *wv.* 'seek (*e-m e-s* s-thing for s-one)' 112/7 (*l. út* 'go out to find'), 'try to cause (s-one s-thing)' 102/8, 'seek (and find), fetch (s-thing for s-one)' 141/5,7.

lengi *adv.* 'for a long time' 35/5 50/6 162/6 (i.e. 'for ever'?); sup. *lengst* 'for the longest time, for a very long time' 41/5.
lesa (las) *sv.* 'express; concoct?' 24/5n.
leyfa (ð) *wv.* 'praise' 81/1 92/4.
leyna (d) *wv.* 'conceal' (with dat.) 28/4.
lið *n.* 'troop, company' (with *fyrir*) 159/2.
liðr *m.* 'joint'; metaphorical ('the right spot (in time)') 66/6n; pl. 'limbs' 113/7; *þér á liðu* 'on to your limbs' 136/6.
lifa (ð) *wv.* 'live' 9/3 16/2 48/2 50/6 54/5 68/6 97/6 120/7; *l. læknar* 'live as physicians' 147/3.
lifðr *a.* 'living, having life'; as subst. 'a living person' 70/1.
liggja (lá) *sv.* 'lie, lead' 34/5; pres. p. 'lying down' 58/4.
lík *n.* 'body' 97/6.
líki *n.* 'body, shape' 92/4.
líknargaldr *m.* 'kindness-spell, merciful charm, mercy' 120/7n.
líknfastr *a.* 'assured of favour' 123/6n.
líknstafr *m.* 'favourable statement, esteem, warm regard' 8/3n.
líta (leit) *sv.* 'look' 129/5.
lítill *a.* (*n.* **lítit**) 'small' 36/2 37/2 53/1,2,3; n. as subst. *í litlu* ('with a small gift') 52/3.
litr *m.* 'appearance, looks' 93/6 107/1n.
ljóð *n.* 'song, incantation, spell' 146/1 162/4 163/6.
ljós *n.* 'light, torch' 100/4.
ljóss *a.* 'bright' 92/5.
ljúfr *a.* 'dear, beloved, welcome'; as subst. 'a beloved person' 35/4 40/5.
Loddfáfnir *m.* 112/1 113/1 115/1–117/1 119/1–122/1 125/1–132/1 134/1 135/1 137/1 162/5.
lof *n.* 'praise' 8/3 9/3 123/6; 'praise' or 'love'? 52/3n.
loga (að) *wv.* 'blaze, burn' 152/2.
logi *m.* 'flame' 85/2.
lok *n. pl.* 'end(ing), conclusion' 163/6.
lopt *n.* 'air, sky' 155/3.
lostfagr *a.* 'delightfully fair, attractive (of beauty that arouses desire)' 93/6.
lygi *f.* 'lie' 42/6 45/6.
lykja (lukða) *wv.* 'enclose (*e-u* in s-thing)' 113/7.
læ *n.* 'destruction, harm, injury' 136/6.
læknir *m.* 'physician' 147/3.
lær *n.* 'ham' 58/5 67/4.
lǫstr *m.* 'fault, defect' 68/6n; 'evil, wickedness, sin' 98/6.

má pres. of **mega**.
maðr *m*. (**mann-**) 'man, person' 3/5 6/2,8 etc.
magi *m*. 'stomach' 20/6 21/6.
magr *a*. (*acc*. **magran**) 'thin, lean' 83/3 ('when it is thin, in poor condition', i.e. so as to get it cheap).
mál *n*. (1) 'measure' 21/6.
(2) 'period of time, season (three months)' 60/6n (acc. 'for a season').
(3) 'time (to do s-thing)' 111/1; 'meal (-time)' 37/6, dat. pl. with neg. suffix *-gi*, '(at) no meals' 67/3.
(4) 'speech' 57/5 (*at máli* 'in speech' or 'in the course of conversation'?) 111/6; 'speech' or 'business, affairs'? 114/3; pl. 'discourse, sayings' 164/1.
málugr *a*. 'continually talking, communicative, affable' 103/4.
man *n*. 'girl' 82/3 92/5 98/3 102/8 161/2 162/3.
máni *m*. 'moon' 137/12.
manngi *pron*. 'no one' 50/5 (nom.) 71/6 84/2 130/10 138/8; gen. *mannskis* 114/5 ('anyone's') 146/3 ('no one's').
mannvit *n*. 'human intelligence, common sense' 6/9 10/3 11/3 79/5.
mánuðr *m*. 'month' 74/7.
manungr *a*. 'girl-young, girlish' 162/3n.
margfróðr *a*. 'knowledgeable about many things' 103/5.
margr *a*. 'many' 32/1 66/2 82/4 104/4; with sg. subst. 'many a' 94/3 102/1; as subst. 'many a one (person)' 30/4 75/3, pl. 'many people' 62/5; n. *mart* as subst. 'much' 27/6,9 54/6, 'many things' 40/6 59/4.
marr (1) *m*. 'sea' 62/3.
marr (2) *m*. 'horse' 83/3.
matr *m*. 'food' 3/4 37/6 67/3 114/4; gen. of respect 39/2.
máttugr *a*. 'mighty'; weak nom. sg. *mátki* 94/6.
með *prep*. (1) with acc. 'into the company of' 27/2 (though the dat. is used elsewhere with the same meaning).
(2) with dat. 'with, among' 5/6 20/5 24/6 31/6 62/5 64/5 68/2 109/6 134/10,11,12 143/1 153/5; 'between' 51/2; 'accompanied by, having' 156/5; 'carrying' 100/4; 'by means of' 52/4,5.
meðalsnotr *a*. 'moderately wise, clever' 54/1 55/1 56/1.
meðan *conj*. 'while, as long as' 9/3 120/7.
mega (má, mátta) *pret. pres. vb*. 'be able, can' 28/5 60/5 (pres. subj.) 123/5 149/5 153/6; p. subj. *mætti* 'could' 4/5.
megin *n*. 'power' 137/6.
meiðr *m*. 'tree' 138/2,7.

mein *n.* 'harm' 151/6 (pl.).
meiri *a. comp.* 'greater'; *n.* as *adv.* 'more (in more ways, of more kinds)' 74/7.
metnaðr *m.* 'pride' 79/4.
mettr *a.* 'fed, full' 61/1.
mey acc. and dat. of **mær**.
mikill *a.* 'great' 6/9 10/3 11/3 34/1 148/2; as subst. 'a great deal' 52/1 (i.e. 'a large gift').
mikilsti *adv.* (= *mikils til*) 'all too, much too' 66/1.
mildr *a.* 'liberal, generous, kind' 39/1 48/1.
minn *poss. a.* 'my' 49/1 96/3 104/5 148/3,5 154/3 163/9.
minnigr *a.* 'mindful, having a good memory' 103/4.
misseri *n.* 'season (of six months)' 60/6n (acc. 'for a season').
mjǫðr *m.* 'mead' 19/2 105/3 140/5.
mjǫk *adv.* 'very' 2/4 142/3,4.
mjǫt *n. pl.* or *f.* 'measure' 60/3.
móðr *a.* 'tired' 23/4.
morginn *m.* 'morning' 59/5 (*um morgin* 'throughout the morning'); dat. sg. *morni* 23/5 101/1.
munnr *m.* 'mouth; cutting or biting end of a tool' 106/1.
munr *m.* 'desire, love, lust' 94/6; 'love, loved one' 96/3n.
munu (mnn, munda) *pret. pres. vb.* 'shall, will' (future) 16/2 32/5 123/5 136/5 142/1 146/5 162/2; 2nd pers. sg. *mun* 162/5, with suffixed 2nd pers. pron. 'you will' 112/3 etc. 123/2; *munu* 'they (*ráð*) will be' 112/4 etc.; subj. *mynda* 'would' 99/5, *myndi* '(it) would be' 67/2; with neg. suffix *-at* 158/4.
munuð *f.* '(physical) love' 79/3.
myrkr *n.* 'dark(ness)' 82/3 (*í* understood from line 1).
mækir *m.* 'sword' 81/3 83/4; with prep. *á* understood from previous line 82/7.
mæla (t) *wv.* 'speak' 27/6,9 29/1 46/5 91/1,4 92/1 104/5; subj. (optative) *mæli* 'let him speak' 19/3; *m. við e-n* 'speak to s-one' 45/4 157/7; *m. sér e-n* 'win s-one for o-self by talking, woo so as to win s-one' 98/3 (or 'betroth s-one to o-self, come to an agreement to possess s-one'?).
mær *f.* (*acc.* and *dat.* **mey**) 'maiden, virgin' 81/4 82/8 (with prep. *á* understood from line 6) 84/1 (gen. sg.) 102/1 163/3 (dat. sg.); 'girl (daughter or wife)' 96/5 97/1n.
mœta (tt) *wv.* 'meet (*e-m* s-one)' 89/2 ('though one meet him').
mǫgr *m.* 'son' 146/3.

ná (ð) *wv.* with inf. 'manage to, be able to do s-thing' 68/5 121/9; subj. (conditional) 30/6n.

nár *m.* 'corpse' 71/6.
nauðr *f.* 'need, necessity' (with *at* and inf. 'to do s-thing') 154/2.
ne *adv.* 'not' 93/5 108/4 121/9 131/10 133/5 135/5 (combined with neg. suffix -*a*).
né *conj.* 'nor, and not' 50/3 58/6 61/6 84/3 88/3 114/3,5 132/5,7 133/6 135/6 148/6 163/3; without preceding neg., 'but not' 63/5, 'and not' 111/8; negating the preceding as well as following element 126/6n 139/2.
neiss *a.* 'shamed, despised' 49/6.
nema (1) *conj.* 'unless' 20/2 27/6 29/5 33/3 72/6 98/5 112/6 126/7; 'except' 163/7; with inf. 'except, without doing s‑thing' 97/6.
nema (2) (nam) *sv.* 'take, pick (*upp* up)' 139/4,5; 'accept, follow' 112/3 etc., subj. *nemir* 'you should accept' 112/2 etc.; 'learn' 120/7 140/2 153/3 162/8 164/7. With inf. 'begin to' 141/1.
nest *n.* 'provisions for a journey' 74/2.
niðr (1) *m.* 'kinsman, relative' 72/6.
niðr (2) *adv.* 'down, below' 139/3.
níu *num.* 'nine' 138/3 140/1.
níundi *ord. num.* 'ninth' 154/1.
njósn *f.* 'spying'; *á njósn* 'on the watch' 112/6.
njóta (naut; *pres.* **nýtr)** *sv.* with gen. '(get) benefit (from)' 71/6 112/3 etc.; pp. *notit* 107/2; subj. 'let him benefit' 164/7; p. subj. with suffixed 1st pers. pron. *nytak* 108/4 ('if I had not had the help of G.').
nótt (pl.** nætr)** *f.* 'night' 23/2 (*um allar nætr* 'throughout whole nights, all night long'), *nætr allar níu* 'through all of nine nights, nine whole nights' 138/3; dat. sg. *nótt* 74/1 112/5 ('at night').
nú *adv.* 'now' 78/3 91/1 104/2 107/5 164/1.
nýfelldr *a.* (*pp.*) 'newly felled, just struck down' 87/4.
nýsa (t) *wv.* 'peer, search, investigate' 139/3. Md. *nýsask fyrir* 'spy (find) things out around o-self' 7/6.
nytak see **njóta**.
nýtr *a.* 'effective, efficient' 100/2; 'useful' 162/8 (n. pl., refers to *ljóð*).
nytsamligr *a.* 'useful, beneficial, advantageous (*e-m* to s-one)' 153/3.
næfr *f.* 'piece of (birch-)bark' 60/2.
nær (1) *conj.* 'when' 38/5; *þat ... nær* 21/2.
nær (2) *prep.* with dat. 'near, close to' (postposition) 72/5 95/2; of time 'towards' 98/1 101/1.
næst *adv.* 'next (time)' 100/1.
nætr pl. of **nótt**.
nøkkviðr *a.* 'naked' 49/6.

óauðigr *a.* 'not wealthy, poor' 75/5.
óbeðit *pp.* (see **biðja**) 'not invoked, not prayed' 145/1 ('it is better that there should be no prayer, it is better the request be not made').
óbrigðr *a.* 'unfailing, reliable'; comp. 6/7.
óbryddr *a.* (*pp.*) 'not ice-spiked, without spikes for ice; without calkins, not roughshod' 90/3.
Óðinn *m.* 98/2 110/1 138/5 (dat.) 143/1.
óðr *a.* 'furious, raging' 90/7.
Óðrerir *m.* 'a vessel, or its contents, the mead' 107/4n 140/6n.
ódæll *a.* 'difficult, troublesome to deal (*við e-t* with s-thing)'; comp. n. as adv. 8/4.
of (1) *pleonastic particle* with vbs. (= um (2)) 14/5 67/2 72/2 100/6 109/7 140/4 145/9 150/6.
of (2) *prep.* with acc. 'concerning' 46/1 111/7.
ofarla *adv.* 'high up (*e-m* in s-one)' 118/1n.
ofblótit *pp.* 'excessively sacrificed, too much offered in sacrifice' 145/2 ('than that too much should be offered').
ofdrykkja *f.* 'excessive drinking, overdrinking' 11/6.
ofrǫlvi *a.* 'excessively drunk' 14/2.
ofsóit *pp.* 'excessively immolated' 145/5 ('than that there should be too much immolation')(cf. **sóa**).
ofvarr *a.* 'too cautious, excessively wary' 131/6n.
ógóðr *a.* 'not good'; n. as subst. *ógott* 'evil' 29/6.
ógǫrla *adv.* 'imprecisely, not quite, not for certain' 133/1.
óhapp *n.* 'misfortune' 117/7 (pl.; *at þér* 'befalling you' or 'arising from you'? '(learn) from you'?).
ok *conj.* 'and' 3/3 4/3,6 5/6 etc. Pleonastic, correlative with *ef* 151/4 (introducing the main clause).
ókunnr *a.* 'unknown, strange' 10/5.
ókynni *n.* 'lack of knowledge (of how to behave), ineptitude, bad manners' 19/4.
ólagaðr *pp.* (*laga*) 'not ready, not brewed' 66/5.
ólifðr *a.* 'not having life'; as subst., 'a dead person' 70/2.
óminnishegri *m.* 'heron of forgetfulness' 13/1n.
ónýtr *a.* 'useless' 89/5.
opt *adv.* 'often' 9/5 20/4 29/6 40/4 44/6 52/3 65/3 93/4 133/1 134/7,8; 'generally' 33/2, 'frequently' 103/6 119/7 125/7.
ór *prep.* with dat. 'out of, from' 134/8, postposition 9/6 108/3; 'out of, from being' 94/4.
óra (ð) *wv.* 'show hostility' 32/6.
orð *n.* 'word' 65/1 84/1 104/4 (dat. pl. '(by) using many words')

118/3 122/5 125/5 (as 104/4) 134/9 141/4,5; 'speech, conversation' 4/6.
orðstírr *m*. 'hǫnour, renown, glorious reputation' 76/4.
orka (að) *wv*. 'bring about'; *o. (til) e-s (á) e-t* 'get s-thing from s-thing, make use of s-thing for s-thing, look for s-thing from s-thing' 82/5.
ormr *m*. 'snake' 86/4.
orrosta *f*. 'battle' 129/6 156/2.
ósent *pp*. 'not sent, nothing sent' 145/4 (cf. **senda**).
óskǫp *n. pl*. 'chaos, disorder, monstrosity, calamity' 98/4.
ósnjallr *a*. 'foolish' or 'cowardly' 16/1n 48/4.
ósnotr *a*. 'unwise, foolish' 24/1 25/1 26/1 27/1 79/1; as subst. 'unwise person' 103/9 159/6.
ósviðr, ósvinnr *a*. 'unwise, foolish' 21/4 23/1 122/7.
óvinr *m*. 'enemy' 1/6 43/4.
óvíss *a*. 'uncertain'; *óvíst er at vita* 'one cannot know for certain' 1/5 38/4.
óþarfr *a*. 'not useful, not beneficial, i.e. harmful (*e-m* to s-one)' 164/4.

rá *f*. 'yard (of a mast)' 74/3.
ráð *n*. 'counsel, advice' (pl.) 9/4 112/2 etc.; ? 'situation, circumstances' 109/3n (see **fregna**); ? 'plan', ? 'interpretation' 111/8 (cf. **ráða**).
ráða (réð) *sv*. with dat. 'rule, have power over, control, determine the fate (development) of' 88/4; 'advise' with suffixed 1st pers. pron. 112/1n etc.; 'interpret' 144/2, pp. *ráðinn* 'interpretable, meaningful' 142/2; with inf. 'decide, determine, undertake (to do s-thing), be able (to do s-thing)?' 124/2 ('goes and ... ').
ráðsnotr *a*. 'wise in counsel, prudent'; partitive gen. as subst. 64/2.
ráðspakr *a*. 'wise in counsel' 102/5.
rammr, ramr *a*. 'strong, stout, powerful' 136/1 151/3.
rangr *a*. 'crooked' 126/9.
rata (að) *wv*. 'travel about, rove' 5/2 18/2.
Rati *m*. name of an auger 106/1.
regin *n. pl*. '(divine) powers'; gen. pl. *rǫgna* 142/7n.
reginknnnr *a*. 'of divine origin' 80/3.
reifr *a*. 'cheerful' 15/4 103/2.
reisa (t) *wv*. 'raise, set up' 72/6 (subj.).
reka (rak) *sv*. 'drive' 71/2.
rekkr *m*. 'warrior, champion' 49/4.

renna (rann) *sv.* 'run'; i.e. 'grow, arise' 138/9.
reyna (d) *wv.* 'prove, demonstrate, find out (by experience)' 96/1 102/4; pp. 80/1, 'tried, tested' 81/3.
reyr *n.* or **reyrr** *m.* 'reed, reed-bed' 96/2.
ríða (reið) *sv.* 'ride'; with dat. 71/1; pres. subj. (optative) 'let (a man) ride' 61/2; 'swing, move from side to side' 136/2.
ríki *n.* 'power, rule?' 64/1; *með ríki* i.e. 'victoriously, triumphantly' 156/5.
ript *n.* 'clothing' 49/5.
rísa (reis) *sv.* '(a)rise, get up' 58/1 59/1 145/8; imp. with neg. suffix 112/5.
rísta (reist) *sv.* 'incise, cut, carve' 142/7 143/5 144/1 145/6 157/4.
ro = *eru* 'are' 73/1 133/3; 'there are' 63/6.
róa (rera) *sv.* 'row, go out in a boat' 82/2.
róg *n.* 'strife, discord' 32/4.
rót *f.* 'root' 138/9 151/3.
rótlauss *a.* 'rootless' 85/6.
rúm *n.* 'space' 106/2.
rún *f.* 'secret, secret wisdom, secret writing, rune' 80/2 111/7 137/14 139/4 142/1 157/5.
rýta (tt) *wv.* 'squeal, grunt, roar?' 85/5 (pres. p.).
rǫgna gen. pl. of **regin**.
rǫk *n. pl.* 'fate, history' 145/7n ('before mankind existed').
rǫnd *f.* 'edge, rim (of a shield)' or the shield itself 156/4.

sá (1) p. of **sjá (2)**.
sá (2) *pron.* 'he, that person' 18/6 44/4 75/6 etc.; *þeim* 'for such a one' 56/6; n. *þat* 'this' 41/3n 163/6, referring to pl. subst., 'they' *(trémenn)* 49/4 (with pl. vb.), cf. 136/5n, *þess* 'of them' 60/3; *sá (...) er* 'that person who, he who, the one that' 2/5 9/1 92/6 etc., 'some one whom' 46/1, 'that guest who' 31/5, 'anyone who' 58/2; *era sá vinr ǫðrum er* 'he is not a friend to another who' 124/6; *þeim er* 'for one who' 37/5, *þeir er* 'those who' 133/2, *þeiri einni er* 'to that one alone who' 163/7, with partitive gen. *þeim fyrða ... er* 'for those kinds of men who' 54/4; *þat (...) er*, *því er* 'what' 84/3 95/1 134/7; for *því at* see **því**; see also **þats, þeims, þeirs**; as demonstrative a. 13/4 19/4 (*þess ... at*) 158/6, separated from noun 152/6 157/6; *sá ... er* 'the ... which' 60/4 136/1, *þau ... er* 'some ... that' 146/1; combined with def. art. for emphasis, *sá inn* 94/6, *þat (ljóð) it* 148/1 etc.; doubled for emphasis *þann hal er ... þann* 151/6; *sá er* as rel. 'who' 3/6, 'which' 50/2 134/10, 'whom' 44/2 50/5, 'those ... who' 147/3,

hverr sá er 'each (one) who' 63/3, *því er* 'of what' (in apposition to *eyvitu*) 28/6 cf. 94/3; see also **þanns**.
saldrótt *f*. 'hall-band, house-guard' (or 'household'?) 101/3.
salr *m*. 'hall, house not divided into rooms' 36/5 152/3; pl. 'premises' 104/6.
saman *adv*. 'together'; *einn saman* 'on one's own' 47/2, *einir ... saman* 'they only between themselves' 98/6, see **einn**.
samr *a. pron*. 'same'; *it sama* as adv. 'likewise' 28/3 76/3 77/3.
sandr *m*. 'sand' 53/1.
sannr *a*. 'true'; 'just(ified)' 118/6.
saurngr *a*. 'dirty' 83/4 ('when it is dirty'; cf. **magr**).
sé (1) pres. of **sjá (2)** 150/2 152/2 155/2 157/2.
sé (2) subj. of **vera (2)** 34/6 39/6 69/2; with subject omitted 33/5 36/2 37/2 72/2; with neg. suffix *-t* (and pp.) 61/3; *eða ... sé* 'or who was' 163/9, cf. note, conditional 126/9n ('suppose ...'); *ok sé* 'and when it is' 90/6; *en sé* 'than that it should be' 10/3 11/3,6 145/2,5, 'than that one should be' 71/5, 'than it would be' 70/2 124/5; (optative) 'let him be' 54/3 55/3 56/3, 'may they (i.e. *ljóð*) be' 162/7.
sefi *m*. 'mind' 56/6 95/3n 105/7 161/6.
sefr pres. of **sofa**.
segja (sagða) *wv*. 'say (*e-m e-t* s-thing to s-one)' 65/2 111/11 124/6; 'tell' 121/9 124/2; 'give information' 28/3 63/1 103/8.
seinn *a*. 'late, slow'; n. as adv. 'slowly, late, not for a long time' (i.e. 'never') 162/2.
sem *conj*. 'as'; 'the same as' 23/6, 'as though' 33/5; *svá ... sem* 'as ... as' 12/2, 'like' 78/5, 'as if (one were to)' 90/3.
senda (nd) *wv*. 'send' 144/7n.
senn *adv*. 'at the same time'; *allt er senn* 'it all happens at once, together' 17/4.
senna (t) *wv*. 'dispute, contend, quarrel'; *s. þrimr orðum* 'dispute using three words (or more)' 125/5 ('don't waste even three words quarrelling').
sér (1) subj. of **vera (2)**, 2nd pers. sg. 126/7.
sér (2) pres. of **sjá (2)** 145/3.
sér (3) *reflexive pron. dat*. 'for himself' 4/5 8/2 20/3 26/3 37/6 76/6, 'for itself' 29/6, 'for o-self' 52/3; 'to himself, his' 24/2 25/2; *einn sér* 'on his own, by himself' 95/3; *una sér*, see **una**.
sessmǫgr *m*. 'bench-, table-companion' 152/3 ('around (my) table-companions').
sétti *ord. num*. 'sixth' 51/5 151/1.
sextándi *ord. num*. 'sixteenth' 161/1.

síð *adv.* 'late' 66/3 72/2.
síðr *adv. comp.* 'less'; as conj. 'lest' 129/9.
sif *f.* 'affinity' 124/1n.
sigr *m.* (*acc.* **sigr**) 'victory' 58/6.
sik *reflexive pron. acc.*; *um sik* 'about himself' ('in his behaviour'?) 103/3.
sinn *reflexive a.* (*n.* **sitt**) 'his' 2/6 6/1 12/6 14/6 15/6 21/6 38/1 39/4 40/1 42/1 43/1,4 56/4 59/3 64/1 68/4; 'one's' 89/1, 'her' 105/6,7 ('for that ... of hers'), 'their' 155/6,7.
sitja (sat) *sv.* 'sit' 2/3 5/6 24/6 33/4 96/2; 'stay put' 35/5; *s. fyrir* 'be present (already)', or 'lie in wait'? 1/7 133/2.
sjá (1) *pron.* 'this (person)' 2/3; n. dat. *þessu ǫllu* 'all this' 89/8; gen. pl. *þessa* 'these' 162/4.
sjá (2) (sá) *sv.* 'see' 111/4,5; with suffixed 1st pers. pron. *sék* 'I see (catch sight of, look at)' 150/6; with acc. and inf. 70/4 118/2 150/2 152/2 155/2 157/2, with acc. and *vera* understood? 78/2; *sjá til e-s* 'look for, expect s-thing' 145/3.
sjaldan *adv.* 'rarely' 6/6 48/3 55/5 58/4 (i.e. 'never') 66/6 72/4.
sjálfr *a. pron.* 'the self, o-self' 76/3 77/3, 'himself' 9/2, 'myself' 143/5, 'themselves', i.e. 'their bodies, their outward appearance' 41/3n; *sjálfum þér* 'for yourself' 126/7; *s. sjálfum mér* 'myself to myself' 138/6.
sjálfráði *a.* 'self-willed, independent, headstrong' 87/2.
sjaundi *ord. num.* 'seventh' 152/1.
sjautjándi *ord. num.* 'seventeenth' 162/1.
sjón *f.* 'sight'; *sjónum* 'by sight, with my eyes' 150/6.
sjór *m.* 'sea' 82/2. Cf. **sær**.
sjúkr *a.* 'sick' 87/1.
skammask (að) *wv. md.* with gen. 'be ashamed (of)'; pres. subj. (optative) 'let (no man) be ashamed' 61/5.
skammr *a.* 'short' 74/3.
skap *n.* 'character' 22/2.
skapa (að) *wv.* 'shape, create'; *skór er skapaðr illa* '(suppose) the shoe is shaped badly' 126/8n; *e-t er skapað e-m* 's-one's s-thing is made' 84/5.
skapt *n.* 'shaft' 126/9.
skarpr *a.* 'shrivelled, shrunk, withered' 134/8n.
skeptismiðr *m.* 'maker of (spear-)shafts' 126/6.
skíð *n.* 'stick, billet' 60/1.
skil *n. pl.* 'distinction, distinguishing features, details (*e-s* of s-thing)' 159/5.
skilinn *a.* (pp. of *skilja*) 'reasonable, understandable, sensible' 134/9 (cf. *ráðinn* s.v. **ráða**).

skip *n.* 'ship' 74/3 82/5.
skipta (pt) *wv.* with dat. 'exchange (*við* e-n with s-one)' 44/5; *s. orðum* 'bandy words' 122/5.
skjóta (skaut) *sv.* 'shoot'; pp. *skotinn* 150/2 (with *flein*).
skjǫldr *m.* 'shield' 82/6.
skoða (að) *wv.* 'look' 7/5 (*e-u* 'with s-thing'); md. *skoðask um* 'look around (o-self), spy around' 1/3n.
skolla (d) *wv.* 'hover, dangle' 134/11.
skór *m.* 'shoe' 126/8; gen. pl. *skúa* 61/4.
skósmiðr *m.* 'shoemaker' 126/5.
skrá *f.* 'skin, hide, piece of leather' 134/11.
skríða (skreið) *sv.* slide, glide' 83/2.
skriðr *m.* '(swift) movement' 82/5.
skúa see **skór**.
skulu (skal, skylda) *pret. pres. vb.*; *skal* 'shall' 2/3 26/5 50/6, 'one shall' 144/1–8, 'shall one' 110/3, 'must' 63/2 92/1, 'has to' 2/5 8/5 37/5, 'is going to' 136/2; (gnomic) 'shall' 137/15, 'one shall' 137/12, 'should' 42/2 43/2 58/1 59/1 94/2 103/3, 'one should' 35/1 81/1 82/1,5 83/1 103/6; 'ought to' 63/5 (with *vita* in preceding line); *ef ek skal* i.e. 'whenever I' 156/2 158/2 159/2; *skulu* 'should, ought' 41/2, 'should be' 46/6, 'must (go)' 21/2; with neg. suffix, *skala* 'ought, should not' 30/2 35/2 38/2, 'one should not' 52/2; *þú skalt* or *skaltu* with suffixed 2nd pers. pron. 'you shall' 98/2, 'you must' 44/4 45/4 46/4 122/6 130/8; with neg. suffix -*at* and suffixed 2nd pers. pron., *skalattu* 'you shall not' 113/6 125/6 129/6; subj. *skyli* 'should' 15/2 42/5 84/2 93/2, 'ought' 33/2 43/5 64/2, 'should be' 15/5 54/2 55/2 56/2, 'one should' 1/3,4; *eða skyli* 'or (as if) one had to' 90/9; with neg. suffix, *skylit* 'ought not' 6/2, 'should not' 40/3, 'one should not' 75/6.
skyggna (d) *wv.* 'peer, spy'; md. *skyggnask um* 'look round (o-self) carefully' 1/4n.
slíkr *a.* 'such (a)' 98/6; n. *slíkt* as subst. or adv., 'like that' 10/6.
slokna (að) *wv.* 'be extinguished, die away' 51/4.
snapa (ð) *wv.* 'snatch, snap' 62/1 (*á e-t* 'at s-thing').
snemma *adv.* 'early' 19/6 66/1; 'soon' 88/3.
snópa (t) *wv.* 'look round hungrily' 33/4n.
snotr (gen. snotrs) *a.* 'wise, clever' 54/3 55/3,4 56/3 95/5; pl. as subst. 'wise people' 5/6 24/6.
snúa (snera) *sv.* 'turn (to another direction), change (the direction of)', with dat. 161/6.
sóa (ð) *wv.* 'kill, immolate' 144/8; pp. *sóit* with dat. object, 'killed' 109/7.

sofa (svaf) *sv.* 'sleep' 19/6 113/6 114/6; pres. *sefr* 59/5, pres. p. 58/6, pp. *sofinn* 'asleep' 101/3; *finna e-n sofa* 'find s-one asleep' 97/3.
sól *f.* 'sun' 68/3.
sólginn *a.* 'famished' 33/5.
sólhvítr *a.* 'sun-white' 97/3.
sonr *m.* 'son' 12/3 68/2 69/3 72/1 78/2 153/5 164/3,4; dat. sg. *syni* 88/3,5 140/2, nom. pl. *synir* 28/5 129/8 147/2, acc. pl. *sonu* 94/5.
sorg *f.* 'sorrow, grief, care' 121/8 146/6.
sorgafullr *a.* 'full of sorrows, sorrowful' 114/6.
sorgalauss *a.* 'free from sorrows, cares'; sup. 56/6.
sótt *f.* 'sickness, illness' 95/4 137/8.
sótta p. of **sœkja**.
spara (ð) *wv.* 'save (*e-m* for s-one)' 40/4.
spjalla (að) *sv.* 'chat' 82/3.
spretta (spratt) *sv.* 'spring' 149/6.
spyrja (spurða) *wv.* 'ask, enquire (*at e-u, e-m* about s-thing, s-one)' 80/2 109/5 (*ef* 'whether').
staðlausa *f.* 'meaninglessness, nonsense' 29/3n.
staðr *m.* 'place' 10/5 35/3 66/2; *leita sér út staðar* 'go out to find somewhere (to relieve o-self)' 112/7.
stafr *m.* 'stave; runic symbol' 142/2,3,4; 'word, statement' 29/3.
standa (stóð) *sv.* 'stand' 50/2 72/5; *e-t stendr e-n* 's-thing afflicts, lies, comes upon s-one, befalls s-one' 154/2. Md. *yfir ok undir stóðumk = stóðu yfir mér ok undir mér* 106/5.
stela (stal) *sv.* 'steal (*e-u e-n* s-thing from s-one), rob (s-one of s-thing)' 13/3.
stinnr *a.* 'stiff, unbending, strong' 142/4; n. as adv. 'hard, inflexibly' 150/4 ('with such force').
stjórnlauss *a.* 'rudderless' 90/8 (dat. sg. n., *skipi* understood).
stóll *m.* 'seat' 105/2 111/2.
stórr *a.* 'large, mighty' 142/3.
stýra (ð) *wv.* with dat. 'control, have command over, possess' 18/5.
stǫðva (að) *wv.* 'stop' (trans.); with suffixed 1st pers. pron. and neg. suffix and 1st pers. pron. added again 150/5 ('that I do (can) not stop (it)').
sumbl *n.* 'drink' (i.e. the mead) 110/5.
sumr *pron. a.* 'some'; sc. *staði* 66/3, sc. *ǫl* 66/5, sc. *rúnar* 143/5; '(a certain) one' 69/3,4,5,6.
sút *f.* 'sorrow, suffering, anxiety' 48/3 146/7.
Suttungr *m.* 104/6 109/7 110/4.

svá *adv.* 'thus' 7/6 100/6 106/6 145/6, 'so, the same' 50/4 62/4, 'as follows' 111/11, 'that' 159/6; *svá ... sem* 'as ... as' 12/1, 'thus ... as (like)' 78/4 90/1 ('as if one should, it is just like driving'); *svá at* 'so that' 113/7, *svá ... at* 'so ... that' 39/2,5 89/7 133/4,6 150/4 152/4, 'in such a way that' 114/1 149/4 155/4 157/4, 'it being the case that, in such circumstances that' 100/1.

svárr *a.* 'heavy' 105/7.

sverð *n.* 'sword' 86/6.

sviðr, svinnr *a.* 'shrewd, wise' 103/3 (*um sik* 'in his behaviour' or 'concerning himself'?) 161/2.

svíkja (sveik) *sv.* 'betray'; *s. e-n frá e-u* 'cheat s.-one of s-thing' 110/4.

svín *n.* 'pig, boar' 85/5.

svinnr see **sviðr**.

svæfa (ð) *wv.* 'lull to sleep, make still' 154/6 (with suffixed pron. *-k*).

sylgr *m.* 'drink' 17/5.

sýn *f.* 'sight' 68/3n.

syni, synir see **sonr**.

sýnn *a.* 'evident, apparent'; sup. 41/3.

systir *f.* 'sister' 163/9.

sýta (tt) *wv.* 'be anxious or troubled (*við e-u* about, when faced with s-thing)' 48/6.

sæla (d) *wv.* 'bless, cheer' 139/1n (subject 'they' understood).

sæll *a.* 'blessed, happy' 8/1 9/1 69/3.

sællifðr *a.* 'having a happy life' 70/2 var.

sær *m.* 'sea, lake' 154/6; gen. sg. *sævar* 62/2, gen. pl. *sæva* 53/2n. Cf. **sjór**.

særa (ð) *wv.* 'wound' 151/2.

sœkja (sótta) *wv.* 'seek, visit, go to see' 104/1.

sǫk *f.* 'cause (of offence)'; 'accusation, guilt' 118/6; '(cause of) dispute, contention, lawsuit?' 146/6.

-t *neg. suffix* with vbs. 6/2 19/1 53/5 61/3,7 75/6 89/7 148/6. Cf. **-a, -at**.

taka (tók) *sv.* 'take (to)' 31/2; 'accept' or 'take up, use (*við e-u* in return for, against s-thing)' 42/5; *t. við e-u* 'receive, absorb, contain, take away s-thing', or 'stand up to, resist s-thing' 137/7,15 ('enclose'?).

tamr *a.* 'tame, tractable'; *illa tamr* 'badly trained' 90/6.

taugreptr *a.* (*pp.*) 'roofed with withies' 36/5.

teitr *a.* 'cheerful'; of a horse, 'frolicsome' 90/5.

telja (talða) *wv.* 'enumerate, list' 159/3.

teygja (gð) *wv.* 'entice, lure, (try to) seduce (*á e-t* into s-thing)'

102/6; imp. with suffixed 2nd pers. pron. 'draw, attract' 115/6, 120/6 (*sér at e-u* 'so as to be one's s-thing, into s-thing with o-self').

tíða (dd) *wv.* impers., *e-n tíðir* with inf. 'one desires, has the inclination to do s-thing' 116/6.

til (1) *prep.* with gen. 'to' 4/2 7/2 17/2 30/3 33/3 62/2 156/2; postposition 6/5 156/6; 'to the house of' 34/2,4; 'for the purpose of, to get' 82/6,8; 'about' 12/6 (see **vita**); as adv. 'for it, on it' 106/6.

til (2) *adv.* 'too' 27/6,9 54/3 55/3 56/3 57/6 61/3 66/3 88/3.

tíundi *ord. num.* 'tenth' 155/1.

tívar *m. pl.* 'gods, divine beings' 159/3.

tólpti *ord. num.* 'twelfth' 157/1.

tré *n.* 'beam' 136/1n; 'tree (used as gallows)' 157/2.

trémaðr *m.* 'wooden man' 49/3n.

troða (trað) *sv.* 'tread (on)' 119/10 (pres. *trøðr*).

trúa (ð) *wv.* with dat. 'trust' 44/2 84/2 ('believe in, put faith in') 88/2 89/8 110/3 119/6, 'have confidence in, rely upon' 74/2; *t. illa* 'mistrust' 45/2 46/2.

tryggð *f.* 'troth' 110/3 (pl.).

tryggr *a.* 'true, trusty, reliable'; gen. sg. (weak) *tryggva* 67/5; 'trusting' 89/7n.

trøðr pres. of **troða**.

tunga *f.* 'tongue' 29/4 73/2 118/4.

túnriða *f.* 'fence-rider, witch' 155/2.

tveir *num.* (*f.* **tvær**, *n.* **tvau**) 'two' 36/4 49/3 67/4; 'two men' 73/1.

tvévetr *a.* 'two winters old' 90/5.

tæla (d) *wv.* 'deceive, delude' 91/6.

ugga (ð) *wv.* 'fear, be afraid of' 48/5.

úlfr *m.* 'wolf' 58/4 85/3.

um (1) *prep.* (1) with acc. 'over' 3/6, 'through' 106/3; 'over, upon' 94/3, 'about, concerning' 24/5 28/6 (or 'upon') 77/6 103/3; 'for, because of' 118/6; 'around' 46/5 (see **hugr**); of time, 'through (-out)' 23/2 59/5.

(2) with dat. 'over' 31/5, 'over, around' 152/3, 'with' 95/3 (with acc.?), 'about' 111/8.

(3) as adv. 'around'; *skoðask um* = *skoða um sik* 1/3, similarly 1/4 17/3.'

um (2) *pleonastic particle* (= **of (1)**) 2/6 4/4 8/2 9/2 17/5 18/3 21/6 29/6 38/6 58/5 59/4 65/3 74/5 84/6 100/3 101/2,3 104/2 105/1 106/2 123/3 129/9 145/6,8 154/2 163/5.

una (ð) *wv.* 'be content'; *una sér e-u* 'be content with s-thing' 95/6.

und *prep.* with dat. 'dependent on, in the hands of' 59/6.
undaðr *a.* (*pp.*) 'wounded (*e-u* with s-thing)' 138/4.
undir *prep.* with (dat. or) acc. 'under' 156/4; as adv. 'beneath' 106/4, see **standa**.
ungr *a.* 'young' 47/1 158/2.
unna (ann, unna) *pret. pres. vb.* with dat. 'love' 50/5; abs. 'be in love' 99/2.
unnit pp. of **vinna**.
unz *conj.* 'until' 15/6 57/2.
upp *adv.* 'up' 70/4 107/5 129/5 139/4 145/8.
uppi *adv.* 'up' 157/2; 'displayed, visible', or 'finished, exhausted' 17/6n.
upplok *n.* '(action of) opening'; *ǫllum at upploki* 'in opening to all, to give entrance to all' 136/3.
Urðr *f.* a norn (cf. *urðr m.* 'fate' and OE *wyrd*) 111/3.
urðut 53/5 see **verða**.
út *adv.* 'out, outside'; *leita e-s út* 'go out to look for s-thing' 112/7.
úti *adv.* 'out(side)' 38/5 70/6.

vá (1) (ð) *wv.* 'blame (*e-n e-s* s-one for s-thing)' 19/5.
vá (2) *f.* 'misfortune' 75/6; 'woe, calamity', or **vá (3)** *f.* 'corner' 26/3n.
váð *f.* 'cloth'; pl. 'clothes' 3/4 41/1 49/1.
vaða (óð) *sv.* 'rush forward, move fast, fly' 150/3.
váfa (ð) *wv.* 'swing to and fro' (intrans.) 134/12 157/3.
vágr *m.* 'wave, sea' 85/7 154/5.
vaka (ð) *wv.* 'be awake, stay awake' 23/2.
vakinn *a.* (*pp.*) 'awake' 100/3.
válaðr *a.* 'wretched, needy'; as subst. 'poor person' 10/6 135/7.
valr *m.* 'the fallen in battle' 87/4.
valtr *a.* 'unstable, unreliable'; sup. as subst., with partitive gen. 78/6.
vamm *n.* 'blemish, fault' 22/6.
vánarvǫlr *m.* 'beggar's staff' 78/3n ('to carry a beggar's staff' means 'to be a beggar').
vanr *a.* 'lacking (*e-s* s-thing), free (from s-thing)' 22/6; 'in need of, deprived of' 162/6 ('have to go without'); *e-m er vant e-s* 's-one goes short of s-thing' 107/3 ('a wise man can get anything').
vápn *n.* 'weapon' 38/1 41/1 148/6 (pl.).
vár (1) gen. of **vá (2)** 75/6; **(2)** pres. of **vá (1)** 19/5.
vara (1) (að) *wv.* 'warn'; md. *varask við e-t* 'beware of, avoid s-thing' 16/3.

vara (2) (ð) *wv.* impers. (*e-n*) *varir* 'one expects' 40/6 ('worse than expected').
vark = *var ek* 13/5.
varr *a.* 'wary' 7/1 131/5, as subst. 'the wary person' 6/6; 'cautious'; sup. *vera varastr við e-t* 'be very wary of s-thing' 131/7.
vatn *n.* 'water' 4/1 158/3.
vaxa (óx) *sv.* 'grow' 141/3, 'increase' 153/4; pres. p. 'rising' 85/7; *e-t vex e-u* 's-thing becomes overgrown with s-thing' 119/8.
vé *n.* 'sanctuary, holy place' 107/6n.
veðr *n.* 'weather' 88/4; *(í) veðri* 'in good weather' 82/2.
vega (vá) *sv.* 'lift, carry, convey', with neg. suffix *-a* 11/5; 'fight' 71/3 125/8 ('attack'? 'strike'?).
vegnest *n.* 'provisions for a journey' 11/4.
vegr *m.* 'way, road' 38/5 119/10; gen. of respect, 'in (my) paths' 47/3; *jǫtna vegir* 'haunts of giants', i.e. 'rocks, mountains' 106/5.
vel *adv.* 'well' 41/6 44/2 61/3 107/1,2 116/7 119/6 135/7 141/3; 'very' or 'moderately, reasonably' 54/6n, 'pretty well, very' 69/6n.
velir pl. of **vǫlr**.
vella (vall) *sv.* 'boil' 85/8 (pres. p.).
velli dat. sg. of **vǫllr**.
vera (1) *f.* 'resort, refuge' 26/3; 'refuge' or '(means of) existence, way (of going on)' 10/6 ('on this depends the poor man's existence').
vera (2) (var) *sv.* 'be' 6/2 15/3 24/2 etc.; 'stay' 35/2; *var mér* 'was to me, for me (my?)' 96/5; imp. *ver þú* 121/6 (*at e-u* 'the cause of s-thing') 131/7, *verðu* 128/6; subj. *sér* 126/7, *þú verir* (optative) 'you should (not) be' 126/5; aux. with pp. (passive) 66/4,5 81/2,3,4,6 84/5 164/1 ('have been'), p. subj. *væra, væri* with pp. of intrans. vb. 'would have' 108/2, 'had' 109/6; *væri þegit* 39/3 see note. See also **er (2), sé (2), ro**.
verða (varð) *sv.* 'become' 14/1,2 35/4 55/5 57/5 75/3 129/8; 'find o-self' 47/3; 'be' 74/1; 'turn out' 41/6; *e-t verðr e-m* 's-thing happens to s-one, befalls s-one' 6/6, 'there comes to be s-thing for s-one' 38/5 ('when there will be') 148/2; p. pl. with neg. suffix *urðut* 'have not turned out to be' 53/5; subj. with neg. suffix *verðit maðr* 'let no man become' 89/7; *v. at e-u* 'become the object of s-thing' 5/4; *v. e-m at e-u* 'cause s-one s-thing' 118/5.
verðr (1) *m.* (*gen. sg.* **verðar**) 'meal' 4/2 7/2 33/1; dat. sg. *verði* 31/5, *virði* 32/3 116/7 (i.e. 'food, provisions').
verðr (2) pres. of **verða**.

verja (varða) *wv.* 'enclose, enfold (*e-u* in s-thing)' 163/8 ('embrace').
verk *n.* 'deed, action, work' 69/6 141/6,7.
verki *m.* 'work' 59/3n.
verpa (varp) *sv.* with dat. 'throw (*á e-n* on to, over s-one)' 158/3.
verr *adv. comp.* 'worse' 40/6.
verri *a. comp.* 'worse' 11/4 95/4 (*e-m* 'for s-one') 125/6 (*e-m* 'than s-one'); *inn verri* as subst. 'the worse person'.
versna (að) *wv.* 'worsen, deteriorate, be spoiled' 51/6.
vesall *a.* 'miserable, wretched' 22/1 69/1.
vex pres. of **vaxa**.
við (1) acc. of **viðr**.
við (2) *prep.* (1) with acc. '(together) with' 44/4 97/6; 'by the side of' 83/1; '(speak) to' 45/4 82/3 122/7 125/6 157/7; 'towards' 32/6 102/3 103/2; 'against, (wary) of' 16/3 131/7,8,9, 'for' 148/3; '(deal) with' 8/4, '(in association) with' 68/6.
(2) with dat. 'at, towards' 46/4, 'in the face of' 48/6, 'against, from' 146/6, 'in return for' 42/3,4,6 (or 'against', see **taka**) 45/6, 'with (by means of)' 139/1,2; *taka við e-u* 137/7,8,9,10,11,13,14,15, see **taka**.
(3) as adv. 'in reply' 26/5.
víða *adv.* 'widely' 5/2 18/2.
viðhlæjandi *m.* (*pl.* **-endr**) 'one who laughs (smiles) at one' 24/3 25/3 ('all those who smile at him, ? laugh with or at him, are his friends').
viðr *m.* (*gen.* **viðar**) 'wood' 60/4 100/5n; 'tree' 82/1 85/6 151/3.
viðra (að) *wv.* 'make weather, be of a certain kind' (of the weather); 'blow' (of the wind)? — *fjǫlð um viðrir* 'there are numerous kinds of weather' or 'the wind changes a lot' 74/5.
viðrgefandi *m.* (*pl.* **-endr**) 'one who gives in return, requiter' 41/4.
víf *n.* 'woman' 102/9.
víg *n.* 'battle' 16/3.
vígdjarfr *a.* 'bold in battle' 15/3.
vígdrótt *f.* 'war-band' 100/3.
víl *n.* 'trouble' 23/6 ('all his trouble is as it was').
vildr *a.* 'wished for, pleasant, agreeable'; n. *vilt* as subst. 'that which is desired, what is pleasant' 124/6.
vili *m.* 'joy, delight'; dat. *vilja* 99/3.
vilja (ld) *wv.* 'want, wish'; with inf. 147/3 161/2, 3rd pers. sg. *vill* 58/2 92/3 103/5, 2nd pers. sg. *vilt* 98/3 130/5, *vill þú* 44/3 (conditional), with suffixed pron. *vildu* 45/3 (conditional); with pp. (*vera* understood) *vill* 'wants to be' 63/3; 2nd pers. sg. with neg. suffix *villat* with direct object, 'will not want' 114/4.

villr *a.* 'wild, astray (*e-s* in relation to, i.e. from s-thing)' 47/3 155/5n.
vilmæli *n.* 'pleasing, beguiling, gratifying speech' 87/3.
vílmǫgr *m.* 'wretch' 134/12.
vílstígr *m.* 'path of wretchedness' 100/6.
vilt (1) n. of **vildr** 124/6.
vilt (2) 2nd pers. sg. of **vilja**.
vindr *m.* 'wind' 82/1 154/4.
vindugr *a.* 'windy' 138/2 (weak dat. m.).
vinna (**vann**, *pp.* **unnit**) *sv.* 'act, perform, achieve, bring it about (that)', with suffixed pron. -*k* 155/4; *v. eið* 'take, swear an oath' 110/2; md. *vinnask* 'last' 60/5.
vinr *m.* 'friend' 6/7 34/2,4 41/2 44/1 51/2 119/5; partitive gen. 78/6; dat. *vin* 42/1 43/1 121/5, *þeim ok þess vin* 'to him and his friend' 43/3; *v. vinar e-s* 'friend of s-one's friend' 43/6; *v. e-m* 'friend to, of s-one' 24/3 (*sér* 'his') 25/3 42/2 43/2 124/6; *erusk vinir = eru vinir sér*, 'are each other's friends' 41/5; *at ins tryggva vinar* 'at the faithful friend's (house)' 67/5.
vinskapr *m.* 'friendship' 51/6.
virði see **verðr (1)**.
virgilnár *m.* 'halter-corpse, hanged corpse' 157/3.
víss *a.* 'certain' 99/3.
vit (1) *n.* 'intelligence, sense' 5/1 9/3 88/5; *vitandi vits* 'having good sense, having one's wits about one' 18/6.
vit (2) *n.* 'visit'; *á vit e-s* 'to visit, inspect s-thing' 59/3.
vita (**veit, vissa**) *pret. pres. vb.* 'know (*e-t* s-thing)' 22/5 26/2 27/8 54/6 63/4 (inf. with *skal*) 63/6 75/2 95/1, 'know about s-thing' 98/5, 'have come, got to know' 91/2; *v. e-t at e-m* 'learn s-thing about (or from?) s-one', or 'experience s-thing at s-one's hands'? 117/7; *v. e-t fyrir* 'have foreknowledge of s-thing', subj. *viti engi fyrir* 'let no one have foreknowledge of' 56/5; with *at*-clause 138/1, *v. þat at* 27/4, *v. hitt at* 22/4, *v. einn at* 77/4 ('one thing of such a kind that, of one thing that it'), *v. hitt hvat* 26/4, *v. hvar, hverju, hvers* 1/5 18/1 133/1 138/8, *v. (þat ...) nær* 21/1 38/4; 2nd pers. sg. with suffixed pron. *veiztu (hvé)* 'do you know (how)' 144/1–8, 'you know, you should know' (equivalent of imp.) 44/1 119/5; with neg. suffix -*a* 75/1, *veita þótt* '(he) does not realise even if' ('does not know but that, whether ... not') 27/7 31/4; with gen., *v. geðs*, also *v. til síns geðs* 'know one's mind, have control over one's mind' 12/4 20/2; pres. p. *vitandi vits* 18/6n see **vit (1)**; pp. *vitaðr* 'allotted, destined, laid down (*e-m* for s-one)' 100/6.

víti *n.* 'penalty, punishment, liability to penalty; injury, misfortune' 6/6n.
vítka (að) *wv.* 'blame (*e-n e-s* s-one for s-thing)' 75/6.
vreka (vrak) *sv.* 'drive'; md. *vrekask* 'quarrel, abuse each other' 32/3.
væða (dd) *wv.* 'clothe' 61/3.
væni *n.* 'expectation'; *e-m er v. e-s* 'one expects, can expect, must be prepared for, s-thing' 73/4.
vætta (tt) *wv.* 'wait for' (with gen.); with suffixed 1st pers. pron., *vættak* 'I waited for' 96/3.
vættki *pron.* 'nothing' 27/8 75/2, 'no creature, no one?' 119/10; with partitive gen. 102/9 (i.e. 'I got her not at all').
vǫllr *m.* (*dat. sg.* **velli**) 'level ground, field, open country' 11/5 38/2 49/2.
vǫlr *m.* 'stave, stick, cudgel'; pl. *velir* 148/6.
vǫlva *f.* 'prophetess, seeress'; gen. sg. *vǫlu* 87/3.

yfir *prep.* with (acc. and) dat. 'over, above' 13/2; as adv. 'over, across (it)' 81/5, 'over' ('whom' or 'me', see note) 108/6, 'above' ('me', see **standa**) 106/4.
yndi *n.* 'pleasure, delight, enjoyment (*e-s* of being s-one)' 97/4.
yrkjandi *m.* (*pl.* **yrkendr**) 'worker, labourer' 59/2.
ýtar *m. pl.* 'men' 28/5 68/2 147/2 164/3.

þá *adv.* 'then' 21/3 47/3 101/4 126/10 141/1; correlative with *er* 23/4 25/4 51/4 64/4 80/1 91/4 96/1 101/3 102/4, with *ef* 17/6 30/4 80/6 89/5; *þá ... hverr er* 124/1 see **hverr**; *þá er* conj. 'when' 6/4 125/8.
þaðan *adv.* 'from there' 139/6.
þáfjall *n.* 'thawing mountain' 90/10.
þagall *a.* 'silent, reserved' 15/1.
þakinn *a.* 'for roofing, roofing-' 60/2n.
þanns = *þann er*, '(one) whom' 45/2 119/6.
þar *adv.* 'there' 104/3; *þar ... er* 'there ... where' 145/8 (or 'there ... when'?).
þarfr *a.* 'needful, useful, beneficial' 162/9 (referring to *ljóð*); n. as subst. 'what is useful' 19/3.
þars *conj.* = *þar er* 'where, when' 67/6.
þats = *þat er* 'that which, what' 40/5.
þegi (1) subj. of **þegja** 19/3 27/3.
þegi (2) subj. of **þiggja** 39/6n.
þegit pp. of **þiggja**.

Glossary 39

þegja (þagða) *wv.* 'be silent' 7/3 29/2 80/6 111/8; with suffixed 1st pers. pron. 111/4; subj. *þegi* 27/3, (optative) 'let him be silent' 19/3; pres. p. 'by being silent' 104/3.

þegn *m.* 'thane, warrior, man' 151/2 158/2 (with *á*).

þeims = *þeim er* 'for him who' 3/2.

þeirs = *þeir er* 'they who' 164/8.

þerra *f.* 'towel' 4/3.

þess- see **sjá (1)**.

þeygi *adv.* 'yet not, nevertheless ... not' 96/6 118/6.

þiggja (þá, *pp.* **þegit)** *wv.* 'receive' 9/5, 'accept' 162/9; pres. subj. *þegi* 39/6n; inf. and pp. as subst. (subject and complement) 39/3n ('receiving was accepting s-thing').

þing *n.* '(legal) assembly' 25/5 61/2 114/3.

þinn *poss. a.* 'your' 121/5 127/7.

þjóð *f.* 'people, nation; the people, the public' 63/6; pl. i.e. 'mankind' 145/7.

þjóðann *m.* 'ruler' (of a *þjóð* 'people') 15/2 114/3 146/2.

þjóðlöð *f.* 'friendly invitation' 4/3n.

Þjóðreyrir *m.* 160/2.

þjófr *m.* 'thief' 131/10.

þó *adv.* 'nevertheless' 19/2 36/6 45/3 162/7.

þola (ð) *wv.* 'suffer, endure' 40/3.

þorp *n.* 'farmstead, hamlet' 50/2n.

þótt *conj.* 'although, even if' 16/6 36/2 37/2 61/3,7 69/2 72/2, 'even though' 34/3,6 89/2 158/5, 'if but' 36/4; after vbs. of perception, 'though, even if' 24/5 ('he does not notice it, even if'), 'but that, whether ... not' 27/9 31/6; 'when' 30/3n.

þrettándi *ord. num.* 'thirteenth' 158/1.

þriði *ord. num.* 'third'; *þat it þriðja at* 'this third thing that' 131/9, *þat ... it þriðja* 'this third one (*ljóð*)' 148/1.

þrír *num.* 'three'; 'three (people)' 63/6; dat. pl. *þrimr* 125/5.

þróask (að) *wv. md.* 'thrive, grow (big), increase (*e-m* in s-one)' 79/4 ('he increases in pride, his pride increases').

þruma (ð) *wv.* 'stand motionless' or 'hover' 13/2; 'remain silent' 17/3, 'sit quiet' 30/6.

þræll *m.* 'slave' 87/2.

þulr *m.* 'sage, seer' 111/2n 134/5.

Þundr *m.* 145/6n.

þunnr *a.* 'thin, stretched (i.e. fine, sensitive), strained' 7/3.

þurfa (þarf, þurfta) *pret. pres. vb.* 'need' 147/2; p. subj. with suffixed 1st pers. pron. 'I needed' 67/3; with inf., p. subj. *þyrfti* 'should, ought' 22/5 ('it would be better for him to know').

þurr *a.* 'dry' 60/1.
þurrfjallr *a.* 'with dry skin' 30/6n (perhaps metaphorical, 'without being caught out').
þvá (þó) *sv.* 'wash'; pp. *þveginn* 61/1.
því at *conj.* 'because, for' 1/5 6/7 9/4 12/4 38/4 53/4 55/4 84/4 91/2 107/4 117/8 119/8 123/1 137/7; *því ... at* 'in these circumstances ... that' 14/4n ('when it happens that').
þykkja (þótta) *wv.* 'seem, be found to be' 10/5; with inf., *e-t þykkir e-m vera* 's-thing seems to s-one to be, one thinks s-thing is' 97/5. Md. 'think o-self (to be), be thought, seem?' 28/1 30/4 31/1 47/4; *þat þóttusk* 'these thought themselves' 49/4; with inf. 'think that one' 26/2 99/2.
þylja (þulða) *wv.* 'chant, proclaim' 111/1; md. *þylsk um = þylr um sik*, 'mumbles to himself' 17/3.
þǫgðu p. of þegja.
þǫgull *a.* 'silent'; as subst., 'a silent, reserved person' 6/4.
þǫll *f.* 'pine, fir' 50/1.
þǫrf (1) n. pl. of þarfr.
þǫrf (2) *f.* 'need, lack (*e-s* of s-thing)' 40/3; *e-s er (verðr) þ. e-m* 'there is (will be) need of s-thing for s-one, s-one needs (will need) s-thing' 3/1,5 4/1 5/1 38/6; *e-m verðr þ. mikil e-s* 's-one has great need of s-thing' 148/2.

æ *adv.* 'always' 32/5 48/6.
æva *adv.* 'never' 29/2 54/3 55/3 56/3 163/2.
ævagi *adv.* 'never' 21/5.

œði *n.* 'disposition' 4/4n.
œpa (t) *wv.* 'cry (out), scream, shout'; pres. p. 139/5.
œrinn *a.* 'enough, plenty (of)' 69/5, 'only too much (many)' 29/1 (with *stafi*).

ǫðrum dat. of annarr.
ǫl *n.* 'ale' 11/6 12/3 66/4 81/6 83/1 131/7 137/5.
ǫld *f.* 'mankind' 32/4; 'class of men'? 53/6n; pl. 'mankind, men' 12/3 27/2 107/6.
ǫlðr *n.* 'ale' 137/7; 'ale-party' 13/2 14/4.
ǫlr *a.* 'drunk (with ale)' 14/1.
ǫrn *m.* 'eagle' 62/3.

øngr *pron. a.* (= engi) 'no, not any'; f. *øng* 95/4; dat. sg. n. 'with nothing' 95/6.
ørlǫg *n. pl.* 'fate, destiny' 56/4.